DUCY

Exploits, Advice, and
Ideas of the Renowned Strategist

By

David Sklansky

Alan N. Schoonmaker, Ph.D.

A product of Two Plus Two Publishing LLC
www.twoplustwo.com

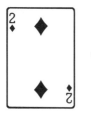 **+** 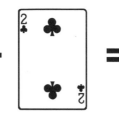 **=**

FIRST EDITION
FIRST PRINTING: JANUARY 2010

Printing and Binding
Creel Printing Co.
Las Vegas, Nevada

Printed in the United States of America

DUCY?
Exploits, Advice, and
Ideas of the Renowned Strategist

Copyright © 2010 by
Two Plus Two Publishing LLC

For information contact: **Two Plus Two Publishing LLC**
32 Commerce Center Drive
Suite H-89
Henderson, NV 89014
www.twoplustwo.com

ISBN: 1-880685-48-5
ISBN13: 978-1-880685-48-8

Table of Contents

About David Sklansky

David Sklansky is generally considered the number one authority on gambling in the world today. Besides his thirteen books on the subject, David also has produced two videos and numerous writings for various gaming publications. His occasional poker seminars always receive an enthusiastic reception, including those given at the Taj Mahal in Atlantic City and the World Series of Poker in Las Vegas.

More recently, David has been doing consulting work for casinos, Internet gaming sites, and gaming device companies. He has recently invented several games, soon to appear in casinos.

David attributes his standing in the gambling community to three facts:

1. The fact that he presents his ideas as simply as possible (sometimes with another author) even though these ideas frequently involve concepts that are deep, subtle, and not to be found elsewhere.

2. The fact that David's teachings have proven to be accurate.

3. The fact that to this day a large portion of his income is still derived from gambling (usually poker, but occasionally blackjack, sports betting, horses, video games, casino promotions, or casino tournaments).

Thus, those who depend on David's advice know that he still depends on it himself.

Other Books by David Sklansky

Hold 'em Poker
The Theory of Poker
Getting The Best of It
Poker, Gaming, & Life: Expanded Edition
Sklansky on Poker
Sklansky Talks Blackjack
Tournament Poker for Advanced Players

Gambling for a Living by David Sklansky and Mason Malmuth
Hold 'em Poker for Advanced Players by David Sklansky and Mason Malmuth
Seven-Card Stud for Advanced Players by David Sklansky, Mason Malmuth, and Ray Zee
Small Stakes Hold 'em: Winning Big with Expert Play by Ed Miller, David Sklansky, and Mason Malmuth
No-Limit Hold 'em: Theory and Practice by David Sklansky and Ed Miller

About
Alan N. Schoonmaker Ph.D.

Dr. Alan Schoonmaker has a unique combination of academic credentials, business experience, and poker expertise. After earning his Ph.D. in industrial psychology from The University of California at Berkeley, he joined the faculties at UCLA and Carnegie-Mellon University's Graduate School of Industrial Administration. He then became a research fellow at The Catholic University of Louvain in Belgium.

Dr. Schoonmaker was the manager of Management Development at Merrill Lynch before starting Schoonmaker and Associates, an international consulting company. He personally taught or consulted in twenty-nine countries on all six continents for clients such as GE, GM, IBM, Mobil, Rank Xerox, Bankers Trust, Wells Fargo, Manufacturers Hanover, Chemical Bank, Chase Manhattan, Ryan Homes, Sun Life of Canada, and AAA of Michigan.

Dr. Schoonmaker has authored or co-authored three research monographs and has published four books on industrial psychology — *Anxiety and the Executive, Executive Career Strategy, Selling: The Psychological Approach,* and *Negotiate to Win,* one book on coping with college — *A Student's Survival Manual,* and four books on poker psychology — *The Psychology of Poker, Your Worst Poker Enemy, Your Best Poker Friend,* and *Poker Winners Are Different.* His books have been translated into French, German, Dutch, Russian, Spanish, Portuguese, Swedish, Japanese, and Indonesian.

Dr. Schoonmaker has published over 100 articles in business and poker periodicals such as *The California Management Review, Expansion, Poker Digest,* and *Card Player.* He has written, and/or played the leading role in four video series. Two were part of the multi-media training programs *Selling: The Psychological Approach* and *Negotiate To Win.* The other two, *Management by Objectives* and *Career Development,* were produced and used by Mobil Oil Corporation and its subsidiary Montgomery Ward. At one time, *Selling: The Psychological Approach* was the world's best selling computer based course for business people.

Dr. Schoonmaker has served as an expert witness about poker psychology in both an administrative hearing and a lawsuit, and played online poker as a member of Royal Vegas Poker's team of experts. He also welcomes personal messages at www.twoplustwo.com.

Acknowledgments

We are lucky to have friends who read our drafts and suggest changes. First and foremost is our publisher, Mason Malmuth. He carefully checks everything.

We would also like to thank Mathew Sklansky, Jim McManus, Michael Kaplan, Dr. Arthur Reber, Lyndsay Haynes, and Roxanne Ormrod for reading the entire manuscript and making helpful suggestions. Steven Metzger read parts of it and made some useful recommendations. Norman Fast didn't read it, but he did have one great idea. In addition, we also thank Sue Marie Woods, Gina Sferra, Brett Stanko and Sharron Hoppe for clerical, administrative, and technical assistance.

For the index, we need to thank Carol Roberts of Roberts Indexing Services. Her website is located at www.RobertsIndexing.com. And finally, we thank Jayson "El Gonso" Hughes from the Two Plus Two forums at www.twoplustwo.com for his terrific cover design.

Prologue

Four middle-aged couples were sitting in the gourmet restaurant at Bob Stupak's Vegas World Casino anticipating that in about an hour one of them would be a millionaire. It was the culmination of a year-long slot tournament that was part of Bob's vacation packages. One member of each couple would go on the stage to play on one of the four machines assigned to them. Whoever did the best would win a million dollars.

Second prize was a steep reduction, $50,000. Third prize was $20,000. Fourth was $10,000. But even the small prizes were big money to these middle-class people who had gotten extremely lucky in this tournament's earlier rounds.

Several months earlier Bob Stupak had hired me as his consultant. As such, I was always looking for ways to make or save Bob's money. While observing these couples, an opportunity to save some serious money became apparent to me. I pulled Bob aside and said "Offer each of them a settlement of $60,000. They will still appear on the stage and go through the motions, but let's see if they will sign a contract specifying that, regardless of the outcome, they will all be paid $60,000."

Bob frowned, shook his head, and replied, "No way would they make such a deal."

But my professional gambling experience had taught me something about human nature. Even though any serious gambler would laugh at this offer, these four couples might see it differently. From their point of view, it might appear better to take an offer that three-quarters of the time would give them more than they would get from playing. So I said, "Bob, just ask them. It can't hurt to ask."

He did, and they all said, "Yes." They agreed to take a total of $240,000 rather than a total of $1,080,000. My simple proposal was about to drop $840,000 into Bob's lap.

Introduction
David Sklansky, A Unique Thinker
by Alan N. Schoonmaker, Ph.D.

You have just seen David's unusual mind at work. Hardly anyone else could suddenly think of a way to combine math and psychology to save $840,000. Those abilities and several others have made him the most respected and influential poker and gambling writer of all time.

Because his books have been translated into many languages, serious poker players and gamblers all over the world have read and been influenced by them. He has consulted with many casinos, and he was the main expert witness regarding the house's edge for the National Gambling Impact Study Commission.

Why Should You Care?

You may think, "So what? I don't gamble. Why read this book?"

To answer this question, this book is not primarily about gambling. Our goal is to improve your thinking and decision-making. We use gambling and non-gambling examples and biographical anecdotes to teach you how to analyze situations and make good decisions.

Successful gambling has little to do with being lucky. If you make good decisions, you should eventually win. If you make bad ones, expect to lose. It's that simple.

David has helped hundreds of thousands of gamblers to make better decisions. His ideas can also improve your decisions about much more important issues such as choosing a career, running a business, supervising subordinates, making major purchases, investing your money, and educating your children.

1

What's Unique About David's Thinking?

As a professor and management consultant, I worked with many brilliant people including Nobel Laureate Herbert Simon. David is as bright as any of them. For example, most children take the Scholastic Aptitude Tests (SAT) when they are about seventeen, and the average score is 500. When he was only twelve, David got a perfect score of 800 on the math SAT. The math exams of The American Actuarial Society are usually taken by college students. When David was a high school junior, he easily passed them. He became a finalist in the National Merit Scholarship competition in high school despite having limited interest in purely intellectual activities.

Nearly all geniuses have narrowly focused interests and abilities. David is one of the few who combines creativity, probability, logic, and psychology. They almost never go together. People who emphasize probability and logic tend to be weak in creativity and vice versa. Few psychologists think probabilistically, and many mathematicians (except for certain types of statisticians) ignore psychology.

David has been called "A Creative Spock." In *Star Trek,* Spock was a completely logical, unemotional, unimaginative, and uncreative being from another planet. He could not understand emotions, and he was never original or creative. He thought perfectly inside his narrow box, but couldn't think outside of it.

David is almost as logical as Spock, but not as rigid. In fact, he often thinks "outside the box," and will help you do the same.

David has the same emotions as everyone else, but works hard to control them. He constantly analyzes the way he thinks, feels, and acts. I urge you to follow his lead.

You will be surprised by some of David's thoughts. When you read other books, you may often say to yourself, "I knew that." When you read some of David's stories, you'll wonder,

"How did he come up with that?" (But, often after he tells you, you'll wonder why you didn't think of it yourself.)

His unusual abilities have produced a unique book. You'll see how combining math, creativity, logic, probability, and psychology can produce much better decisions than you can make with a narrower approach.

How Did His Thinking Develop?

He has had an unusual life. From early childhood his father, Prof. Irving Sklansky, taught him how to think mathematically and logically. His father used to tell him, "If you really know math well, you can be good at almost anything." He wanted David to have the ability and freedom to exploit opportunities that most people never even consider.

Professor Sklansky's teaching went far beyond mathematics and logic. He wanted David to think clearly about everything, and he constantly looked for teaching opportunities. David remembers his father's teaching him a lesson about human nature while driving. "Watch, David. I'm going to wave at total strangers, and they will all wave back." David was surprised by this. His father explained that, despite not recognizing him, they weren't going to risk offending someone they might know just to avoid waving to a possible stranger. As you will see, this lesson influenced one of our major themes: Keep in mind other people's perceptions of their risks and rewards.

Dinner was the time for tutorials. The subjects included math, logic, psychology, history, science, and whatever else his father believed would develop David's mind. He often included puzzles that the young Sklansky was expected to answer by the next dinner.

If David had followed the path of most prodigies, he would have gotten a Ph.D. and become a professor or scientist. But as a rebellious kid, he escaped from the Ivory Tower's constraints by dropping out of college. While his early life developed the rigorous logic and thoroughness of academia, his premature departure from academia prevented it from imposing its narrow, rigid constraints.

These type of constraints are among my worst flaws. Despite being out of academia for decades, I often think the way psychology professors are supposed to think, while David thinks like a brilliant eccentric whose mind roams freely. Academic constraints can be so powerful that many professors at well-respected universities can be narrowly-focused specialists who don't care much about other subjects.

David resembles what I think Richard Feynman would have become if he had decided to leave physics when he was twenty. Feynman won a Nobel Prize in physics, but he thought and wrote creatively about many other subjects. Scientists, mathematicians, and engineers, etc. naturally focus on their specialty. But the better ones could have thought of many of David's points if they focused more on the real world.

After David dropped out of college, he entered the gambling world. Virtually all gambling is intensely mathematical, and poker also requires psychological skills. You must understand odds and so on, but you must also be able to get into the other players' heads, understand how they think and feel, and manipulate them into believing whatever you want them to believe. His years as a professional poker player have sharpened all these skills.

David's mind can roam so freely because he has fewer demands on his time than nearly all highly intelligent people. Since he doesn't have a job, David can think about whatever he wishes. Even when "working" (playing poker), he has usually folded his cards and can think about whatever he likes.

David once called me to discuss a serious subject. Conversations with him are demanding because he thinks so quickly and his ideas are often complicated. He was talking rapidly, and it was difficult to keep up with him. Then he said, "Wait, Al, I'm in a hand."

"What? You're playing poker?"

"Yeah"

"What stakes?"

"$200-$400."

I was astonished. I've never played for such high stakes, but if this was to happen, my concentration would be on the game. However, for David, playing for those stakes was just "another day at the office," and since his mind often wanders into other subjects, he decided to talk to me.

We don't claim that all his ideas are original, but his way of applying them often is. Well read people will recognize that some of his ideas were proposed by other fine minds, sometimes even centuries ago. And some excellent poker players will often say, "I already knew that." Poker develops certain ways of thinking that can solve countless problems.[1]

What Kind of Person is He?

David is a professional gambler with most of a successful professional's characteristics. They are unemotional, calculating, and brutally realistic. They constantly look for an edge, and then they ruthlessly exploit it.

David doesn't look for issues to discuss even though this book covers an extremely wide range of topics. Their common factor is not their importance, but that he thinks they have not been analyzed properly. Whenever he encounters bad thinking, David feels obliged to comment.

I have known him for eight years, but he had a huge impact on my poker playing and writing even before we met. His

---

[1] The appendix, "Poker Is Good For You," summarizes the way poker develops valuable abilities.

rigorously logical approach was the similar to what I had encountered in academia. All first class universities emphasize logical thinking and solid evidence. If you relied on gut feel, as so many people do, your chance of success will probably not be what it could be.

David is a popular writer with many best-sellers, but he is not always well liked because he confidently takes controversial positions and is involved in debates. If you like, dislike, or don't understand something another author says, you usually can't do much about it. Not so with David. You can ask him questions, express your feelings, or debate with him on the forums at www.twoplustwo.com where David has over 6,000 posts (as of December, 2009). Some of the discussions there have included hundreds of posts from people in America, Europe, Asia, and just about everywhere else.

Many people believe that since he does not have a degree, it's arrogant to comment on abortion, the criminal justice system, economics, and other non-gambling issues. These critics don't understand the primary meaning of the word "arrogant."

If David claimed to have qualities he doesn't have, he would be arrogant. Since he can back up his claims, he just *looks* arrogant, rarely taking a position without thoroughly analyzing the situation. In fact, David often avoids stating his own opinions and values. Instead, he focuses on the poor thinking that causes so many people to take inconsistent positions.

But David always thinks about costs and benefits, not about what feels right or what the authorities say is right. The critical issues are not whether an individual's or government's actions seem morally right. They are:

1. What are the costs and benefits?

2. Are your positions logically consistent with each other?

You may believe that some of his views are mean-spirited, and David does insist that some ends do justify debatable means. He is always concerned with efficiency and with taking actions that lead to the best consequences. Thus we expect outraged reactions to recommendations of positions that, if they thought more clearly, many people would support. These include:

1. Punishing the police for illegal searches, but using the evidence in criminal trials.

2. Allowing healthy people to pay to use handicapped parking spaces

3. Using a dollar standard to resolve disputes about legalizing drugs and prostitution, bailing out sub-prime borrowers, giving amnesty to illegal aliens, conducting embryonic stem cell research, providing condoms to your teenaged children, and supporting gun control laws.

4. Varying punishments for identical crimes so that they fit the criminal's finances and personality.

5. Permitting solo drivers to pay for the privilege of using car pool lanes

Some of his recommendations violate our values, but they are all driven by David's desire to get the best results. For example, if letting healthy people use handicapped spaces will help both them and the handicapped, we should do it, even if it seems "unfair."

Neither of us pays much attention to ideology, and we regard all types of political correctness as nonsense. We expect criticism from liberals, conservatives, and others because many people are not pragmatic. They want to do "the right thing," without dispassionately analyzing the costs and benefits of all their alternatives. We reject this sort of thinking and our main concern is helping you to make decisions that produce the best results by your standards.

I said your standards because David is not trying to force you to accept his. He rarely discusses the goals, opinions, or values you should have. That's your job. In fact, he will surprise you by saying that it's okay to have irrational goals as long as you understand and accept the consequences of having them. Hence, David focuses on the way you should think, not on what it is you're trying to accomplish.

A critical step toward achieving goals is accepting responsibility for the consequences of your actions. Accepting responsibility is a traditional American virtue, but it has gone out of fashion. Today people expect to be given things. No, they demand them due to the belief that they are "entitled."

David constantly asks the central question of winning poker players: "Will it work?" If so, let's do it regardless of how it looks to most people. Poker is a ruthlessly results-oriented game, and that same emphasis upon effectiveness can improve your thinking about much more important subjects.

However, David is not remotely as serious as some people believe. While writing this book, we often laughed about his "crazy exploits" and "quirky mind." We once disagreed about an issue and exchanged several emails. I was shocked one morning by an email that said he had sent an article to *Psychology Today* about "our theory" that completely disagreed with my position. I wondered, "What the hell is he doing?" Then I realized it was April Fools' Day.

Our working environment is exceptionally relaxed. We meet in restaurants, the UNLV student union, The Bellagio Poker Room, and his home. His cats climb onto our laps demanding attention, and they get it. His parrot flies around, perches on his shoulders, plays with the cats (honest, it really does), walks across our working area, and occasionally poops on our papers.

Still, David is not a sympathetic person. He believes that if you are too dumb[2] or lazy to analyze situations thoroughly, you *deserve* to be exploited by casinos, advertisers, and politicians. Nor is he sympathetic to stupid or lazy casino owners. When casinos create situations which allow smart people to beat them, it's management's own fault. If they can't do their jobs properly, that's their tough luck.

Why am I Involved in this Book?

When David offered me a chance to collaborate, my emotions were mixed. I was eager to work with the smartest man in poker, but had never been the "junior partner" in a creative project. This book is based on his ideas. My responsibilities are to:

1. Help David present his ideas

2. Help you apply his ideas to yourself and your situation (mainly through the "Al's Comments" section of many chapters).

One reason for taking this role was to improve my own thinking. David has helped me see many subjects differently, (but I still have a long way to go).

Parts of this book may be irritating or challenging, but reading it should help you to break out of the narrow box of your own thinking, analyze situations in new and creative ways, and make immeasurably better decisions.

---

[2] David is quite sympathetic to slow learners and other handicapped people. It's not their fault. He does, however, believe that many "stupid" people have consciously chosen to be that way by refusing to educate themselves, and also believes that people who have problems with complex thinking should at the very least pay more attention to renowned thinkers.

Why This Book?
by David Sklansky

I was born with a very good brain. Obviously I deserve no credit for it, but it's still true. My mother is a near-genius, and my father was unquestionably a genius. Half of my uncles and cousins have Ph.D.s from great universities and/or have written several books. Many are professors. My second cousin, Prof. David Sklansky, even clerked for Supreme Court Justice Harry Blackmun (after graduating with honors from Harvard Law School and before becoming a distinguished professor of law at UCLA and Berkeley).[3]

I was lucky to inherit good genes, but my father worked hard to help me make the most of them. During my childhood he spent countless hours teaching me about subjects that are usually taught only to much older people (and often aren't taught at all). He focused primarily on science, math, and logic, but also taught me about other things such as understanding how other people think and feel. He wanted me to go beyond just knowing subjects to truly understanding them. Above all, I should *think clearly and creatively* (while maintaining the ability to think in a childish, simplistic way when the situation called for it.) Many people who knew him would agree that he was one of the greatest teachers who ever lived.

Unfortunately, I did not put the things he taught me to very good use. I was a National Merit Scholarship finalist and so on, but never even graduated from college (University of Pennsylvania). Instead, I became a professional gambler, and, of course, the black sheep of the family. Naturally, this makes me

---

[3] If you're afraid that someone may criticize you for reading about the ideas of a professional gambler and semi-scoundrel, you can claim that you thought you were reading one of Prof. Sklansky's books.

feel uncomfortable about not using his genes and training more productively. But these feelings have created a sense of having a *mission* of repaying my debt to my father by doing for others what he did for me.

That mission is a big reason for writing poker and gambling books. Those books did not just teach gambling strategy, they also taught many people how to think better. This book is an expansion of that mission. It goes far beyond gambling to teach you how to think better about nearly everything.

The title, *DUCY?*, was taken from our forums at www.twoplustwo.com. Since one of my goals is to have people think better, I often did not tell them the answer to one of my questions. Instead, my reply would be, "Do you see why?"

I did it so often that some of our posters shortened it to "DUCY?," and used it repeatedly. It became so popular that it was defined in the Urban Dictionary as "Abbreviated form of 'Do you see why?' Commonly used on online forums; Originated from the Two Plus Two Poker Community."

Since I believe you learn best by figuring things out for yourself, I will sometimes ask, "DUCY?" When you see it, stop and try to work out the answer for yourself. Active learning is immeasurably better than passive reading.

My wide-ranging experience and free time have helped me to think about things that I believe many people would like to read about. It includes stories, observations, thoughts, and "stuff" I have come up with that you probably don't know, but would like to know. Some of these thoughts and stories will be merely entertaining, and some you should find useful. And a few of these chapters just might change your life.

Part One

My Years with Bob Stupak

Introduction

Our first chapters describe my work as a consultant to Bob Stupak, one of the most colorful builders of modern Las Vegas. Every resident and visitor repeatedly sees Bob's permanent monument, The Stratosphere Tower.

Just before this book went to press, we got the sad news that Bob had died. I wish he could have lived a little longer to read what we wrote about him. Al and I did have a chance to discuss it with him, and he was looking forward to reading it.

Our book focuses on the ideas I gave him, but he was much more than just my client. In fact, he was one of those men you could correctly call, "larger than life." He was often outrageous, but never boring. To give you a clearer picture of who he was and how much impact he had, I asked John L. Smith, his biographer, for permission (which he graciously granted) to reprint a column he published in the September 27, 2009, issue of *The Las Vegas Review-Journal*.

Las Vegas May Have Lost One of Its Last Characters, But Huckster's Dreams Live On

Come on, Bob Stupak. Give us a sign. From up above or down below, tell us how you placed your life's final bet.

Because as surely as this community will miss your insanely colorful character, those of us who knew you also know that you couldn't have resisted making a play on your life's final day.

That day came Friday at Desert Springs Hospital after a long battle with leukemia. He was 67 and turned in his body with some very high miles on it. Bob embodied the Vegas adage, "Anything worth doing is worth overdoing."

And overdo it he did.

The son of Pittsburgh gambling boss, Chester Stupak, Bob was born with a huckster's heart and was a tireless self-promoter. He rarely let silly things like rules and regulations get in the way of a good pitch, whether he was running a backroom dice game as a teenager, selling coupon books in Australia as a young man, hustling "VIP Vacation" customers at Vegas World, or seeing his dream project, the Las Vegas Stratosphere Tower, become a reality just prior to his business bankruptcy.

Bob was an audacious dreamer who never ran out of plans to boost himself or his casino. He worked more angles than a geometry book. With his ninth-grade education, he had a head for numbers a college professor would have envied.

"I never had a steady job," he once told me. "All the jobs I had were self-inflicted."

"He was the last of the mavericks," Huntington Press publisher Anthony Curtis said Friday.

Curtis published my 1997 book, "No Limit: The Rise and Fall of Bob Stupak and Las Vegas' Stratosphere Tower."

"He called himself the Polish Maverick, and indeed that's what he was. He didn't put on any airs. He kind of tightroped it a little bit. He was kind of an anti-corporate guy, a casino boss who did it by his guile and answered to himself."

Occasionally, Stupak also was compelled to answer to the authorities. His "VIP Vacation" program was extremely successful and made the gaudy Vegas World, which squatted in a terrible location on Las Vegas Boulevard, a big moneymaker. It also generated complaints to the Gaming Control Board from several attorney generals, a particularly humorless lot if you ask me.

They should have smiled a little and felt almost honored to be involved in a Stupak hustle. Over the years, we all were hustled by Bob. Frankly, I came to appreciate it.

In his youth, Bob dreamed of being a teen idol. His problem was simple. He couldn't sing. But that didn't stop him from playing clubs and cutting a Christmas record called "Jake the Flake."

Stupak was a gutsy, kamikaze-style poker player who won a World Series of Poker bracelet, but he made far bigger headlines when he went head to head against a super computer — and won.

Stupak would gamble on anything, but news of his $1 million bet in Super Bowl XXIII circled the globe. And if, confidentially, it was a publicity stunt, well that was just Bob being Bob.

There was the time Bob hired the Native American fellow to jump off the top of Vegas World onto a cushion for $1 million — and charged the guy a $990,000 landing fee.

There were Bob's forays into politics — always with bets on the side. He nearly won the mayor's job and helped bankroll a couple of his kids' campaigns. One Election Night, after celebrating early and then losing, he slapped one reporter and tried to kiss another on camera.

Bob was the kind of guy who would bet you he could do between "two and 300 push-ups," and after reeling off three say, "I win. Three is between two and 300."

When I insisted on writing an unauthorized biography of Stupak during construction of the Stratosphere, Bob offered me $10,000 to go away. I wasn't offended. A bribe? He was just being Stupakian.

With numbers guru David Sklansky checking his math, Stupak developed angles on dice and blackjack he called "crapless craps" and "double exposure 21." The games drew raves from customers, who were having too much fun to fully appreciate they were getting worse odds.

"He understood the gambler's instinct as well or better than anybody," Curtis says, placing Stupak's casino savvy high in the great green-felt pantheon.

Even the VIP Vacation program, which Curtis called "the Swiss cheese of all casino deals," gave short-pocket customers value if they played their cards right and read the fine print.

Not many people would call him a handsome guy, but Bob was never short on bravado. Singing legend Phyllis McGuire admired that about him. She called him her "Peck's Bad Boy." He once sent her enough roses on Valentine's Day to cover a parade float.

That, too, was pure Bob.

"When I think of Bob Stupak, what pops to my mind is that he was the best ever at making something out of nothing," Curtis said. "It didn't matter. He'd take any idea and figure out a way to promote it."

Stupak's friend of 35 years, Mike Flores, says, "It's the end of an era." Even Bob seemed to appreciate that one night a few years ago as we sipped whiskey at Fellini's.

"The days of characters are gone," he said. "There's no more Jay Sarnos around. There are no more me's around. It's over."

But who will be able to drive past the Stratosphere and not smile at the idea that an angle-shooting big dreamer with a ninth-grade education made that amazing tower become a reality?

I'd say you won your bet, Bob.

I Meet Bob

It was the late 1970s and Bob had just built his Vegas World Casino-Hotel a few hundred yards south of the Sahara. I had never personally met him, but was vaguely aware of him, primarily because his casino offered a new, interesting game, Double Exposure 21. It allowed players to see both of the dealer's cards in return for losing ties and getting paid only even money on blackjack (versus the usual 3-to-2).

One day he showed up at the World Series of Poker at Binions' Casino. Back then there were only about 15 tables, and his appearance caused a stir. This unconventional casino owner had decided to learn how to play poker. I saw an opportunity and grabbed it. I walked up to him and said, "Mr. Stupak, you don't know me, but I know more about gambling than anyone in the world, so you ought to know me."

My brashness earned me a seat at his booth during lunch. At the time I had written only one or two books, and they were not yet national best sellers. Since Las Vegas is full of con men, he was naturally skeptical about whether I was really that knowledgeable. He tested me by asking, "Okay, David, I'm putting a new game into my casino. I call it Crapless Craps. Can you can tell me how big my edge is?"

"Okay Bob, tell me the rules, and I'll give you the answer."

"It's simple enough. Seven is an immediate winner. All numbers except seven are points. Two, three, and twelve are no longer automatic losers, and eleven is no longer an automatic winner. People love this game because, if they make place bets or come bets, they can have long streaks of hitting numbers before they get their seven. So, what's my edge?"

I went off by myself for about twenty minutes and came back with an answer that struck most people as amazing. Many of you know that the edge in regular craps is 1.4 percent. But for Crapless Craps it was about 5.4 percent.

There are two ways to arrive at the answer. The first way is straightforward calculating and adding up of the probabilities. There are various ways of winning:

1. You can roll a 7. It happens $\frac{1}{6}$ of the time.

2. You can roll a 2 and then make it. How often does that happen? The 2 on the come-out (first roll) will occur only 1 out of 36 times, and then there's only one way to make it compared to 6 ways of making a 7, so the chance that a point of 2 will win is $\frac{1}{7}$. Thus a 2 followed by a win is $\left(\frac{1}{36}\right)\left(\frac{1}{7}\right)$. The same math applies to 12, so double that number.

3. A 3 for your come-out followed by a win is $\left(\frac{2}{36}\right)\left(\frac{2}{8}\right)$. The same math applies to 11, so double that number. (But remember that 11 is normally an instant winner.)

4. A 4 is $\left(\frac{3}{36}\right)\left(\frac{3}{9}\right)$. The same math applies to 10, so double that number.

5. Continue along this path for 5 and 9, and 6 and 8.

6. Each of these chances is independent of any other meaning that you can add all of them together to see how often you will win and you'll get an answer of about 47.3 percent. This means that you will lose 100 - 47.3 = 52.7 percent which gives the house an edge of 5.4 percent.

$$5.4 = 52.7 - 47.3$$

When Bob saw my answer, he was impressed. He had been given the same answer when someone else had suggested the game and had been skeptical. "Okay, David, your answer agrees with what I was told, but you have to tell me why it comes out this way. The 11 is no longer an automatic winner, but 2, 3, and 12 are no longer automatic losers. It looks like I'm giving more to players than I'm taking away from them. Since 3 comes up as often as 11, they should cancel out, and now I'm giving the player the chance to win on the 2 and the 12. So why is the edge greater, let alone so much greater?"

His question gave me a chance to show off both my teaching ability and my math aptitude by drawing on the second way of calculating his edge. I said, "Your mistake, Bob, is not realizing that what you are taking away on the 11 is more than you are giving back on 2, 3, and 12 combined. The eleven was a 100 percent winner, and you have turned it into only a 25 percent winner. That's 75 percent of what had previously been a $\frac{2}{36}$ shot. Three does not make up for it because a 3, while also being a $\frac{2}{36}$ shot, has moved up only from a 0 percent winner to a 25 percent winner. The two and the twelve are really no big deal; they were 0 percent winners, and you've turned them into 14 percent winners; furthermore, they don't occur very often. If you calculate the additions and subtractions, you get a net subtraction of about 2 percent. That's why the players win only about 47.3 percent of the time (as opposed to 49.3 percent in regular craps), giving you an edge of 5.4 percent."

I didn't bore Bob, nor will I bore you with the precise calculations. If you're interested, you should be able to figure the exact subtraction yourself. But I did show Bob why taking away the eleven was the key component, and it convinced him that Crapless Craps was a good game to offer and that I was a good guy to hire.

Al's Comments

One evening David called me while I was playing poker. He and Bob had just finished playing in a poker tournament, and he wanted to introduce me to Bob. After hearing so much about him, I naturally wanted to meet him, and, of course, agreed to do so.

I was wearing my usual, rather unkempt, poker-playing clothes and considered going home to change. Since David had said that Bob did not dress that well, I decided to go without changing. So after we said, hello, what were his first words?

"You dress even worse than David."

Fortunately, I laughed comfortably because Bob was just testing me and having a little fun. If I had apologized or gotten flustered, Bob probably would have most likely dismissed me as a lightweight. He tested me a few more times by making obvious mistakes to see whether they would be picked up. He didn't like "Yes Men." I must have passed because after David left, We talked until 2 a.m.

Bob was delighted that our first section would be about him and David, and enjoyed reminiscing about the good old days. He loved being Mr. Las Vegas, getting on TV frequently, playing with The Harlem Globetrotters, pretending to marry a movie star, introducing new games and promotions, and being an "A-list" celebrity. I'm not sure how much of the real Bob was encountered — Bob was a gifted huckster. But everything I saw and heard was as fascinating as his public persona.

My First Days with Bob

When the World Series was over, Bob invited me to his casino and said, "I want you to be my gambling consultant."

I told him, "Bob, you would be wasting my talents if you use me only for gambling problems." I suggested that he retain me as his all-around personal consultant and said I'd do it for a salary plus a free suite.

He thought a minute and said, "In other words, you want to be my resident wizard."

I smiled and replied, "That's as good a name as any." And that's what my position was. To this day I have kept many Vegas World business cards with the title "Resident Wizard." (When Bob ran for Lieutenant Governor of Nevada, his ads said that he would appoint me as "Nevada's Resident Wizard.")

Two things came up in those first days that convinced Bob that my outside the box thinking would be valuable for non-gambling problems. One was fairly easy to figure, but the principle was important. It involved diamond rings, cheap ones, but still real diamond rings. Bob had just started giving them to guests who came in on a special package. When he advertised them, his sales jumped 20 percent, and he calculated that the amount of extra money which came in was about four times what it cost to give people this ring. Unfortunately, he was not calculating the cost of giving it to people who would have come anyway.

Again, I won't go into the technical math, but, for some reason, he had missed this essential principle. When I explained it during our first meeting at his place, it reinforced his belief that he needed somebody like me.

This principle is elementary, but business owners sometimes make the same mistake when putting items on sale. You must always consider the cost of putting something on sale to someone who would have paid full price. It's much better to come up with promotions that offer the better price only to those who will not buy at full price. Since I first taught Bob this principle, many businesses (such as Orbitz and Travelocity) have converted it into a science. But back then most people didn't think this way.

What really convinced Bob of my value was an experiment we conducted a few days later. I could see that most of the Vegas World employees were unmotivated. They were just doing their jobs to get a paycheck. Two days earlier I had seen a pit boss call a porter to clean up a tiny spill on the blackjack table instead of just grabbing a rag and doing it himself. Almost everybody just wanted to get through the day with no real concern for the overall hotel and casino. To prove this to Bob I said, "Let's go over into the casino, sit at the bar, and see how long it takes before somebody picks up this newspaper that I will put on the floor."

As suspected, nobody picked it up. Dozens of employees walked right by, and none of them reached down to pick up and throw away a spread open newspaper right in the middle of the casino floor.

Bob was appalled. But then I said, "It's even worse than you think, Bob." I took a stool from in front of one of the slot machines and put it on its side. Again, dozens of employees walked by until one of the slot supervisors finally stooped down and put it right.

I asked Bob, "Why did you think so many people ignore the newspaper and the stool?"

"I don't know, but I don't like it.

"They think, 'That's not my job,' and they don't really care about anything except getting a paycheck. They don't identify with you or the company. They see themselves as waiters or dealers or pit bosses, not as parts of a team that works together to make the whole business succeed. We have to make them care about the casino's total success."[4]

"Do you think you can change that attitude?"

With all the confidence of youth my reply was, "Sure."

He said, "Do it," and I set about planning ways to change their attitudes about their jobs and the casino. We had a series of meetings with the entire staff where everybody was told, "You see yourself as being in the maid business, or the waiter business, or the bartender business, but we are all in the casino business. Gambling pays for everything, including our salaries. We all have to do everything we can so our customers are happy and spend their time gambling."

I was only moderately successful. Because Bob didn't pay well, we didn't get the cream of the crop. But whatever improvements were made would not have happened if Bob hadn't seen the newspaper on the floor and the stool on its side.

---

[4] A few days later Bob and I went to a fancier strip casino and put a stool on its side. Within a few seconds, someone set it upright.

Our Free Keno Promotion

Bob's package deals had a problem: They were not profitable for us unless people gambled with their own money in our casino. Some people would stay at our hotel, eat their free meals, gamble only with the special chips we gave them, and then spend almost all of their time in other casinos.

After Bob explained this problem, I combined human nature and mathematics to fix it using the simple game of keno. Many unsophisticated guests could not bear the thought of missing out on a major score. So why not give everyone an automatic chance to win a lot of money every few hours — with a catch? They had to be there to claim their prize.

The easiest way to do this was to use our keno board. We would have special games just for our guests. Nobody else could play. The special games would be at noon, four, eight, and midnight, and the winners had only 20 minutes to claim their prize.

Bob had two concerns. First, it seemed that having so many guests complete and submit keno tickets would be a logistical nightmare. After a few minutes thought, I said, "Bob, forget about having them fill out tickets. We'll assign specific numbers to each room and post them on their hotel room's door. Guests will have those numbers as long as they remain in the room." I believe that we used an 8 spot, so each room got a different set of 8 numbers.

Bob's second concern was that most keno pay outs were too small to keep people in the casino. They wouldn't care about risking the loss of a few dollars. So we made the payoffs different from the typical $1 keno 8-spot ticket. Specifically, all the smaller payments were eliminated and the three highest payments were substantially increased. I don't remember the details, but they were something like $100 for 6 out of 8, $1,000 for 7 out of 8, and $50,000 for 8 out of 8.

Real keno could not offer such payouts because players expect to receive frequent small payments as well as occasional large ones, just like they get from slot machines. But since our guests weren't paying for their tickets, these small payments wouldn't matter much, and they wouldn't stay in the casino just to prevent losing a few dollars. Eliminating the small pay outs allowed what seemed to be great ones for the higher prizes.

They may have seemed great, but, when you do the math, we were paying approximately $.60 to each person who went into the casino to see whether he had won. In most cases those people would have been in their rooms or in another casino. Many patrons did, in fact, come down, stay longer, or came back from other places to find out whether they won, and a decent proportion of them then played slot machines or other games.

I was quite proud of this idea because it combined several of my concepts. The main one was that people can't stand the idea missing a giant win. We increased that fear by announcing and displaying the name of anyone who did not claim his prize. So there was little chance they could avoid hearing about it. "Harry Johnson would have won $1,000, but he didn't claim his prize. Make sure it doesn't happen to you."

Mathematically, people who did not stay to hear the keno results were losing about $.60, and they would never have stayed if someone paid them a mere $.60 to do it. But the thought of missing out on a possible big score once they were given a ticket was too much for many people to bear.

The second concept involves the fact that small payoffs comprise most of the EV of this kind of bet. (This concept of EV is defined on page 76 in the chapter "A Short Lesson About Thinking.") Whether we're speaking of insurance, slot machines, casino rebates, or this promotion, eliminating small payoffs allows a surprisingly large increase in other payouts.

Finally, I was pleased to have thought of a way to eliminate the logistical problems of all those paper keno tickets. Assigning numbers to rooms not only eliminated this difficulty, it also made it extremely easy to know and announce who would have won, but failed to claim a prize.

This promotion was very successful. Every free keno drawing attracted about 200 patrons, and many of them would not have been there. Plus, some of them stayed and gambled, which was exactly what we had hoped for.

The Trump Challenge

Bob understood the importance of getting his name into the news as often as possible. Millions of people saw his newspaper and magazine ads and received his direct advertisement mailings. If they recognized his name, they would be much more likely to buy his packages.

Don't get me wrong. Bob loved publicity for its own sake, but there was always that marketing element: He wanted publicity to help his business. His very brief stint with the Harlem Globetrotters was a perfect example. Another was his $1 million bet on the 1989 Super Bowl. (He took seven points with the Cincinnati Bengals and won his bet when they lost by four.)

It was probably the first $1 million legal bet ever made with a Nevada bookie, and it garnered him the publicity he sought. Several months later, Bob asked me to think of new ways to grab publicity. He thought that perhaps another million dollar football bet would do it. But I had a better idea.

A new board game had recently hit the scene, "Trump: The Game." Donald Trump was even better known than Bob, and his image was very positive. He was seen as brilliant because everything he touched seemed to turn to gold. He had been cashing in on his notoriety by writing books, getting on TV, and now by putting his name on a game.

The ads for this game included a statement (that supposedly came directly from "The Donald"). I don't have the exact words, but they were something like: "This is a great game for aspiring businessmen and entrepreneurs. How you play it will show whether or not you've got what it takes. If you're a winner at this game, you'll know that you've got it. If not, well, you can still go home and enjoy the wife and kids." Obviously, those words, while slightly nasty, were tongue in cheek.

I had seen this ad, but didn't originally pay too much attention to it. I wasn't interested in Trump or his game. But, when Bob said he would bet another million to get publicity, a light went off in my head.

"Bob, don't just bet a football game. Challenge Donald Trump to play *his own game* for a million dollars. Challenging him will certainly get you great publicity. It would not just highlight that you're a gambler. It would say that you're a better strategist than Trump."

"But I have no idea how to play that game."

"So what? First of all, it's extremely unlikely that he will accept your challenge. Second, if he does, I'll read the rules, and it's very likely that, with coaching from me, you'll be better than him. But winning isn't the point. Regardless of who wins, you'll get great publicity."

Bob agreed. A few days later we put full page ads into *The New York Post* and *The Atlantic City Press*. We picked those papers because Trump owned several luxury buildings in New York and was Atlantic City's biggest casino owner. Bob was always great at wording ads, and with my help he came up with terrific verbiage. It said something like: "Donald Trump has arrogantly gone on record that this game is a good indicator of your talents for business and wheeling and dealing. Well, I say that I'm better than you, Mr. Trump, and I'm willing to bet a million dollars on it." There were several other comments, and the ad ended with, "But don't worry, Donald. If I beat you, you can still go home and enjoy the wife and kids."

The scheme worked exactly as expected. Trump did not ignore the challenge, nor did he accept it. When the media asked him why he wouldn't accept the challenge, he gave lame excuses. So he looked a bit foolish and gave Bob the publicity we had hoped for.

As an amusing footnote to this story, Trump could have very easily deflected the challenge without making him look like he was afraid of Bob. All he had to say was, "I can't play Mr. Stupak because this game requires a minimum of three players." Luckily for us, Trump apparently didn't even know the rules for his own game.

Al's Comments

Bob got an immense amount of publicity by challenging Trump, and it cost him very little. He did the same with his phony wedding to a movie star and various other "pranks." I put "pranks" in quotation marks because they weren't pranks at all. They were masterful public relations coups.

Bob recognized and brilliantly exploited the media's hunger for material. The television producers and newspaper editors have to fill up their time and pages, and there is not enough genuine news to do it. So they look for anything that their readers will consume.

Bob knew that it was much better, and immeasurably cheaper, to do things that the media publicized than to buy advertising. Of course, he spent a fortune on advertising, but he got more value from his advertising dollars by getting so much publicity. And he got it by his "pranks."

The lesson for you is: *If you want publicity, don't be afraid to be outrageous.*

Experto 21

Bob was always looking for new games that would bring more money into the casino than the ones we usually offered. Nowadays, most casinos offer many different games, but back then all you could normally find would be craps, roulette, and 21. Even before Bob met me, he had come up with two new variations that attracted customers: Crapless Craps and Double Exposure 21.

Crapless craps was discussed earlier, and Bob copyrighted both that name and "Double Exposure 21." He picked it because the dealer actually showed both his cards. In return for this information, the players lost ties and were paid only even money on blackjack. Bob did quite well with these games because they had three things going for them:

1. The house edge was greater than for most casino games.

2. The house edge appeared to be smaller than for normal games.

3. The games were fun to play, perhaps even more fun than the original game they were based on.

For the first few years, Bob made millions from these games, especially Double Exposure 21. Many high rollers from fancy strip hotels made special trips to his place to play a game they thought they could beat.

But as the years passed, such scores became fewer and farther between. Players smartened up, or perhaps they just noticed they didn't do as well as they did in the routine games.

So Bob asked me to come up with something new, something with those three characteristics. I fulfilled his wishes by inventing the game we called "Experto 21." The rules were simple. It was played just like regular 21, except that we used only one deck and we dealt all the way to the bottom. Unlike other single-deck blackjack games, we reshuffled only when all the cards were gone. (We did burn one card to prevent most "end play" possibilities.)

These rules added a big advantage to professional blackjack players and a smaller advantage to amateur counters who thought they were experts. In return for helping them, we changed only one thing: We paid even money on blackjack instead of the usual 3-to-2. (To temper this slightly, we paid the players even if their blackjack tied the dealer's blackjack.)

This game worked well for us because the vast majority of blackjack players were too dumb to realize the implications of even money on blackjack. And "dumb" is exactly the right word. It's incredibly simple to calculate that you will be dealt a blackjack approximately 5 percent of the time.

$$.05 = \left(\frac{16}{52}\right)\left(\frac{4}{51}\right) + \left(\frac{4}{52}\right)\left(\frac{16}{51}\right)$$

Therefore, taking away half a bet means that you will be shortchanged $2\frac{1}{2}$ bets every hundred hands. Only very accomplished counters who used a high bet spread (that we sometimes forbade) gained back that $2\frac{1}{2}$ percent. Thus, what we gave customers did not nearly make up for what we took away from them, but they did not realize it.

Thousands of wannabe counters thought we were giving them a game far preferable to a typical game with a shoe of 4 or 6 decks. But most did not come close to gaining back the $2\frac{1}{2}$ percent we were taking away from them. And, of course, non-counters didn't get any of it back. Our Experto 21 tables won more than twice as much as the regular blackjack tables — approximately 4 percent of the total action versus approximately 2 percent for the normal game. And, unlike Bob's Crapless Craps and Double

Exposure 21, they continued to earn Bob a fortune during all the years we worked together.

Al's Comments

These games made Bob millions by taking advantage of people's tendency to rely on their instincts about mathematical facts. You can't take advantage of people's misunderstanding about something that appears to be a good deal if they know how to calculate and will do the work. But most people can't or won't do the calculations.

David told me that laymen don't realize that even mathematicians can instinctually think that something is one thing when it's actually something else. But mathematicians don't rely on instincts. They do the calculations before making their decisions, while most laymen will just rely on their gut feelings. And their gut feelings will often be wrong since many probabalistic events are counter-intuitive to most people.

That is, even though the mathematicians' instincts are better than laymen's, they will not trust them. But most laymen will trust their inferior feelings rather than do the calculations. Since your gut feelings are not as good as a mathematician's, the lesson for you is quite simple: When making significant decisions about anything with a probabalistic component (not just gambling), don't trust your instincts. *Learn how to do the math, and then make the calculations.*

The same principle applies to non-mathematical problems. Learn how to analyze situations and make a thorough analysis before committing yourself. It's easy to see how casinos exploit their customers' failure to analyze situations well, and countless other businesses and virtually all politicians do the same thing. They have become extraordinarily skillful at manipulating people, but they rarely manipulate people like David because they take the time to do the proper analysis.

If you get into the habit of analyzing situations thoroughly, you will develop some immunity from the constant efforts to exploit and manipulate you. In other words, never make a significant commitment without thoroughly analyzing the situation.

Playing Chicken

Game theory is not just for poker and other games. The logic and math first developed by John von Neuman and John Nash can solve an extremely wide range of problems. One of the more amusing examples relates to a game called "Chicken." It's an outlandish contest involving silly courage and fast cars that I've seen only in the movies and on television. Two people drive straight toward each other at high speed, and the one who veers off first loses. Does game theory propose a winning strategy?

Actually, it does. Throw your steering wheel out the window (where the other driver can see it). Obviously, unless he is suicidal, your opponent has no choice but to veer off. He knows that you can't.

To apply this solution to real life situations, you must convince your opponent that you won't budge, regardless of the consequences. Either you're irrationally committed to your position, or you're flat out crazy. When I told Bob how to beat Chicken, he loved it. In fact, without knowing this game theory solution, he had already used it. After I told him about it, he did it again.

Not Enough Shrubs

Bob first "threw his steering wheel out the window" a few years before we met. Since he had used every dollar he could beg, borrow, or steal to build Vegas World, he didn't care much about spending on little frills. For instance, he planted very few shrubs around his hotel. And though it may sound trivial, Bob had violated a regulation.

A few months after his place opened, he received a letter from the government telling him to plant more shrubs. The letter essentially said, "If you don't plant these shrubs within the next two months, we will close your casino."

Bob could have afforded to buy the needed shrubs, but that was irrelevant. The threat was what mattered to him. So he wrote back something like this, "I will not plant these shrubs in the allotted time. You said that, if I don't, you will close me down. I would love to see the newspaper headlines the day you do it: 'City's government puts 600 people out of work. Not enough shrubs.'"

When the city's bureaucrats got this letter, they were afraid that Bob was crazy enough to actually call their bluff. Since they realized that couldn't push him around, they backed down. For quite a while Vegas World remained a relatively shrubless place.

The Nevada Power Deposit

This confrontation occurred after I told Bob how to play Chicken. Nevada Power normally requires its new customers to make a deposit before their electricity is turned on. After the customer has paid his bills regularly for a while, the deposit is returned. For Vegas World this deposit was $50,000. After paying his bills promptly, Bob got his refund. But a bit later he received a letter asking him to redeposit that money.

I'm not sure why they asked for that redeposit. Perhaps they were concerned about Bob's "eccentric" reputation. The problem was that their request contained a threat: "If you don't give us this deposit, we will shut off your electricity." Shutting off the electricity obviously meant shutting down the whole casino-hotel.

Perhaps Bob was thinking of the shrubbery incident or my lesson about Chicken. In any case, he called them and said, "I'm not making this deposit. Shut off my electricity. Then you can explain to The Gaming Commission, the city government, and the voters why you put 600 employees out of work." The electricity remained on, and Bob never did make that deposit.

Al's Comments

Bob's reactions to threats from the local authorities and Nevada Power can teach you two lessons.

1. **It sometimes pays to appear to be irrational.** If people believe that you are angry or irrational enough to act in ways that harm both you and them, you have a huge advantage.

   While teaching negotiations, I coined a term, "The Law of Irrationality." "Sane people are at a disadvantage because they are much more restrained than madmen... For example, if you and a lunatic are locked in a room, and you both have hand grenades, who has the power? He does! You are too rational to use your grenade, but you can't tell what he will do.[5]

2. **Don't make threats that your targets won't believe.** Bob didn't believe the threats made to him, and he was right not to. On the other hand, the local authorities and Nevada Power backed down because they did believe that Bob would allow his casino to be closed. If they had not believed him, his threats could have been counter-productive. The other people might have become so angry that they acted rigidly and stupidly. Because he had an "eccentric" reputation and was known to love publicity, his threat was believable, and they backed down.

---

[5] See pages 138-139 of Schoonmaker, Alan, *Negotiate To Win: Gaining The Psychological Edge,* Englewood Cliffs, NJ, Prentice-Hall, 1989.

Move the
Line, Not the Spread

The greatest fear of a bookie is to be middled. One team starts out as a $3\frac{1}{2}$ point favorite, and people bet so much money on it that the spread is increased to $4\frac{1}{2}$ points. With that move everybody starts betting the underdog. If the favorite wins by four points, it's a bookie's nightmare because he pays almost everybody.[6]

Soon after Bob put in his sports book, something exactly like that happened, and he took a huge loss. He was so upset that he said, "David, I'm thinking of closing the whole damned sports book."

I replied, "Don't close it. There's a way to avoid being middled. Just keep the point spread the same regardless of the action. If there is too much action on one side, move away from 11-to-10 on both sides. If you move the odds enough, you will get action on both sides without risking the catastrophic payouts of being middled."

He did it and made a bundle from his sports book. There are technical downsides to doing things this way, but unless bookies have giant bankrolls, it's often correct, especially when easily hit numbers are involved. For instance, if a 3-point favorite has lopsided action, it is very often mathematically wrong to move the line to $3\frac{1}{2}$ or $2\frac{1}{2}$. Keep it at 3, and make the money line a

---

[6] If you don't bet with bookies, you may not know that they almost always prefer to have the same amount bet on both sides. They are then guaranteed a profit because both sides lay odds of 11-to-10. They change the odds and/or point spread to encourage people to bet on the side with less action.

-120/even or -130/+110. In fact, nowadays that's what almost all bookies do. To the best of my knowledge, Bob did it before anybody else because of my idea.

The Five Gifts

This story doesn't involve much money, but I'm including to illustrate an interesting logical point that you may find useful. Some of our packages let customers choose from a menu of five gifts when they arrived at the hotel. Because we bought them in bulk, we got a good deal. Even though they cost us about $40, we could legitimately claim that their retail value was over $100.

When the manufacturer of one gift went out of business, we were forced to shop for a replacement. Bob did a little market research by asking our customers which one of several prospective replacements they would choose. I don't remember all the details, but let's say that he had four options that he wanted to whittle down to one. He asked hundreds of our guests, "Which one of these four do you like best?" He planned to fill out his menu by choosing the one that got the most votes.

But his logic was flawed because the test's winner was not necessarily the best choice. Remember, the one he chose would go onto a menu of five gifts, and customers would pick only one of those five. The winner of Bob's test might not be the gift that had the most likely chance of being chosen if it were placed on the five gift menu.

To illustrate, suppose that one of the four candidates was a specialty-type gift that did not interest many people, but was very enticing to a small percentage of our guests. For example, I suggested a baseball autographed by Willie Mays. Bob said, "Most people wouldn't want it."

"So what? A few people would love it. Let's say that only 15 percent of the market research group would choose the baseball, and the winner might be a jacket. But, on the main menu, that jacket would almost never be picked because it comes in second to our microwave. Meanwhile, if the baseball were on the main menu, 15 percent of the guests would pick it over everything, including the microwave. That makes the baseball the better choice for our menu."

This principle is quite important in many situations, including selecting candidates for elections, especially ones that don't have a runoff feature. DUCY?

Two Small Lessons
from One Little Room

Because of Bob's marketing strategy, he needed as many hotel rooms as possible. When he couldn't accommodate all the guests on certain packages, he had to send them to nearby motels. Of course, some guests complained. Worse yet, it substantially reduced our profits; we had to pay for those motel rooms, and the people we sent to them spent less time in our casino, which defeated the purpose of our promotions.

So Bob built a new hotel tower with 24 rooms on each of its 22 floors. Shortly before the tower opened, Bob and I toured the structure. He noticed that each floor had a small room, oddly shaped, that was about the size of three or four typical bathrooms.

He asked, "What will this room be used for?"

"It will be a storage room for the maids."

Bob mused, "It's a shame it's not bit bigger. We need every room we can get."

I then said, "Bob, I think we can make this a regular room. Well, not exactly a regular room, but one we can use for guests."

"Why would guests accept such a small space?"

"Most won't. But if we make it special, a few people will love it."

"Are you serious? There's barely enough room for a bed. How can we make it special?"

"A round bed will fit easily. If we add mirrors on the ceilings and walls, we can make it our 'Naughty Room' or 'Love Nest.' Some people are tired of the same old blah hotel rooms. They'd love to have their own little playroom."

Bob slowly nodded his head and said, "Maybe, you're right." He checked the feasibility with his builder. Shortly thereafter, we had 22 more rooms than originally planned.

Two Small Lessons from One Little Room   43

This idea came to me because I again refused to think inside the box and applied a specific marketing principle: We didn't need to make everybody happy; we just had to please a small percentage of our customers. We needed to have only about one out of every twenty customers like this room more than a normal one. This principle is somewhat similar to choosing that fifth gift we just discussed.

Anyway, we made these rooms so nice and unique that even I would have been happy to stay in one with a woman who also liked it. Unfortunately, the front desk screwed up. Some people liked them, but most didn't. Instead of seeing that the rooms went only to those who liked them, the front desk kept them aside until they ran out of regular rooms. Then they put people into those tiny rooms, and many of them complained.

Upon hearing their complaints, I investigated and found out how inefficiently the front desk was using these rooms. They shouldn't be held back until all other rooms were filled. Rather, they should be offered in a way that only the people who wanted them would get them.

I told Bob, "We're not doing it right. Don't give those rooms to the last few people. Make it a special deal so that some people want them, and then give those people what they want."

Bob smiled and said, "Of course you're right." He made big posters with a gorgeous picture of the room and the words, "Ask about our Love Nest."

This new approach was a spectacular success. Since only 5 percent of the rooms were these little Love Nests and more then 5 percent of our customers wanted such a room, we solved the problem. Sometimes, we even got complaints from guests who tried to get into a Love Nest but were turned down because they were sold out.

The lesson here is that, if you have a product or item that most people won't like, but a small percentage will like a lot, make sure that those who like them get them and those who don't, don't.

The Front Desk

On busy days we normally had about ten people working at Vegas World's front desk. Each got paid about $80 per day, $400 per week. It wasn't bad for the 1980s, but it was certainly less than the strip hotels' average.

Because we used packages to fill up our hotel, we had very few check-ins or check-outs on three days every week. We had some success with making our people's days off coincide with those super-slow days, but there was no way to do it completely. As long as all our front desk employees worked a five day week, on those three days we had several of them sitting around, doing almost nothing.

Since the cost was fairly trivial, this problem might never have reached me had I not noticed all these people doing nothing most of the time. I asked their supervisor why they weren't put on a four day week. He replied, "They need five days' pay. If we cut them back to four days, most of them would be demoralized, and some would quit."

I accepted that answer, but knew that there had to be a way to avoid wasting money. We had been paying four or five employees for each for those three days, but we needed no more than two. So we were throwing away perhaps $600 a week. It wasn't a big deal in the overall picture, but if it could be fixed, why not do it?

I realized there was a simple way to save some of that money. We did not have to upset our employees by forcing them to take an extra day off. Nor did we have to waste $600 per week by paying them to sit around, doing nothing. We could make a win-win compromise by offering them an amount they would be glad to accept to take a day off.

I believed that the figure was about $40. When we were scheduling a week in advance, we would ask people, "Who wants an extra day off at half pay?" They wouldn't give up the $80 that they would get for working, but some of them would be glad to get paid $40 and have the day off. If $40 wasn't enough, we would increase the amount. If too many people wanted the day off, we would decrease it.

Obviously, my technique can be applied to far more important situations. In fact, large companies already occasionally do something similar when they need to reduce their workforce. Instead of just firing or laying off people, they offer financial inducements to encourage people to retire, resign, or reduce their hours.

I think that our whole country may soon have so many surplus workers that my method will be needed. As I am writing this (November, 11, 2009), the stock market is making a big comeback, but unemployment continues to rise. One reason is that productivity per employee has increased because companies are becoming more innovative, especially in their use of technology. Even when the economy fully recovers, America may not need to have all our able-bodied people working full time.

Until recently the unemployed consisted mainly of children, senior citizens, lazy people, and those who for some reason were unqualified to hold jobs. But robots and other technology have become so common and so useful that even healthy, motivated, younger people will not be needed to make the country run smoothly. If so, some variation of my front desk solution may be needed to reduce the resulting unrest.

The Slot Tournament

We started this book by telling you about the astonishing settlement that the four slot tournament finalists were willing to take. At first, Bob was flabbergasted by their decision. Why would they take so much less than their EV?

As time passed, he realized something that I had known for years: Average gamblers disregard and misunderstand EV, especially when serious money is involved. Don't gamblers want to take risks? Nobody forces them to play slot machines, craps, and so on. They do it because they get a kick out of it. But, when the money gets serious, they get scared. I'll have a lot more to say about attitudes toward risk later. For the moment, let's finish the story.

Because of my suggestion, the finalists threw $840,000 of EV straight into Bob's pocket. Alas, he threw it right back at them. Don't ask me why. In fact, a few hours later he was kicking himself.

Our attorney told Bob that there was a reasonable chance that the ostensible winner, the man or woman who won on the stage, would later claim that he was under some sort of duress and would ask for the full million dollars. (None of the other entrants would sue because they all would have received more than their official prize money.)

For some strange reason Bob agreed with his attorney, let the tournament go forward, and paid all four winners the original prizes. Do you realize why it was a bad decision?

Because the upside reward was much greater than the downside risk. If his attorney was right, and the winner sued and won, Bob would have paid $100,000 more: $50,000 extra to fourth, $40,000 extra to third, and $10,000 extra to second. If the attorney was wrong, he saved $840,000. Thus he was getting 8.4-

to-1 odds. And he would not lose unless three low-probability events occurred.

First, the winner had to sue. Since most people don't welsh on their deals, there was a good chance this wouldn't happen.

Second, if he did sue, he would have to prove to a judge or perhaps a jury that he was under some sort of duress. I have been told that proving duress is generally difficult, and there were three witnesses who would probably testify that this was not the case.

Third, because there was no skill involved, and slot machines' results are related to the moment the handle is pulled, he could not prove that he would have won had the tournament gone on as planned.

Whenever more than one event must occur, the probabilities of each one must be multiplied (assuming the events are independent). Even if each of these three events had a 50 percent chance of occurring (which is much higher than my estimate), we are still left with a $\frac{1}{8}$ chance of losing an extra $100,000

$$\frac{1}{8} = \left(\frac{1}{2}\right)\left(\frac{1}{2}\right)\left(\frac{1}{2}\right)$$

versus a $\frac{7}{8}$ chance of saving $840,000.

$$\frac{7}{8} = 1 - \frac{1}{8}$$

Since his upside was much larger and much more probable than his downside, he should have paid each finalist $60,000.

I Invent "Caribbean Stud"

Since Bob had made millions from and was therefore receptive to new games, I recommended introducing a table game based on poker. Back then no such animal existed, and Bob encouraged me to invent such a game by promising to provide his casino for the legally required ninety day trial period.

The game needed to simulate poker decisions, but the dealer had to play a fixed strategy. (Casino patrons would not play if they had to go against a dealer who could vary his strategy, nor would The Gaming Commission allow such a game.) In fact, that strategy had to be stated in writing right there on the table.

Wouldn't that give the good player an edge? I realized that the answer was "not necessarily." First of all, if the dealer acted last, it would help him a lot. (It's his only edge in blackjack.) More interesting was the little known fact (at the time) that divulging your strategy is no big deal if that strategy is derived from Game Theory.[7]

With these concepts in mind, it was easy to develop a simplistic five card poker game that I called "Casino Poker." It had an ante and one round of betting. Each player antes an amount of his choice before the cards are dealt, and the dealer "matches" that ante (not physically though). After looking at his five cards, the player either folds and loses his ante, or bets the "pot" (which is two antes). The dealer scoops up the antes of the folded players, calls with his qualifying hands, and folds the others. Since I wanted the dealer to call with approximately the top 50 percent of his hands (to satisfy the game theory), the rules clearly stated that the dealer would call with ace-king high or better.

---

[7] See my book, *The Theory of Poker,* Henderson, NV, Two Plus Two Publishing LLC, 1999.

If the dealer didn't call, any player who had not folded would win one ante. If the dealer called and lost, the player would win three antes. If the dealer called and won, the player lost three antes.

So what's the house's edge? The easiest way to calculate it is to assume that the player never bluffs (bets a hand worse than ace-king). It's a reasonable assumption because he gains nothing by doing so. (If the dealer will call half the time, bluffs will break even in the long run.) With that assumption,

• 50 percent of the time the player will fold and lose one ante

• 25 percent of the time the player will bet, and the dealer will fold, giving the player a profit of one ante.

• 25 percent of the time will be a wash. Both the player and the dealer will have ace-king or better, and they will break even in the long run.

This calculation is a bit inaccurate because the dealer's hand will be ace-king or better slightly more than half the time. I chose that calling criterion rather than "any pair" because I didn't want the players' optimum strategy to be the simplistic "bet every time."[8] If the dealer would fold more than half the time, the players should always bet.

Despite having a fixed and publicized strategy, the preceding explanation shows that the house's edge was a whopping 25 percent of an ante. That's way too much for a casino game. Since the house's edge is usually between 1 and 5 percent, hardly anyone would play a game with such a huge edge. In fact, it would be almost impossible for a player to win for more than a few hours, and if players almost always lost, they wouldn't play. But that huge initial edge was actually okay because it allowed me to

---

[8] Assuming that there were no exposed cards.

give back most of that 25 percent while making the game more interesting.

This was done in two ways. First, I exposed two of the dealer's cards. Thus, the player wouldn't bet small pairs if he was beaten in sight. Also, he could make profitable bluffs if he saw two "rags." Surprisingly, though, exposing those cards did not have much effect. It gave good players a few percentage points, but the house still had an enormous edge that needed to be reduced much further.

Second, I added substantial bonuses for high hands, starting with three of a kind. Bonuses were paid, even if the dealer did not have a "calling hand" of ace-king high or better. (Caribbean Stud uses the term "qualifying hand.") When everything was included, Casino Poker had about a four percent house edge.

Bob put the game on trial at Vegas World, and I set about trying to patent it. But my attorney told me that games like this could not be patented, and only the name, not the game could be protected. I believed him, and to this day he claims that his advice was accurate at the time. He says the patent rules changed shortly thereafter. The trial was a success, but because I could trademark only the name and also had a personal tragedy, I chose not to go through the arduous lengths required to get the Nevada Gaming Commission's full approval.

But that trial did not go unnoticed. A professional poker player tried and enjoyed it, and a few years later he mentioned it to his buddy who had just opened a casino in Aruba. They put in the game with a few modifications: Show only one card, pay bonuses only if the dealer qualified, and add a one dollar side bet for a progressive Royal Flush Jackpot. They then got it patented, called it Caribbean Stud, and sold the game fifteen years later for about thirty million bucks.

Oh well.[9]

---

[9] Actually, when the smoke cleared, I still indirectly made several hundred thousand dollars from my invention. It's not thirty million, but

The Chinese Restaurant

Bob had a problem. Besides bringing all these people into his admittedly mediocre hotel, his packages included one free meal per day. Not surprisingly, as our business expanded, our restaurants became overwhelmed, and we needed a new one.

At first, Bob was slow to react. Eventually, he showed me a spot that could become a restaurant. But it was fairly small, and there was no kitchen nearby. Building a kitchen would take about three months, and the kitchen would take space we needed for tables. Nevertheless, since we had no other places available, there did not seem to be any other solution.

As usual, I racked my brain, looking far outside the box, and came up with a wild idea. I wasn't sure it was legal, but it was worth investigating. The room Bob had picked for his new restaurant was at the back of the casino, and it had a door towards the back street. One block away there was a tiny, somewhat seedy, Chinese restaurant that had reasonably good food. We all know that Chinese restaurants get much of their business from take-outs, and this restaurant was probably no different. So I said, "Bob, how about having it be our kitchen?"

He looked at me like I was crazy, but I continued, "People come into our new restaurant and give the waiter their order. He walks through the door, ostensibly to the kitchen, but it's actually just a tiny room with a phone. He calls the Chinese restaurant, and they scurry over here through that back door with the meal."

Bob has had more than his share of bizarre ideas, but even he was surprised by this one. After thinking about it for a few seconds, Bob shook his head, and said, "You're nuts, David, but it just might work."

---

it ain't bad.

I had been afraid that it might be illegal, especially if customers weren't aware of what was going on, but apparently it wasn't. It took Bob about five days rather than the three months he thought it would take to do the construction, and we had ourselves a very popular and surprisingly good Chinese restaurant.

Money in the Envelope

Bob's packages typically included "$600 worth of special chips when you arrive at the casino." They were not real casino chips. They were one-time-play chips that could be used only for even money bets. You made your bet, and you were paid if you won. But whether you won or not, they took the chip. Because of the house edge, you would win slightly less than half the time. Since each chip was worth about 48 percent of its face value, we essentially gave every guest about $290 of expected value.

I came up with an idea that took advantage of many people's greed and inability to compute their EV. Instead of giving them their chips when they arrived, we would give them an envelope containing two $100 bills. Stapled to those bills would be a note saying, "Take these bills to the cashier's cage to pick up your special gambling chips."

The note did not say they could keep the cash because such wording could create problems. Without that wording, we could not be blamed if some people did not exchange the bills for chips. They would be disobeying our instructions. Still, I was sure that many people would do exactly that. Believe it or not, one-third of our guests pocketed the money. We had 10,000 guests per month, and about 3,300 of them gave us $90 each! My little idea added almost $300,000 per month to our profits.

The Bob Stupak Porter

Now I'll tell you about an idea that did not succeed, but could have worked if Bob had backed it up. Despite not succeeding, it contains important lessons (including understanding why it didn't work). Al will do most of the teaching. I'll just tell the story.

Shortly after we did those experiments with the newspaper and stool on the floor, we were discussing other, similar problems. Specifically, I wondered about little jobs involving minor clean ups or repairs. In a hotel-casino, they happen all the time and, if they aren't fixed promptly, they create a bad impression.

One of my father's more interesting lessons was that businesses should never neglect little things like burnt out letters in their signs or dirty bathrooms. Although he couldn't prove it, he adamantly believed that the negative impact on customers was worth far more than the cost to fix them promptly. When a letter in the Vegas World sign would occasionally burn out, I would alert Bob. The first time I did it, he said, "Don't worry, David, the sign company comes once a week and automatically fixes it."

"But we need to fix it right now."

"To get them to come immediately would cost an extra $500."

Remembering what my father had told me, I insisted that the effect it would have on our customers was worth more than $500.

As far as dirty bathrooms are concerned, I recently saw an interviewer ask a MacDonald's restaurant manager, "What's the most important thing you do?"

Although the interviewer and audience probably expected to hear something about their food or prices, he said, "Making sure that the bathrooms are immaculate." Obviously, they had done research before reaching this conclusion and it gave me great pride by indicating that my father's idea was proven correct. I am

54

equally confident that he was right about burnt out letters in a sign.

Unfortunately, at Vegas World those little jobs often did not get done promptly. As we saw with the newspaper and the stool, most employees ignored even obvious problems, and hardly any of them would care about a small stain on the carpet or a burned out light bulb. And, if someone did notice a little problem, he might assume that it had already been reported. Even if he filed a report, it might take days or weeks before the maids, porters, electricians, etc. got around to fixing it.

I'm not sure how luxury hotels deal with such things, but I had my own idea. We should have one person whose sole job was to walk through the casino and hotel, looking for any sort of small job that needed to be done. If possible, he would do it right then. If it required more expertise than he had, he would report it directly to maintenance, housekeeping, or other appropriate department.

We expected him to get through the entire hotel and casino every few days. He would enter nearly every hotel room, closet, hallway, and so on. The important point was that, even though his job did not require much skill, his reports should be regarded as a high priority. In fact, he was to receive deference when he tried to correct anything wrong.

For instance, if a maid was not cleaning a room properly, he could mention it to her. Essentially, he should be treated as if he were Bob Stupak. If he saw a problem and reported it, other people should deal with it and without complaining, just as if he were Bob.

I thought we would get the best results if this employee was given as much deference as possible. Bob liked the concept, and we came up with the name, "The Bob Stupak Porter." To emphasize our point, we had him wear a badge that said, "I am Bob Stupak." We sent a memo that told all our employees to treat him essentially as if he were Bob himself.

For this job we chose a young guy who seemed smarter and more ambitious than the other porters, and we gave him a small raise. He was Hispanic and had a fairly thick accent, but we didn't care. We told him to walk around looking for anything that needed cleaning or fixing. If he saw something wrong, he should immediately repair it or file a report. Also, if our special porter saw someone making a trivial mistake, he should suggest improvements. That button gave him the authority to tell people what to do.

He loved the job, and it was going exactly according to plan. It may not have been the way that a mega-casino would operate, but it worked well for us. Then one day we had a problem. We got a call from the head of the housekeeping department that the Bob Stupak Porter had told a maid she was doing something wrong. This manager was upset and insisted, "Tell the porter to call me if he has problems. If I agree with him, I'll pass it on to the maid.

When hearing of her complaint, I argued with Bob. "He is The Bob Stupak Porter. He is you. You wouldn't tell the head of housekeeping if you saw a maid doing something wrong. You'd just tell the maid what to do. For something trivial you wouldn't worry about the chain of command."

"Yes, David, that's true, but this fellow is not me, and the head of housekeeping resents the way he is reducing her power and status. So I'll have someone tell the porter that, in cases like this, he needs to tell the department manager."

A few days later the porter quit. Bob was surprised because he had been making more money than the other porters. But I understood that once he was forced to submit to the chain of command, the job was no longer satisfying.

I know that violating protocol can cause problems, but thought in this situation it should be okay. The head of housekeeping should have understood and supported the general theory behind The Bob Stupak Porter. Didn't she want the maids to do their jobs well? Perhaps Bob was afraid she would quit if she felt her authority and status were being undermined. But it's still my belief that this was a good idea, and I'm sorry that it was not implemented the way it was envisaged.

Al's Comments

The maid's boss probably wouldn't admit it, but she cared more about protecting her "turf" than about making sure that the rooms were cleaned properly. She would probably rationalize that the best way to ensure cleanliness was to work through her. But she was really saying, "I'm the boss, and nobody, especially not a porter, is going to tell my people what to do."

If she hadn't complained, some other turf-protecting bureaucrat would have done it. Her attitude is everywhere, from the highest government levels to the smallest Mom & Pop store. Egotism and bureaucracy killed David's great idea.

We Elect Dina Titus

Dina Titus was elected to the U. S. Congress in 2008, after losing an earlier Nevada gubernatorial race to Jim Gibbons. Many people feel that she may someday become our governor or a U. S. Senator. I have no reason to doubt that she is a hardworking and competent public servant who deserves her success. But she might not have attained it without me.

Let me explain. When Bob was dabbling in politics, he started a small, weekly newspaper, *The Las Vegas Bullet.* It specialized in news and commentary that were somewhat outside the mainstream. He usually wrote a column, and he sometimes let me be a guest columnist.

During an election we got a "tip." A married state assemblyman had been having an affair with a Las Vegas stripper. As the election neared, he tried to get her to leave town, but she refused. The stripper herself told us this story, and she presented evidence that made it undeniably true.

The incumbent was about 5 percent ahead of his opponent, Dina Titus, who was then a professor. Since there was only a brief period between the stripper's revelation and election day, the incumbent was a giant favorite to get re-elected if the story was not made public.

Evidently, the stripper had brought her story to several other media outlets, but they had all declined to run with it. Bob's first inclination was to do the same. But then Tom Pitaro, an attorney representing the incumbent, asked to meet with Bob. I was at that meeting. Pitaro implied that there would be negative repercussions if Bob published the story. He also argued that his client's personal life would not affect his ability to perform his assemblyman's duties and that the news would affect the votes of only the shallow thinkers.

I butted in and said, "That's not for newspapers to decide. The fact is that this information might affect enough votes to change the election. Whether these voters are or are not shallow thinkers is irrelevant. Adults who aren't crazy or criminals have the right to vote. Therefore, if we possess information that might make them change their vote, we should not suppress it."

Mr. Pitaro disliked my statement, but it had an impact on Bob. And as we saw with the shrubs as well as Nevada Power, a threat, even a veiled one, would not work with him. We went with the story, and after we broke it, the mainstream media, including television, made a big deal about it.

Dina Titus won that election and went on to become a state senator as well. Years later I had some correspondence with her, reminding her of the *Bullet* story. Of course, she knew about it, but did not know about my influence on the decision to publish it and she did not dispute that we were probably the catalyst for her victory.

Because she is talented and hard working, losing that election might not have been the end of her political career. But it's still neat to think that I may have had a major impact on her eventual success.

Building the Stratosphere Tower

Although I think the two most profitable ideas Bob got from me were "putting the money in the envelope" and Experto 21, he says my best one was pushing him to start building the Stratosphere Tower. He may be right, even though it didn't take most of my skills to come up with that recommendation.

As the years went by, Bob found it harder to sell his packages. Many lavish hotels had been built on The Strip, and his somewhat run down place just couldn't compete with them. He offered more and better perks, but it wasn't a cost-effective strategy. He could have renovated the hotel, but it would have cost tens of millions and would have been of uncertain value because the hotel was in a bad location. The heart of the Strip had moved further south, and people wanted to stay there.

But Bob thought of something better. In his travels he noticed that observation towers were always financially successful. There's the Eiffel Tower, the Toronto Tower, the one in Australia, and even the one in Moscow; so why not Las Vegas? After looking at some of his data, I realized he was almost certainly right and became a big supporter.

He got the country's best architects to design it, and he planned to build it right next to his hotel. Such an attraction would bring more people to his address and they would pay to go up to the top of the tower and patronize the tower's shops and other attractions, and some of them would gamble downstairs. The only problem was that building it would cost about $50 million.

Since Bob didn't have that much cash on hand, he decided to entice investors. He had a few ideas for attracting them that did not work out. As he was lamenting this, I realized that prospective investors were worried that the tower would never be built. Bob's slightly nutty reputation could put off serious investors.

I told him, "Bob, they're afraid you'll take their money, but not build the tower."

He was a bit offended, but could see my point. So he asked, "How can we solve that problem?"

I asked, "Bob how much of that $50 million is to build all that stuff at the top?"

"Almost all of it."

"Could we get it half way up for just a few million?"

"Sure, but what good would that do?"

"Bob, if you invest a few million to put it up half way, they would realize that you're not going to walk away. What good is half a tower? At that point there would be no problem getting the rest of the money."

"That's easy for you to say, David. But, if I sink $5 or $10 million into it, and we don't get the rest of money, I've got big problems."

"I can't tell you what to do, but it's inconceivable to me that you won't get the money if you just build that thing. People can't help seeing it 300 or 400 feet up, and they will be eager to invest."

Bob took my advice, and the rest is history. He built the tower and walked away from the project with a nice profit.[10] As I said, he credits me for that. If he wants to give me the credit, I'll take it.

---

[10] The Stratosphere Corporation later had problems because they borrowed and spent so much money to renovate and expand the hotel. But that was not Bob's original idea. I'm sure that the tower itself was always profitable.

Part Two

More Exploits, Ideas, and Advice

Introduction
by Al

You have just seen how David's creative and quirky mind solved a wide range of Bob Stupak's problems. Now let him do for you what he did for Bob. The next few chapters will teach you how to think in new, creative, and sometimes unique ways that will result in better decisions. He will even teach you how to increase your will power so that you can implement those improved decisions.

Some topics have immense implications such as stem cell research; others are trivial such as whether he should go to a burlesque show or play Frisbee. But the discussion of each topic can teach you how to think better.

You'll read biographical anecdotes that contain useful lessons from how to get a great deal on a new car to how to parallel park it perfectly, and even how to deal with an armed home invasion as David did recently. And you'll read his thoughts about dozens of other different topics including:

- Why some people who object to the Morning After Pill should stop doing so

- Why we should install parking meters to let healthy people use handicapped parking spaces

- Why background probability causes The Rookie Of The Year's "Sophomore Slump" and the FDA's approval of worthless drugs

- Why so many multiple stage projects come in behind schedule and over budget.

The next few chapters should be read in order, and you may want to return to them from time to time. After that, you can read the chapters in any order since we have deliberately mixed them up, interspersing heavy and light chapters, stories and lessons, and even a bit of humor. If a chapter looks interesting, you can jump ahead to it. If a chapter doesn't look appealing, you might just skim or skip it.

But don't be a passive reader. Whenever you see DUCY?, stop and try to figure things out for yourself. In fact, even if you don't see DUCY?, you should occasionally stop. If you're confused about what either one of us says, or you disagree with it, or you wonder how you can apply an idea, *stop and think.*

Page intentionally left blank

A Short
Lesson About Thinking

Before getting into more enjoyable and interesting stories and ideas, I have to become a bit academic for quite a few pages. I promise that the later chapters will be more fun to read and much shorter. Despite the originality and ingenuity of some of my ideas, they would not exist without certain fundamentals. If you know these fundamentals, you can skim this chapter. Otherwise, read it carefully.

You have just seen how combining creativity, logic, probability, and psychology enabled me to help Bob Stupak solve a wide variety of problems. Here is a tiny primer on those subjects.

Creativity

From age six to ten my father made sure that almost every dinner included a short lesson, often in puzzle form. One of those early lessons involved the nine dots shown here.

Your task is to connect those nine dots with four continuous straight lines. You cannot lift your pencil off the paper. Before turning the page, try to do this puzzle.

Answer:

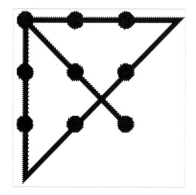

I'm guessing that you did not solve this famous puzzle. Now that you see the solution, it should be obvious what stopped you. You assumed that your lines had to be within that square. But, I never said that you had to stay within it. You simply assumed it, and that assumption constrained your thinking. As you read this book, you will see that many of my ideas, including some you have already read in "My Years With Bog Stupak," are similar. You have to think "outside the box."[11]

Here's a similar puzzle. You've just gotten a big hint, so your chances of solving it should have increased. With six toothpicks, form four equilateral triangles with the sides of each triangle being the length of the toothpick. Again, think about it for a while before turning the page.

---

[11] I believe the saying "outside the box" comes from this exact puzzle. The saying used to be "outside the lines" and it somehow changed recently into what it is today.

Answer:

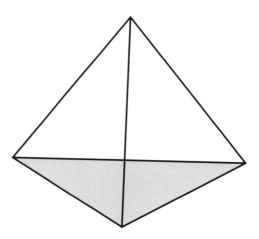

Did you get it? If you didn't, you probably thought that all the triangles had to be on the same plane. As you can see, to solve this puzzle you again had to think outside the box. Don't assume that you are constrained by rules that don't exist.

Here's one more. You have a life-threatening disease that requires two different pills a day, both taken at noon, to keep you alive. Miss a dose or take two doses at once, and you're dead.

Unfortunately, the two pills look identical. You have them separated into two different vials labeled A and B.

You have five of each pill left and will not be able to replace them for five days. In other words, if you lose one, you're dead.

One day you get careless. Instead of taking one at a time, you shake pill A into your hand and then shake two pill Bs into the same hand by mistake. How can you guarantee survival even though you can't differentiate between the pills in your hand?

Answer: Cut the three pills in half. Take one of each of those halves. Cut one of the four pills in Vial A, and take that as well. Do the same the next day.

Again, you had to think outside the box. If you did not get it, you probably did not consider the possibility of cutting the pills in half. So our lesson from these puzzles is quite simple: *Don't restrict your thinking by assuming you have to stay inside boxes you have mentally created.*

Logic

Now we will switch gears. Some people actually claim that they think outside the box as an excuse to think illogically. But you should never think illogically. Creative thinking does not mean you disobey logic's rules.

So let's discuss some of those rules and the ways that people violate them. The two biggest and most common types of illogical thinking are called *affirming the consequent* and *denying the antecedent*. They sound complicated, but they're not.

About 2,400 years ago, Aristotle invented a simple type of thinking sequence called a "syllogism." It had three lines. The first and second lines said something that you should assume was true. The third line gave a conclusion that was supposedly based on the first two lines. For instance:

1.   All men are mortal.
2.   Socrates is a man.
3.   Therefore, Socrates is mortal.

This syllogism obviously ends with a valid conclusion. But you must realize that valid conclusions can be deduced even if the assumptions are untrue. If you changed "mortal" to "wealthy" and "Socrates" to "Sue," the conclusion, "Sue is wealthy" is valid, even if it's not true. The conclusion is valid because it's consistent with the first two lines, but it may not be true because the assumptions may not be true.

(Before going further, please note that I could have changed the first line to, "If you are a man, then you are mortal" and it would have had the same meaning. The word "all" and the words, "if … then," are essentially the same when dealing with syllogisms.)

Let's take another example.

1. If someone never eats sweets, he will live to be 100.
2. Steven lived to be 100.
3. Therefore, Steven never ate sweets.

Is our conclusion valid? The answer is a resounding "No!" If you think it is, you have committed the fallacy of "affirming the consequent." Just because X implies Y does not mean that Y implies X.

Think about it for a while. There are many examples in real life. "If Judy uses heroin, then she sometimes uses marijuana," does not imply that "if Judy sometimes uses marijuana, then she uses heroin." She may use heroin, but you can't conclude it from the premises.

Here's another one:

1. All those who don't eat sweets live to be 100.
2. Marie does eat sweets.
3. Therefore, she won't make it to 100.

Is this valid? Nope. If you thought so, you committed the crime of "denying the antecedent." You can't say that, if X implies Y, then "not X" implies "not Y."

What about this one?

1. Those who don't eat sweets live to be 100?
2. Roxanne did not live to 100.
3. Therefore Roxanne did eat sweets.

Is this a valid conclusion? Yes. Think about it. The technical term for this restatement of the syllogism is the *contrapositive*.

The contrapositive is always valid. If X always implies Y, then not Y always implies not X.

There is a lot more to logic than what I just wrote. But almost all of it can be manipulated into the form of Aristotelean syllogisms, these two fallacies, and the valid contrapositive. It really is fairly simple which is why my father knew he could explain it to me over the dinner table when I was 7 or 8.

Gut Reactions

My father also opened my mind to other thinking processes which were sharpened by my experiences as a gambler, especially a poker player. Perhaps gambling's most important lesson is: *Don't trust you gut reactions.* I've seen many intelligent people make terrible mistakes because they relied too much on their gut reactions instead of doing the calculations and observing the facts.

Even Aristotle made that mistake. Despite his invention of syllogisms, I'm not one of his bigger fans. He set back our understanding of gravity for centuries by proclaiming things to be true that weren't. Worse yet, he could have come up with the right answers if he had been willing to do a few experiments or to think more creatively and thoroughly. His most notorious error was saying that heavy objects fall faster than lighter ones.

Not only was he too lazy to do a simple experiment that would disprove that common sense idea, he didn't think of a thought experiment that would have accomplished the same thing. Take two rocks and attach them with a string. You would then have an object that weighs twice as much, but it obviously falls at the same speed as it did before. We will discuss gut reactions in greater detail in "Trust Your Instincts?" starting on page 84.

Probability

I won't attempt to seriously teach you even elementary probability. If you want to learn that subject, the best place to start would be the first seven chapters of my book, *Getting The Best Of It*. But I do need to give you a little introduction because one of the biggest and most common decision-making mistakes is not taking probability into account. If you don't properly evaluate probabilities, you often can't make a good decision.

Probability is measured by a fraction between 0 and 1. A zero probability means that something is impossible. A probability of one means something is certain to happen. A probability of one-half means something is as likely to happen as not to happen. If you flip a fair coin, the probability you will get a head is one-half. You can also use decimals or percentages and it's more common to use percentages or the term "out of." If I throw one die, the probability that it would be a four is $\frac{1}{6}$ or 1 out of 6, or .167 or 16.7 percent. Use whichever works best for you.

The general probability principle is to make a fraction by putting the number of successful outcomes over the total number of possible outcomes. For instance, what is the probability of being dealt the five of spades if you are dealt one card? The answer is obviously $\frac{1}{52}$. What about the probability of being dealt any five? Hopefully, you will see that it's $\frac{4}{52}$. When you use fractions, you can simplify them by reducing them to the lowest terms. So you could change $\frac{4}{52}$ to $\frac{1}{13}$.

What is the probability of getting a red number on a roulette wheel? If you play roulette, you know that the answer is 18 out of 38. There are 18 red, 18 black, and 2 green numbers. However, to do this kind of problem without any additional calculations, each possible outcome must be equally likely. An unbiased roulette wheel satisfies this condition. We can therefore say that the probability of getting a red number is 18 out of 38 because we can assume that each of these numbers will come up as often as any other one. But, if the wheel is biased in some way, we can no longer conclude that 18 out of 38 is correct.

Here is another example. What is the probability of throwing a total of three with two dice? You cannot simply say that there are 11 different possible totals from 2 to 12 and that the chances of throwing a three is 1 out of 11 because three is one of those possibilities. DUCY?

You can't do it because certain totals don't come up equally often. Certain totals are easier to hit than three, while others are harder. You can make a three only two ways: 1 & 2 and 2 & 1. You can make a seven six ways: 6 &1, 1 & 6, 5 & 2, 2 & 5, 4 &3, and 3 & 4. You can make a two or a twelve only one way (1 & 1 and 6 & 6). Other numbers can be made in three to five ways.

Probability problems become tougher when they involve more than one event. For instance, if you win only if both of two events occur, you have to calculate each event's probability, and then multiply those probabilities. If you want to know the probability that the two cards you deal me will both be aces, you have to do a little math. You would multiply $\frac{4}{52}$ times $\frac{3}{51}$. Some people may think you just multiply $\frac{4}{52}$ times $\frac{4}{52}$. Many probabilities problems are like that, but not this one. The second probability changes a bit since the second card comes from a deck with one less ace.

The other type of probability problem involving more then one event requires adding rather then multiplying. It happens when you need one event to occur, but don't require both. If at the start of the season the Yankees have a 10 percent chance and the Dodgers have a 5 percent of winning the World Series, the probability that one of them will win is 15 percent. Sometimes it's a little bit trickier, but I'm not going to go into that here. I just want you to get a very simple feel for what mathematicians do when solving probability problems.

One reason to have some feel for probability is related to a very important concept called "mathematical expectation" which is often called "expected value." Many people, especially gamblers, call it "EV."

EV is the amount of money that you will win or lose on average per bet. One way to calculate your EV is to multiply each of your possible results times the probability of each result and then add up all those individual products. Let's say there is a 10 percent chance you will win $50 or:

$$(.10)($50) = $5$$

a 20 percent chance you will win $20 or:

$$(.20)($20) = $4$$

and a 70 percent chance you will lose $5 or:

$$(.70)(- $5) = -$3.50$$

You would add $5+$4 and subtract $3.50, giving you an EV of $5.50.

$$$5.50 = $5 + $4 - $3.50$$

Notice that your chances of winning is well below 50 percent, but you still have a positive EV.

A bunch of our posters on www.twoplustwo.com renamed the EV of gambling decisions "Sklansky Bucks." So in the above example, you would theoretically be earning 5.50 Sklansky Bucks, regardless of what actually happened.

Expected value arises most frequently when you must make financial decisions about uncertain outcomes. However, it's also useful for other types of decisions if you can convert the alternatives to numerical values.

If you don't convert, you may be unable to compare two or more uncertain possibilities. But when you use EV, you convert your decision into a comparison between specific numbers, and then usually, but not always, select the alternative with the highest EV.

Here's another example. Suppose I tell you, "I will give you $120 if you take this die and roll a three." That's nice of me, but exactly how nice is it? Hopefully, you will see that I am as nice as a person who hands you a $20 bill.

That $20 was the EV of my offer. If I let you roll six times, you would have gotten (on average) my gift of $120 the one time that you rolled the three. Since it takes (on average) six times to get $120, each roll was worth an average of $20 to you. The normal way to calculate this to multiply your reward of $120 times $\frac{1}{6}$.

Let's say that, instead of being totally charitable, I said, "I'll give you $120 if you roll a three, but you have to give me $12 if you roll any other number." You have no longer gotten a certain gift in real money, but I have still given you a gift of Sklansky Bucks. We can easily determine how many Sklansky Bucks are coming your way. First, multiply your reward times its probability:

$$(\$120)\left(\frac{1}{6}\right) = \$20$$

Second, multiply your punishment times its probability:

$$(-\$12)\left(\frac{5}{6}\right) = -\$10$$

Third, subtract your expected punishment from your expected reward:

$$\$20 - \$10 = \$10$$

So this proposition gives you ten Sklansky Bucks.

Thus, you see that this proposition is still worthwhile in the long run even though you are far more likely to lose than to win. So you should do it. But should you always choose the alternative that gives you the most Sklansky Bucks?

No! Sometimes you should not. The general principle is that you should give up some EV if the higher alternative is risky, and your bankroll forces you to worry about the risk. This principle will be explained in more detail in "A Bird In The Hand Is Worth Several In The Bush," starting on page 130.

But here is a simple example. Let's say that you have a choice between two business propositions. Proposition A has a 60 percent probability of making you $2,000,000 or $1,200,000:

$$\$1,200,000 = (.60)(\$2,000,000)$$

and a 40 percent probability of costing you $1,000,000 or -$400,000 :

$$-\$400,000 = (.40)(-\$1,000,000)$$

Your EV is $800,000.

$$\$800,000 = \$1,200,000 - \$400,000$$

Proposition B has a 90 percent chance of making you $700,000 or $630,000:

$$\$630,000 = (.90)(\$700,000)$$

and a 10 percent chance of costing you $200,000 or $20,000.

$$-\$20,000 = (.10)(\$200,000)$$

Your EV is $610,000.

$$\$610,000 = \$630,000 - \$20,000$$

You probably should not choose Proposition A if your net worth is under several million dollars. You can't afford to accept the 40 percent risk of losing $1.000,000

On the other hand, sometimes you must choose an option with negative expected value. If there are only two such alternatives available, you should normally pick the one whose negative EV is closer to zero. Keep in mind though that every once in a while you might not do that because of the risk and bankroll issues mentioned earlier. (In other words, you sometimes pick the more negative EV alternative if it avoids a substantial risk.)

There are actually two different kinds of probability: those involving the nature of the event and those involving your knowledge of the event. Some mathematicians may object to this distinction, but we won't worry about them.

By "nature of the event" I mean the uncertainties inherent in the contest. By "knowledge of the event" I mean that you are not quite sure of the alternatives. For instance, you may say that John has a 20 percent probability of beating Bob because you think there is some luck involved in the competition or because you are not sure that Bob is better.

For example, suppose John and Bob decided to play a round of golf and then to run a 100 yard race. You may think that John has a 20 percent chance of winning the golf match even if you are certain that he doesn't play as well as Bob. Golf has luck in it and sometimes the better player doesn't win. But in the 100 yard dash the faster runner will virtually always win (unless they are almost equally fast). So what would you mean if you said, "John has a 20 percent chance of winning the 100 yard dash against Bob?" Your statement makes sense only if you are not sure that Bob is better.

Here's another way to look at it. Suppose they played golf and you were surprised to find out that John won by one or two strokes. Then they played again the next week. You may still think that John has only a 20 percent chance because you know them well enough to be confident that John got lucky. However, if you were surprised to learn that that John won the 100 yard dash and then they raced again the next week, you would almost certainly reverse yourself and make John the favorite. That one event was enough to change your opinion. The bottom line is that probability can emanate from the luck inherent in events or, even if luck is not a factor, from your limited knowledge.

You should realize that either type of probability can affect your decisions. You must often choose between two or more alternatives. To make the best decision, you need to know not only which is more probable, but also the risks and rewards. And then, unless your bankroll forces you to adjust, you should simply pick the one that gives you (or saves you) the most Sklansky Bucks.

When calculating probabilities, consider *all* the possible outcomes. Far too many people, in gambling and real life, don't think deeply enough. Or they dismiss unlikely possibilities even if they involve a big number. They consider only one, two, or three possibilities, when there are really four, five, or more.

Psychology

Although I took and did well in a couple of college psychology courses, this is obviously not my area of expertise. And unlike logic and probability, there are not clear cut fundamental precepts that you can quickly master. However, I still want to share with you some important tidbits that I learned from my father, poker, and classes.

You have already read that my father waved to strangers as if he knew them while we were driving. Every single one waved back because the error of ignoring someone they knew was much greater than the error of showing recognition to a stranger. My father did this to show me how to get into other people's heads.

During one of his dinnertime lessons, he told me that Leo, who weighed 300 pounds, brought enough candy for all ten people at a meeting. My father said that Leo almost certainly did this so that he wouldn't feel so bad about his unhealthy eating habits when his coworkers all joined in. He told me I would see this trait in many people, and he was certainly right.

One of his most memorable dinnertime lessons was about a dispute over grades. Even though he got the correct answer to a test problem, his math instructor marked it wrong. She claimed that he used the wrong method. He went to the head of the math department to try to get the decision reversed. After he explained his method and the instructor's, the department head said, "Sorry Irving, but the instructor's way is clearly better."

Then my father replied "I know that, sir. That's actually the way I did it. The instructor did it the other way." I have never forgotten this lesson about how bias influences people's thoughts and decisions. This book will frequently discuss ways to reduce the effects of bias.

One of the simplest examples of applying psychology to poker occurs when you're playing no-limit hold 'em and there are four of a suit on board, but no pair (or straight flush possibility). You bet with the second best possible flush and someone raises a large amount. You should probably not suspect a bluff. No matter how courageous they may be or how sure they are that you can be bullied, most players would not attempt such a daring bluff.

Only one card can give a player a cinch. If they don't hold it, there's a good chance you do. Therefore, it's probably correct to fold your second best hand. You got into your opponent's head and deduced his thoughts.

Sometimes you can deduce someone's thoughts about a third person. You often have to do it in both poker and real life. My father first introduced this idea to me over the dinner table by using a puzzle. Three men are brought into a room blindfolded and get their foreheads painted either black or white. They all know that. They also all know that all three of them are reasonably intelligent. When the blindfolds are removed, they are instructed to raise their hand if they see two black foreheads. The first guy who can figure out the color of his own forehead and explain his reasoning wins $100. All foreheads are painted white so no one raises his hand. After about fifteen seconds one of the men announces his forehead is white and explains why.

How did he do it? I won't insult you with the answer that I had little trouble with all those years ago. Think about it. If you are having trouble, the hint is to imagine what would happen if your forehead was painted black. Anyway this puzzle was one of my first introductions to how logic and psychology go hand in hand.

Intermittent reinforcement was one lesson from a psychology classroom that actually had a lot of impact on me. We'll start by contrasting it with continuous reinforcement, which means that every correct response is rewarded. If rats are rewarded with food pellets every time they press down on a bar, they quickly learn to press it. When the food stops coming, they fairly quickly stop pressing.

The pattern was very different for intermittently rewarded rats. If they sometimes were rewarded, but sometimes were not, the learning was much slower. However, when the rewards stopped coming, they kept pressing the bar for a long time. The type of intermittent conditioning affects both the speed of learning and the number of times that the rats would press when food stopped coming. For example, if every fourth press was rewarded, the learning would be slower than if every second time was rewarded. If the rewards were delivered randomly and then stopped, the rats kept pressing for very long periods.

I found this piece of information both illuminating and useful, Its application to gambling is obvious, especially to those pitiful slot machine addicts. It also explains quite nicely why many women keep on going back to their exciting, abusive, repentant boyfriends. I will let the reader come up with other examples.

Al's Comments

It isn't always easy to understand and apply some of David principles. You are so used to thinking a certain way that changing your thinking can be both difficult and uncomfortable. But it can also be immensely rewarding since you should become able to solve problems that previously appeared unsolvable.

Here's an anecdote from a tennis magazine. After trying to hit a backhand the way his coach taught him, the student says, "It doesn't feel natural."

The coach replies, "Of course, it doesn't feel natural. You're used to doing it wrong."

When first trying to think the way David recommends, you may feel just like that tennis student. You have been making various thinking mistakes for so long that they seem right and natural. Trying to think David's way can make you so uncomfortable that you revert to your old ways.

Trust Your Instincts?

Many people say that you should trust your instincts when making a decision, and it's often the worst advice possible. If you have ever seen an optical illusion, you should realize that your instincts can be inaccurate. They tell you that line A is longer than line B, but their lengths are identical. It's just one example of how your mind can play tricks on you, and I'll describe several more.

I don't have a problem with using your instincts if there is no alternative. But you often have one or more such as using a ruler with that optical illusion. Unfortunately, you must sometimes do much more to get the right answer, and not taking those extra steps can easily get you in trouble. This is truer today than ever before because some highly skilled specialists make lots of money by identifying and exploiting people's instincts, emotions, and gut feelings.

Take jury consultants. They are adept at predicting which way jurors are likely to vote based on their answers to questions and their body language during the jury selection process. These consultants wouldn't get high fees if they couldn't influence verdicts, and they are aware that many people will come to conclusions for reasons other than a purely logical analysis of the evidence. *I don't want to be one of those people. And neither should you.* If you seriously disagree with this point, there is little reason to read this book.

No one, including me, is immune to the tricks the mind can play. But some tricks are actually good. For instance, you wouldn't enjoy a movie if you actually saw thirty-two different pictures per second. And your whole world would be different if your brain did not integrate the slightly different views from your left and right eyes into one three-dimensional image. So I'm not angry with my brain for sometimes trying to fool me. I just need to be aware of this fact to protect myself when necessary.

If Aristotle had been more aware of the way his mind deceived him, he might not have jumped to the conclusion that heavier objects fall faster than lighter ones or that a body in motion will slow down of its own accord. Because he trusted his instincts and other people believed him, Aristotle messed up some parts of physics for over two thousand years. And, as already stated, his mistakes were especially shameful because he could have easily conducted experiments that would have disproved his conclusions.

If you're not publishing an opinion for the world to see, your thoughts or actions can be based on a gut reaction without your knowledge of it. For example, I recently read a study that found that human resource employees are more likely to hire a person if they just had a cold drink instead of a hot one. Surely, you would not want something like this to affect your decision. But if you were unaware of this study, it probably would.

Hence, you can't make yourself immune from this sort of reaction, but its effects can be minimized. First, just acknowledging that you may be influenced by irrational influences may temper their impact. Second, you can establish objective procedures and be willing to stick to the resulting decision (especially if it's close), even if you "feel" it's the wrong one. For instance, you can't be sure that the reason you picked Mary over Sarah isn't that Sarah was wearing a similar shirt to the one your fiancé wore when she dumped you. So if a thorough analysis of the objective information says to hire Sarah, do it.

The general technique of being aware of hidden influences and developing methods to try to dull them should probably have a name. Perhaps we can call it "Sklansky Introspection" or "SI" for short.

A good example of SI occurred in the biographical movie, *A Beautiful Mind*. John Nash, the Nobel Prize winning and schizophrenic mathematician, was beset for years by a group of imaginary friends. They were so real (to him) that he wouldn't believe the doctors who insisted they were mere delusions. Then one day, on his own (at least according to the movie), he announced to his family that these friends were "not getting any older." Therefore, even though they continued to haunt him, he knew that they were not real.

Unfortunately, incidents like this are not as rare as you might think. Even people who appear to be mentally healthy sometimes succumb to an outlandish trick of the brain. For example, some stroke victims insist that they can move the side of their body that is really paralyzed. They say that they just don't want to move it right now. Assuming that it would be wise to do so, somebody adept at SI might learn to admit that he was, in fact, paralyzed. I believe that scientists who have strokes are less likely to maintain this delusion.

This syndrome shows that your senses cannot always be trusted and that you should strive to double check them with thought. On a lighter note, here are three examples of similar syndromes and how to deal with them.

When I was kid and hit a baseball by tossing it up in the air and then swinging the bat, it always popped up. It's still not clear to me why, but, if I aimed to hit the ball squarely, my swing was an inch too low and it drove me crazy. As I got older, I shrugged my shoulders, accepted it, and aimed an inch above the center; which resulted in beautiful line drives. In a similar vein, when screwing around at a golf driving range, if I try to hit the ball, it doesn't work. But if my swing is aimed two inches behind it, I can hit some decent shots. If my goal was to become a good golfer, this shortcut would have to be abandoned. But for now, I acknowledge that my eyes and brain are playing tricks on me and adjust accordingly.

I once had an opportunity to profit from this syndrome. An acquaintance's football picks were terrible. Despite studying every aspect of the games, he won only three bets out of seven. It's not clear to me why this was the case, and it really doesn't matter. He had enough wires crossed in his brain that betting against him showed a profit, even after laying 11-to-10. Eventually, after making some money with this information, I suggested that he admit the truth to himself and turn his liability into a profitable asset by betting against himself. He just couldn't do it despite all the evidence. So please don't be like him. If you've got a destructive quirk, admit it and take corrective action.

Getting more serious again, it's important to realize that advertisers are extraordinarily skilled at manipulation. Someone out there has determined that you are more likely to buy his product if his ads have a blue background rather than a red one, or something along those lines. Luckily, almost all brands are about the same. So it's no tragedy if you are manipulated in this way.

But what if you're reading or watching an ad for a presidential candidate? The same advertising agencies that manipulate you into making bad purchasing decisions make the political ads. Wouldn't it bother you greatly if your vote was changed because one candidate was bald? or he walked on the beach just like you used to do with your father? So use some SI.

Ever since my youth, I have asked myself what my thoughts would be if the year was 1850 and my home was a southern plantation, or it was 1940 and my residence was in Germany.

Nowadays, everyone agrees that those people's thoughts about slavery or Jews were flat out wrong, period. And I totally agree. But despite this obvious truth, the vast majority of the people living in those situations believed that their thoughts were right.

They resembled the stroke victims discussed earlier. Psychological pressures pushed them into believing irrational ideas, and they didn't dispassionately try to think their way out of these beliefs. Instead, they succumbed to social pressures. My goal has been to make sure that I could never become one of those people.

Al's Comments

"Don't trust your instincts" is a dominant theme in this book and most of David's other work. Everybody wants to believe that our instincts are accurate. It's part of a larger tendency that relates to all sorts of misjudgments. While we were writing this book, David told me, "People are at the mercy of their brain's tendency to try to make them feel better about themselves and the world. Our brains go to great lengths to keep us from feeling pain."

Because David constantly analyzes his thinking and strives to be dispassionately logical, he is much less likely to yield to his brain's attempts to deceive him or to oversimplify things. Unfortunately, many people don't even try to be logical and objective.

Our desire to reduce pain often causes us to deny evidence that would make us distrust our instincts. Then, our selective memories reinforce this error. We remember the times that our gut feelings were right, but forget our mistakes.

David, like most mathematicians and scientists, distrusts his instincts and emphasizes logic because it has three great advantages over instincts (which are often called "gut feelings" or "intuition"). Logic is correctable, easily teachable, and additive.[12] These advantages are discussed below.

Advantage No. 1: Correctable. If you make a mistake, you and other people can see why it occurred because the entire process is completely visible. If your basic premise was wrong, it can be changed. If your reasoning process was faulty, you can retrace

---

[12] Schoonmaker, Alan N. *Your Worst Poker Enemy*, NY, Kensington Publishing, 2007, p. 25. My comments are based on pages 19-60 of that book. Because quoted and paraphrased materials are combined, quotation marks have been omitted.

your steps, see exactly where you went wrong, change your method, and get it right.

Because intuition is not clearly defined or visible, it's often hard to say why a mistake was made. So the same mistake can be made again and again.

Advantage No. 2: Easily teachable. The decision process is broken into a series of small, clearly defined steps that other people can learn and duplicate. It took Euclid, an exceptional genius, many years to develop geometry, but high school students learn it fairly easily and quickly. The same can be said for many other areas of our intellectual data base. They took a long time to develop, but today are easily learned and understood.

Advantage No. 3: Additive. Because logic is correctable and teachable, it's also additive. We can build upon the works of earlier people. Newton, one of history's greatest physicists, said it best: "If I have seen further than other men, it was by standing on the shoulders of giants."

Because great instincts are so rare, and our minds deceive us about our own instincts, you must work very hard to overcome their deception. Here are some ideas to be aware of:

1. **Don't assume that you have great instincts.** Unfortunately, because you want to believe it, you may think you have them but be utterly wrong.

2. **Recognize your vulnerability to expert manipulators.** Advertisers, salesmen, con artists, and politicians are extraordinarily skilled at manipulating people. If you don't know how to recognize and resist them, you can be manipulated into making self-defeating actions.

3. **Understand that political manipulation, which can have serious consequences, is everywhere.** If you read William Riker's *The Art of Political Manipulation,* Bryant Welch's *State of Confusion: Political Manipulation and the Assault on the American Mind,* Darrell Huff's *How to Lie with Statistics,* or other appropriate books, you might be shocked at how devious and effective the manipulators can be. Hopefully, you will become more able to recognize and resist them.

4. **Recognize and adjust to your limitations.** Do what David did and that losing sports bettor refused to do: See what you're doing wrong and, if you can't correct it, then adjust for it. This recommendation applies to almost everything. For example, if you tend to be too optimistic, adjust your expectations downward.

5. **Develop your ability to think logically:** Even if you have good instincts, you should work on this ability. It's extremely valuable and our educational system does not usually develop it well. Students learn how to memorize material so they can pass multiple-choice exams, but, except in engineering, mathematics, and scientific programs, they may not learn how to think logically. If you have not been trained in logic or analytic methods, ask a professor or librarian to suggest ways to develop your skills. Of course, this book also contains many suggestions.

6. **Develop and use Sklansky Introspection.** Because you are vulnerable, you must develop your defenses, and SI is an effective one. Repeatedly ask yourself, "Why am I doing this, and what am I gaining and losing by it?" Then you will be much more able to resist manipulation by other people or your own irrational desires.

7. **Develop a relationship with someone who will help you to recognize and correct your mistakes.** Because manipulators can be so skilled, and you want to trust your instincts, help from another person will occasionally be needed. Do whatever it takes to build a relationship with someone who will tell you painful truths, especially when you don't want to hear them.

8. **Train yourself so that the rational, mathematical, logical part of your mind overcomes irrational feelings.** I won't say any more except that it's this book's primary goal.

The Acceleration Effect

My years as a poker player have helped me see that we often measure our happiness irrationally. Our feelings of happiness, sadness, contentment, or well-being greatly depend on how today compares to yesterday. In other words, the difference between the two days (or even shorter periods) has more impact on how we feel than our actual situation.

We don't just compare today to yesterday. We also compare it to what we expected today to be like. If our situation is somewhat better than it was yesterday, but we expected it to be much better, we will probably be disappointed.[13]

I'd guess that this syndrome is a product of evolutionary forces. People in bad situations who manage to improve their lives slightly need the reward of a bit of happiness. If they remained miserable because their situation was still poor, they could lapse into an interminable depression.

There may be a technical term for this reaction, but I call it "The Acceleration Effect." Sometimes it's a good thing, but sometimes it's quite destructive. One negative case involves a person whose life is good. He is financially successful, has achieved most of his personal goals, and is well liked by his family and friends. It's a shame that somebody like that will feel badly because the CD he wants is sold out.

Let's take a more extreme case, billionaires who commit suicide because they used to be multi-billionaires. At least two of them did it recently. Adolf Merckle of Germany threw himself in

---

[13] There is a similar pattern which I'll call "The Neighbor Effect." Our feelings depend to some degree, not on how we are doing, but on how our lives compare to our neighbors. Some of this chapter also applies to The Neighbor Effect.

front of a train, and Thierry Magon de la Villehuchet of France slit his wrists. There may be others.

They still had more money than you or I can ever hope to have, but they had much less than they once did. They may also have felt guilt and shame for hurting other people such as their investors and family, but I believe that the Acceleration Effect was their main reason for killing themselves.

A more common example is a business or project with many ups and downs, such as selling big ticket items or playing poker. Most salesmen feel good after making a big sale, even if they remain far below their yearly quota. Conversely, they can be far above quota, but feel terrible if they lose a sale they expected to make.

Mood swings are particularly severe in poker because everybody has winning and losing days. I have little doubt that, if a machine could measure your "happiness," it would find you happier after two $100 losing days followed by a $500 winning day (net = +$300), than after two $500 winning days followed by a $400 losing day (net = +$600), even though the second situation is twice as good.

The Acceleration Effect increases our natural tendency to over-emphasize the short term, especially when things are going badly. There are at least two reasons why you should not overreact to recent setbacks. Sometimes you can't concentrate well enough on the next thing. That's bad, but it can become even worse. You may incorrectly go to great lengths to fix that last thing. For instance, if you are playing poker and you lose a pot, you may play a bad hand because you're trying to get that money back immediately.

The Acceleration Effect is a serious problem for poker players because it pushes them towards destructive strategies and tactics. Specifically, it makes them put undue emphasis on daily results. Even more specifically, they will tend to quit profitable games as small winners rather than risk going home a loser.

Conversely, if they are losing, they may stay in a bad game, hoping to get even. If they are losing heavily, they may even play wildly because it's the only way they can get even for the day. It's called "going on tilt," and it has happened countless times, frequently with disastrous results.

Of course, most pros don't make these mistakes. They grind out as many hours as they can in easier games and avoid the tougher ones. If they get far behind in an easy game, they will keep playing their solid strategies, expecting to get back only some of their losses.

Now that we have defined this effect, let's discuss ways to fight it when it harms you. As always, I think the first step is to look at yourself. Acknowledge its existence and its effects. You're not immune to it; neither am I. But I watch myself and encourage you to do so. Learn how to recognize when you're over-reacting to a small downswing.

If you are trying to accomplish something and have a temporary setback, don't dwell on it. Don't let it affect what you're doing now. That's ridiculously obvious, yet people do all sorts of dumb things for emotional reasons.

If you see that you're over-reacting, give yourself a little pep talk. If things are generally going well, remind yourself of it. If you're in a business that requires the best decisions at all times, remind yourself of that as well. If you're engaged in endeavors that depend on the power of probability, fully embrace the concept of expected value. Making a good bet is a win, even if it loses. (As our posters at www.twoplustwo.com put it, you have won Sklansky bucks.)

These tricks will reduce your natural inclination to feel the Acceleration Effect. Unfortunately, nothing can completely eliminate it. So you'll have to learn to cope with it.

Of course, when The Acceleration Effect helps you, do whatever will provide the maximum benefit. Embrace it, even if it's a little bit irrational. Some studies have shown that depressed people can't do it. They can't enjoy their little successes and victories. Obviously, I don't advocate extreme, irrational optimism even if it makes you feel good, but a little optimism can pay big dividends. So when things are going poorly, but one small thing is going well, use the Acceleration Effect to help you feel better by focusing on the good thing. You can improve your chances of doing it by having lots of irons in the fire. The more you have, the more likely that at least one of them will go well.

I'll give you two personal examples. First, I keep a diary and rate seven aspects of my life. I make columns labeled HMDBFWT: H is health; M is Matt, my son; D is dreams; B is bankroll, F is Friends and Family; W is women (when I'm single); and T is Total. At the end of every day I come up with a numerical rating of how those things went so that if one or two things are going badly, and everything else is going well, I'm still happy. That is, I try to keep a balanced perspective instead of yielding to the Acceleration Effect and focusing on the one or two things that are going badly.

Second, I take steps to overcome negative feelings. For example, if my poker session went badly, something else may give me a sense of accomplishment. It could be an attempt to break my personal best in the mile run or the study of a previously unknown subject.

Sometimes you can get a bit quirky and use the Acceleration Effect for revenge or punishment. Remember, it's the difference between expectations and reality that affects people. So you can hurt someone by creating a false expectation and then not fulfilling it.

I once did it to get revenge on a beautiful, but annoying woman. I repeatedly asked her out, and she never said, "No." She just stalled and stalled: "Maybe next week." or "Call me on Thursday."

Finally, I had enough and said, "I'll pay you $1,000 for just a date. We'll go to a great restaurant or anyplace else you like, then say 'Good night.'"

She said, "Sounds great. When?"

"I'll call you."

Of course, that call never came. So she started calling me, and I was never available.

Here's an example that you may find more acceptable. You have probably gotten emails from scam artists offering you millions from a Nigerian bank account or a lottery. If it really annoys you, string the scam artist along by pretending to be fooled. Ask for directions on how to send the money. Keep him hooked by saying that you'll do this, that, and the other thing.

Then send him an email saying, "You're an imbecile. I was never fooled." That will bother him almost as much as if you stole the same amount he was expecting to get from you. He will visualize getting and spending your money and feel that you've taken it out of his pocket.

You can also pull the opposite trick to reward others. Make someone expect a disappointment, but give her a pleasant surprise. For example, I recently lost my safe deposit box key and a woman had to drill out the lock in my presence. She recognized me and asked, "Will I see a World Series of Poker Bracelet in this box?"

"No."

Then, when she opened the box, two bracelets were right in front of her. She got a much bigger kick out of seeing them than she would have gotten if she knew they were there. I'll give you an even better example in "People As Presents" starting on page 146.

The Acceleration Effect can be either your friend or your foe. With some practice, you should learn when to use it and when to fight it.

A Short
Lesson About Will Power

Thinking well enough to make good decisions won't do you much good without enough will power to stick to resolutions. Despite not studying the subject, I am fairly sure that you can benefit from two of my insights.

First, when a person does something that he knows is foolish (eat too much, drink too much, play queen-jack offsuit under the gun), his emotions have overwhelmed his logical mind. It happens frequently because people's emotions are often stronger than their thinking minds (especially when the issue is debatable or "rationalizable").

One way to prevent this mistake is to train yourself to obey your thinking mind rather than your feelings. Some types of people have been trained to do it — astronauts, battlefield commanders, and emergency room physicians. In fact, if their minds can't control their emotions, they can't get through the demanding training. I haven't had that sort of training, but did develop a shortcut. Rather than fight my emotions, I developed a philosophy of sorts that gives me pleasure from sticking to my resolutions and pain from violating them.

I first thought of this technique many years ago after asking my friend, Jay Heimowitz, "Why didn't you enter the main event of the World Series of Poker?" Jay is an excellent player, and he has had great results in the WSOP and other tournaments.

He replied, "I always resolve to win the entry fee in side games. This year I didn't do it, so I'm not entering."

Because he can certainly afford the entry fee, I thought he should not have made that resolution. So I said, "You're such a good player that the Main Event is clearly positive EV. It seems silly to pass up the opportunity for so little reason."

He didn't deny it, but then said, " I told myself I wouldn't enter if I didn't win the entry fee, and I will not lie to myself."

That conversation helped me to realize that if you can make sticking to your resolutions more important than it's subject matter, your emotions can reinforce your commitments. If sticking to resolutions creates pride and not sticking to them causes instantaneous pain, these feelings can be just the help you need.

I practiced this technique with video games. Even though they're trivial, I wanted to improve my ability to apply this technique. So I would play a game and resolve that if my score wasn't above a certain amount, I wouldn't have dessert, go to the movies for a week, or whatever. And I stuck to it even though there was no rational basis for the resolution. It was just an exercise in sticking to resolutions.

Second, make your resolutions when you feel the urge in question. For example, if you want to give up sweets or fatty foods, resolve to give them up while you're craving them. If you do it at other times, you can easily bite off more than you can chew. Don't swear off the foods you love right after you have gorged yourself, even though that's often when people do it.

Al's Comments

As you will see, David constantly urges you to have your thoughts dominate your feelings (as least when making important decisions). There is nothing new about this position, but most people don't tell you how to do it. And a few of them simply exhort you to think, think, think!

Unfortunately, as David pointed out, your feelings are often stronger than your rational thinking abilities. If you have any doubt, just look at your own errors. Far too many of them were probably caused by letting your feelings dominate your intellect.

Harnessing emotions is a skill, and it's literally impossible to develop this skill without practice and feedback. So practice harnessing your emotions whenever possible. That's what David did with video games.

One final point: If you need to enlist willpower for an ongoing battle (as opposed to a one time decision like Jay Heimowitz's), don't be too ambitious. Start small and slowly work your way up.

Let's say that you want to lose weight, and, like most people, you have failed repeatedly. You know your favorite foods are fattening, but you just can't resist them. If you resolve to completely do without your favorite foods, you will probably cheat, become discouraged, and give up. So resolve to pass on only one of them. Then apply David's technique of being proud every time you pass it up and ashamed every time you cheat.

Then, after you have proved to yourself that you can stick to this resolution, become more ambitious. Resolve to give up another food or make a resolution about a completely different issue. If you carefully apply David's techniques and practice enough, you will increase your control over your emotions and life.

Money as Measurement

"Would you sleep with Mike Matusow to save the lives of thousands of starving African children?"[14] I'm guessing that most women would reluctantly say "Yes." This question was actually asked during a World Poker Tour tournament. A very attractive, well known female poker player was being ribbed by some of the fellows at her table. But they weren't asking about starving children. There actual question was, "Would you sleep with Mike for $5 million?"

Her answer was a resounding, "No."

I don't know whether to believe her since many women would have done it for nothing. That's a different subject that we won't pursue. I'm discussing this exchange only because Michael Binger, a Ph.D. in Physics and a rising star in poker, applied one of my techniques.

After overhearing this conversation he immediately said to her, "But wait a second. With that $5 million you could save the lives of thousands of starving African children." She didn't like being put on the spot, but she reluctantly said, "Well, now that you put it that way, I guess I would have to do it and just donate the money to save those children."

Michael was clearly using dollars as a measurement, and she was honest and courageous enough to admit the validity of that technique and change her mind. Michael converted the dollars into something she valued highly, which enabled her to see and accept the flaw in her thinking. I admire the way both of them reacted.

This story clearly illustrates how helpful it can be to assign a monetary value to the choices facing people. They would then

---

[14] Some people regard Mike as so obnoxious that they call him, "The Mouth." Personally, I enjoy his company.

become more objective, and their emotions would be less likely to steer them to decisions that contradict their own philosophy or values. When this woman was teased into answering the question ("Would you sleep with Mike for $5 million?"), she immediately went with her gut reaction. After Michael Binger helped her to see that $5 million would save lives, she realized that her first reaction contradicted her own values.

Let me add that there is nothing sacred about using money as the standard for comparing one decision to another. Money is merely the most convenient standard. I could just as easily ask how many lawns you would mow or how many fingers you would cut off to avoid something unpleasant. I'm using money because we know what it's worth and can easily compare alternatives.

Please note that I generally don't suggest how highly people should value their alternatives. That's their decision. What's important is to help people recognize the internal inconsistencies of their thoughts and actions, and using dollars helps them to make rational comparisons between their alternatives.

Here's a different kind of example. A friend spends a lot of time trying to get the cheapest air fares. He succeeds, but the time spent may not be justified. I asked him, "How much would you have to be paid to spend x hours researching air fares to find the lowest one" His answer was much higher than the hourly rate he was essentially getting for finding those fares.

It can be a useful psychological trick to think in terms of money when you or somebody else faces unpleasantness. As we discussed in "The Acceleration Effect," the human psyche does a poor job of measuring degrees of happiness or unhappiness. If you spill ketchup on your shirt, your instantaneous reaction will be almost as bad as if you get into a mild car accident even though the car accident is at least twenty times worse.

Therefore, I soften the effects of a mild irritation by putting a dollar figure on the annoyance and the time it would take to correct it. If I spill something on my shirt and can quickly replace that shirt for $50, then there is no reason to feel any worse than from losing a $50 bet. And, if the shirt can be cleaned for $3, and I can easily grab a similar one, getting severely upset is really silly. Since many of life's annoyances would go away or be fixed for a small amount of money, there is no reason to feel any worse than you would feel if you lost what it costs to fix the problem.

I have been using this technique for so many years that it comes automatically. It's particularly valuable when I am with somebody who has just had some sort of irritating event (such as losing their glasses, breaking their heel, or hearing that a store they were planning to go to is closed). I say to them, much like Michael Binger did, "You are awfully upset, but for $30 everything would be back to normal. And you're much more upset than you would be if you lost $30." Saying something like this usually calms down that person.

Let's take another example. You're a passenger when the driver is on his way to an important meeting. After getting cut off by an aggressive driver, he chases him to flip him the bird which makes him late for the meeting. I would ask him, "How much is it worth to you to express your anger? How much is it worth to get to the meeting on time?" Unless expressing his anger has a higher value, his actions are irrational. And converting the alternatives into dollars should help him to see his irrationality.

Even though there is nothing wrong with this technique, some people will have a negative gut reaction. They will think that converting issues into dollar terms seems "cold-hearted," "unfriendly," or "unfair." They may also say things like, "I won't base my decisions on money."

They are wrong at least 95 percent of the time. Perhaps I couldn't persuade you to send your child to Western Kentucky State rather than Harvard by giving you a million dollars, but it's likely I could persuade you to watch *Snow White* for the seventh time for far less then that.

Money can be used as measurement for a wide range of important subjects. Governments should use it much more than they do when making policy decisions. For example, how much money should a city spend to make sure that two of its hospitals have the most esoteric medical equipment? It's ridiculous to say, since this equipment will save lives, that the money should be no object. The amount you save by not buying the second set of equipment can be spent in ways that might save even more lives.

Many controversial issues that normally have both sides talking past each other, might be resolved if they were willing to place a monetary value on having or not having whatever they seek. Later chapters will use this method to make decisions about many different subjects.

My method can also help to compare decisions regarding uncertain events. It may seem that, if there are probabilities associated with each outcome, it's almost impossible to make good comparisons. How do you multiply a 25 percent probability times a moral principle or a highly personal choice? But, when you estimate the dollar values and probabilities of specific events, you can do it.

Let's say that you were trying to decide whether to eat at Denny's or McDonald's because of two waitresses you plan to ask out. Debbie at McDonalds is slightly cuter, and you would pay $100 to take her out, and since Judy at Denny's is not quite as cute, you assign her a value of $80.

You think there is a 50 percent chance that Debbie is working today and a 90 percent chance that Judy is also at work. (Let's assume that both will accept your offer.) We have now reduced this decision to a gambling problem, and your EV of $72 for Judy clearly trumps the EV of $50 for Debbie. So you go to Denny's. Anyway, I hope you see that this method can not only help you get a date, but can also help achieve world peace. DUCY?

Guarding
Against Silly Feelings

The Bicycle Club poker room used to have people going to each table to sell lottery tickets. You paid a dollar and then scratched off the covering over numbers to see if you won. You could be an instant winner of as much as $10,000. The tickets' actual EV was only about $0.50. A player at my table bought several. Just before he started to scratch one off, I said, "Don't do it. Here's $3 for it."

He shook his head, frowned, and said, "No way."

Then I offered him $5. He still wouldn't take it. He knew that I would scratch it off in front of him, and he couldn't bear the thought the ticket might be a big winner while he was watching me. Even though I offered him ten times his EV and an immediate profit of five times his investment, his fear of feeling badly made him reject my offer.

About 25 years ago, while showing a pretty girl around Circus, Circus, I almost yielded to a similar feeling. Just to show her how things worked, I bought a keno ticket. In those days you had to cash your keno ticket within twenty minutes.

The ticket cost seventy cents, and the big prize was $25,000. I bought the ticket, we walked around to see some other things, and then left. When we were about 200 yards away, my thoughts were, "Oh, my God, I didn't check to see if this keno ticket was a winner. We have to go back."

My next reaction was, "What's wrong with me? Of course, we shouldn't go back. This ticket's EV is about fifty cents. How much would someone have to pay me to walk back to the casino? Probably $10." So we kept walking.

This story shows that I sometimes have the same silly feelings as other people. I'm not a robot, and our bodies and minds are hard-wired to have these feelings even though I've just trained myself to fight them. Many professional gamblers, mathematicians, scientists, paramedics and pilots have done the same thing. We train ourselves to have the rational, mathematical, logical parts of our minds overcome irrational feelings.

I constantly examine myself to see whether my thoughts and actions are irrational. If so, I usually force myself to act rationally. It's okay to factor feelings into your decisions, but do it consciously, and make sure that there is a rational relationship between the amount you allow for feelings and your objective gain or loss. Try to put a number on your feelings. Otherwise, you can't make objective comparisons between your alternatives. If you suspect that feelings are making you act irrationally, *stop and think!*

A Little Creative Thinking

On a Friday night several years ago every poker table in the Bellagio was full with a waiting list. I was playing $200 - $400, which was then the biggest game in the room. In walked a bunch of high rollers, all friends of mine, but not usually competitors. They looked around, hoping to start a huge game, but were told that no table was available.

My friends were not used to being turned away. They were $2,000 - $4,000 players and they did not mind greasing palms or whatever else it took to get their game started quickly. They wanted to start playing so that hundreds of thousands of dollars could change hands. Because there was no table, they were planning to go to a different casino.

When they were preparing to leave, I walked over to Chip Reese and asked, "Chip, what are you doing? Think! You're not thinking."

Since Chip was one of the world's greatest players, hardly anyone told him that he wasn't thinking, but he was smart enough to listen to me. He replied, "What can I do? Every table is full. I know they're small players, but I can't tell them to quit."

"Of course not. Don't tell them to quit. But don't you think that if you go up to a $1 to $4 game and give every player a $100 bill, they will gladly quit?"

He immediately realized that it was a simple and good idea. He got $100 from everyone in his group. Ten minutes later they were playing $2,000 - $4,000, while the $1 to $4 players had smiles on their faces.

A similar incident occurred when I was playing $100 - $200 hold 'em. The first name on the waiting list was a truly terrible player with lots of money. Everyone in the game was a good, solid player, and we were all licking our chops about the money we would take from this fish. In cases like this management will occasionally add another chair, but this time they wouldn't do it.

So we were pushing chips back and forth, waiting for someone to quit. We slowly realized that nobody would quit because we all wanted a piece of the twenty or thirty thousand dollars he would probably lose. But if he didn't get into the game quickly, our target player would leave.

So I piped up, "Let's have an auction!"

"An auction? What kind of auction?"

"I'll quit if each of you gives me 800 bucks."

And then, of course, they realized that somebody would say, "Well, I'll take $750." And someone else would probably say, "I'll take $720 per person."

When the smoke cleared, one player took something like $300 from everybody else. He walked away with over $2,000 in his pocket, the live one got in the game, and lost his $20,000. So again we were all happy.

What both these stories have in common is that you have to free your mind up from the shackles of routine thinking. It's the same process you had to follow in those puzzles I gave you earlier. Don't constrain your thinking. Once you free your mind, the solution can become quite obvious.

Al's Comments

As we will say in "Even a Kid Can Recognize Fallacies" starting on page 180, children can often see things more clearly than adults because they have not yet developed what David calls "the shackles of routine thinking." That is David is less constrained than most people, and his thinking often has childlike, unshackled characteristics.

We are used to thinking in a certain way, feel comfortable about it, and recognize its limitations only when we are forced to do so. For example, you have certainly become annoyed for not thinking of something that seemed so obvious after seeing someone else think correctly. You angrily asked yourself, "How could I be so stupid? or "Why didn't I see that?"

Unfortunately, you may not ask those questions until it's too late, or may ask them rhetorically, but not really try to answer them. To protect your ego, you may not even want to know why your thinking is weak.

Motivation is critically important. The desire to think well needs to be stronger than the desire to be comfortable. You will have to work, and some of that work will be uncomfortable.

We don't usually recognize our shackles. If we did, they would be easier to break. The first step is to identify your personal constraints, and that step can be quite painful. But it can also be worth it. David frequently states that he examines his own thinking, and you should follow his example. Self-examination is always valuable, but it's particularly useful when you need to think creatively. Take a hard look at your own thinking and ask yourself, "When do I act on autopilot?"

If you seriously try to answer this question, you will likely see that you often do it, and that it probably occurs in certain kinds of situations. Then ask yourself the next question: "Why do I do it here, but not there?" You may find that you essentially stop thinking when encountering situations that are:

- So commonplace that you just act habitually

- So emotionally troubling that you don't want to think about them

- So outside your control that you believe that there is no value to thinking about them

There are almost certainly other factors that prevent creative thinking. The more deeply you analyze your thinking, the better your chances of moving away from a routine approach, and the more you will be able to break out of the box they create.

Background Probability

This is an important chapter, especially if your decisions are partially based on statistics. It will show you why statistical evidence can't always be trusted. The general principle is: If the background probability or statistics are a lot different from your specific results, you should be suspicious of those results.[15] For instance, if your records show that you're winning an average of $100 per hour in a $10 - $20 casino poker game, don't assume that your win rate will stay at that level.

Even if your data, that is, your standard deviation indicates that you can be confident your win rate is at least $60 an hour, this should still be seriously questioned. Since you know that the world's best players win only $40 per hour at those stakes, that extra piece of information essentially trumps your statistical analysis. There are innumerable examples of this syndrome. Let's look at a few.

There's a myth that when you cash out on an Internet poker site, that site will start giving you worse then random cards. Thousands of players swear that they did well, cashed out, and then did much worse, and the number of players who continue to do well after their first cash out is much smaller.

In baseball there is something called the "sophomore slump." The Rookie of the Year almost always does worse his second year. The "slump" is often attributed to psychological factors, such as pressure, excessive expectations, or whatever, when it should probably be attributed to background probability.

Possibly the most important examples of the need to consider background probability are clinical trials of drugs, food, vitamins, and so on. Again and again reports have been made about benefits

---

[15] Those mathematically inclined will recognize that I'm talking about Bayes Theorem.

that had to be retracted when more evidence became available. Vitamin C, Vitamin E, Selenium and even fiber have turned out to be much less beneficial than was originally thought. How can this be? Weren't all of them tested thoroughly? Didn't they all meet the clinical trial's criteria for being called "efficacious?" Yes, they did, but again background probability was not considered.

The next example will clarify what you just read. Suppose a local radio station holds a foul-shooting contest, using a basket which is two inches smaller in diameter than usual. Whoever hits the best out of twenty wins a nice prize. If you had been a pretty good high school basketball player, you might decide to practice at this special basket to see whether you should enter the contest. You still have your touch and make 75 out of 100. The general statistical equations indicate that your results point to you having over a 90 percent chance of hitting two-thirds of your shots. Without any other information, it's a reasonable conclusion.

The problem is that you were only a 68 percent free throw shooter with a normal basket! This conflicting information should raise doubts. Perhaps you improved your abilities since high school, or the smaller basket may have made you shoot better. Those explanations are unlikely, but you can't totally eliminate them. Still, it's more likely that you just got lucky. Background probabilities and logic should steer you seriously in that direction despite the statistical analysis. With these thoughts in mind, let's examine the previous examples more thoroughly.

The batting average of most second year major league baseball players is likely to be as good or better than their first year results. That's just common sense. But, even though most players hit better their second year, you can bet that the average of the rookie with the highest batting average will drop. Why should he be an exception to the general principle? Shouldn't he get better, just like everyone else? Actually, he does get "better," even though his batting average usually gets worse. This contradiction can be explained by saying that he probably got lucky his first year.

Why do I say that? A batting average is mainly skill, but 30 or 40 points of it is luck. Sometimes, a batter hits the ball perfectly, but a fielder makes a great play. Sometimes he hits badly, but the ball luckily goes into the right spot for a hit. The Rookie of the Year was probably at the upper end of his luck and can be expected to regress to average luck the following year. So even though his skills improve, his batting average will probably go down.

For example, suppose he rated to hit .280, got lucky, and hit .320. The next year he improved and rated to hit .295. That means his sophomore average will probably be close to .295, significantly below his rookie average.

Because luck plays a more obvious role in poker, it's usually easier to see this principle than in baseball. If the first time you played online, you won half your pots, there is no reason to believe that you will continue to win so many.

The "jinx" against those who cash out is basically the same principle. If someone plays briefly and withdraws his money, he probably was lucky and quickly won enough money that he wanted to take some of it. But we must remember that most first time online players are losers. Therefore, we should not be surprised that the players who win quickly do not continue to do as well. The change in their results has nothing to do with their cashing out.

They picked a time to cash out and then compared their before and after results. But I could just have easily said that most first time players will lose after they eat a shrimp cocktail. Of course, there is no relationship between what you eat and how much you win. And it's true that even a short-term winner has some evidence that he is a winning player. But that evidence is not enough to overcome the background probability that most new online players lose. So he should expect to do worse after his first cash out. The fancy name for this pattern is "Regression to the Mean."

Background probability is more important in clinical trials of drugs. A drug is regarded as worthwhile if the trial's result indicate that there is less then a 5 percent chance that a placebo could have gotten the same results. That is, if the drug's positive results would occur only one-twentieth of the time with a placebo, the test is regarded as successful.

Here's the problem. Thousands of drugs are tested. Let's say that, as a background probability, 1 in 100 is eventually successful. If we clinically test a thousand drugs, about sixty of them will meet the statistical standards: The ten drugs that deserve it and the fifty drugs that were lucky. (Although the ten good drugs probably had stronger results than most of the fifty lucky ones, they are all deemed effective.)

Buying a New Car

You might enjoy hearing how I sometimes go to a bit of trouble to get a great price on a new car (plus this story contains a greater lesson). Don't think you can determine a dealer's rock-bottom price simply by using the Internet or consulting reference books. That research can produce valuable information such as the dealer's normal costs and profit margin, but you still won't know whether a particular dealer will accept an even lower price (or how to drive him to it).

He may be getting a rebate you don't know about. He may be desperate enough to accept a small profit or even a loss. Conversely, the car may be such a hot seller that he won't accept anything but a large profit.

Since this information is not known, how can you be sure that you're getting the best deal? I'll tell you my approach, not just to save you hundreds or even thousands on your next car, but to illustrate a general principle that I also cover in other chapters.

First, find two independent dealers who directly compete with each other to sell virtually identical cars. The closer their locations and the more intensely they compete, the better. To make things simple, I'll call them "Joe's Buick" and "Harry's Buick."

Second, you need some *chutzpah.*

Third, you must be willing to spend some time.

A car salesman will often ask, "What do I have to do to get you to buy this car right now?" Basically, he is asking, "How much do I have to take off the sticker price to get you to stop shopping and buy instantly?"

I hope you see that if you give him a price and he immediately accepts, he almost certainly would have taken less. In fact, if he accepts it too quickly, you might recognize your mistake and decide to bargain harder or keep shopping. That's why salesmen are trained not to accept offers quickly. Even if they are delighted with it, they will often look dubious, ask for a bit more, or say, "I don't think my boss will go for it. Let me check." Then he will usually come back with a counter-offer.

If the salesman rejects your first offer, you can't be sure that he isn't bluffing. Frequently, he would accept that price, perhaps even be delighted with it, but tries for more and you may then make a higher offer. Does that ring a bell?

However, if two competing dealerships have almost exactly the same car, and you're willing to spend a few hours, I can virtually guarantee that you will get a great deal. Because I have lots of *chutzpah* and enjoy beating other people at their own game, I was willing to spend those hours.

I was at Joe's Buick, looking at a Park Avenue with a sticker price of $30,000. A salesman walked over, and we talked about the car for a few minutes. Then he asked, "What do I have to do to get you to buy it right now?"

"Well, I'll give you an absurd number. I'm sure you won't take it, but that's okay because, after you turn me down, I'm driving over to Harry's and offer a few hundred dollars more. If they turn me down, I'll come back here and offer another few hundred. So, if I can't get it from Harry's, I'll be back."

He asked, "What's your number?"

"$23,000"

He looked shocked, shook his head, and said, "Oh, come on, that's just out of the question."

My nonchalant reply was, "I thought that was the case, but you wanted a number, and that's where I'm starting. If it's really that outlandish, Harry's won't accept my offer of a few hundred dollars more. So I'll probably be back."

I then drove to Harry's, looked at the identical Park Ave, and told the salesman, "I just left Joe's place and offered $23,000 for that car."

"Well I can't blame them for turning you down, nobody will accept that price."

"I know, so I'm going to offer you $23,500.

"No way. I can't do it."

"Okay. I'll go back there and offer them $24,000. I'm going to buy this car from one of you. If they don't take $24,000, I'll come back here and offer $24,500.

When Joe's salesman heard my $24,000 offer, he realized I really was sticking to my plan. But he still said, "$24,000 is simply too low. We'd lose money and can't consider it."

"No problem, I'll probably be back."

I went back to Harry's, told them that Joe's turned down my $24,000 offer, and offered $24,500. Now both dealers knew what I was doing. They may have resented my strategy, but didn't want to lose a sale to their primary competitor.

Harry's salesman became visibly uncomfortable when he heard my $24,500 offer. He shook his head sadly, hemmed and hawed, and said, "Nope, it's just not possible."

When I went back to Joe's for the third time and offered $25,000, the salesman was clearly ambivalent. He couldn't accept my offer, but knew that if he rejected it, Harry's would probably accept my next offer. He thought for a minute and said, "I have to talk to my boss."

A few minutes later he came back and said, "Look, sir, we just can't do it. But we see what you're doing and know that you're going to offer Harry's $25,500. They won't be happy, but will probably find a way to accept your offer. They will know that, if you don't make a deal at $25,500, we will let you have it for $26,000. But we just can't sell it to you for $25,000."

I believed him. If $25,000 was acceptable, they would have sold it to me because otherwise, Harry's Buick would still sell it to me for $25,500. So I said, "$25,300. Take it or gamble that I will be back later to offer you a little more."

"Make it $25,500. We'll let you buy it at the price you would have offered Harry's"

I smiled, turned away, and said, "Goodbye."

He let me take several steps to see if I was really leaving, and just as I was walking out the door, he ran after me and said "Okay, you've got a deal."

You may wonder, "Why didn't David take the $25,500 offer since he was willing to pay Harry's that much?" Well, why not try to save another $200? I wouldn't recommend being so hard-nosed with people you must relate to on a continuing basis, but buying a car is a one time thing.

You may think my principle of spending money to save time and hassles was violated. In fact, if all I did was save a few dollars, that principle would have been violated. But it was also fun to see how far I could push them, and it produced a good story to tell.

Even though they didn't want to have an "auction," I forced them to have one. And it worked out quite nicely for me. If you think outside the box, you can certainly find many other opportunities to create auctions, and they can save you lots of money.

Al's Comments

"Most people dislike negotiations, especially highly adversarial ones. ... your discomfort can cause you to avoid negotiating, settle too quickly, [or] miss the other side's signals."[16] But David proposed an elegant way to achieve the two primary bargaining tasks: learning the other party's bottom line, and then driving him to it. To scientists and mathematicians, an elegant solution to a problem is simple and precise, and that's exactly what many of David's solutions are. Instead of spending a great deal of time researching the dealers' costs, etc., he forced them to

---

[16] Schoonmaker, Alan, *Negotiate to Win: Gaining The Psychological Edge*, Englewood Cliffs, NJ, 1989, pp.viii-ix.

bid against each other, thereby driving them down to a minimum price.

Actually, in some situations (although probably not this one) you can get an even better price — lower if you're buying, higher if you're selling. People occasionally become so intent on winning the auction that they go well beyond a profitable price. The auction becomes a form of war, and winning it becomes more important to them than their economics.

Several other chapters contain auctions, and you can benefit by applying three of David's principles:

1. Whenever possible, get people to bid against each other.

2. Look for and exploit other people's irrational motives.

3. Develop enough *chutzpah* to do whatever it takes to get what you want.

Changing Their
Risk-Reward Equation

I believe that almost everyone looks out for themselves rather than for those who count on them (except for family or friends). This principle is especially true when the matter is unimportant to those who depend on them. (Maybe I'm a bit biased because so many Las Vegas politicians go to jail, usually for taking bribes involving strip clubs or zoning or other things that they feel aren't important to the public.)

The unpleasant fact is that if they expect to get away with it, most people will look out for themselves rather than for their constituents, bosses, investors, etc. who trust them. They feel that no one really cares whether they bend or break the rules a bit to favor themselves. But regardless of their reasons for acting selfishly, I try to figure out how to profit from their selfishness. Four stories illustrate how to do it.

When I originally wrote the book that is now called *The Theory of Poker*, it had a different title, *Sklansky on Poker Theory*, and was published by The Gamblers Book Club. When it stopped publishing books, it was necessary to find another publisher. So in 1981 I sent it to Prentice-Hall and it was given to a low level editor I'll call Don Harrison.

After a few weeks this person called me and rejected the book. He said that it was a little too technical and specialized for them, but thought it would be a nice book for someone else. I realized that he was making a bad decision for Prentice Hall, but thought it was a good decision for himself.

In those days poker books did not sell well. So Harrison believed that, even if it was successful, sales would be only moderate. He expected no special credit for accepting a moderately successful book. However, if it sold poorly, he could get in trouble. So it was clear that Harrison didn't care that publishing it was somewhat positive EV for Prentice Hall. Since it had very little upside, but significant downside, his personal EV was negative. So I just changed his personal "equation."

My reply was, "Okay, Mr. Harrison, if that's how you feel, I'll find another publisher. But this book has already sold thousands of copies. It's very highly regarded by advanced players, and the intermediate players are starting to buy it. I've been told that it's destined to be a classic.

"I'm sure some other publisher will take it and get good sales, and then will certainly be interviewed and asked why I changed publishers from Gambler's Book Store to Random House or whatever. I'll tell every interviewer, 'I originally went to Prentice Hall, but their editor, Don Harrison, turned me down.'"

After a five second pause Harrison said. "Let me reconsider." He did not even protest my thinly veiled threat. I didn't feel guilty about making it because the book was good and he was turning it down for personal reasons. I know that because, if Harrison really expected the book to fail, my threat would have been meaningless. Yielding so quickly indicated that he knew that the book was probably good enough to be accepted by a major publisher, turn into a good seller, and result in interviews. He originally rejected it because he did not want to take the slightest chance that it would not sell well. Prentice Hall published it for a while, and then 2+2 wound up with the rights. The rest is history.[17]

A similar incident also occurred in the 1980's when I requested a safe-deposit box in a branch of the First Interstate Bank of Nevada. It was right next to the Stardust where I played regularly. Despite writing a few books, I was still mainly a professional poker player and often carried a lot of cash.

When she heard my request, a teller said, "We rent boxes only to customers who have checking or savings accounts."

---

[17] Total sales have now surpassed 250,000, and it has been translated into six languages as of Dec. 1, 2009 with more translations on the way.

"Okay, I'll open a checking account. Here's my driver's license."

"We need a second piece of identification. Do you have a credit card or passport?"

"No, but here's a copy of my book with my picture on it."

"I'm sorry, but we need a proper piece of identification."

The branch manager, we'll call him "Todd Jones," came up and asked, "What's the problem?"

I explained what was going on and said, "This is silly. Here's my book with my picture. Here's my driver's license and $1,000. I just want to open an account to have a safe-deposit box. Surely, you should have no problem with that."

He replied, "I'm sorry, but we're not going to do it."

I said, "Is this an unbreakable rule? Are you forced to abide by it, or can you choose to break it?"

"No, I could break this rule, but choose not to."

That was his mistake. He could have easily gotten rid of me by saying he had no choice, but he wanted to show that he had power, that he wasn't just a functionary. His words opened the door for me. You may think that my response was out of line, but I don't. Mr. Jones was not looking out for his bank. He just didn't want to take even the tiniest chance that something would go wrong and that someone would see that he broke the two pieces of identification rule. He was looking out only for himself.

So I didn't mind saying, "Well, sir, you should understand that, because of my gambling books, I have become friendly with quite a few Las Vegas big shots — Steve Wynn, Bob Stupak, Jack Binion, etc. I'll tell them that even though it's obvious who I am, you decided to assert your power for no good reason and not let me have this account. Then my request to them will be to withdraw all their money from First Interstate. When they are asked why, they will say, 'Because my friend David was mistreated by Todd Jones.'"

Of course I was bluffing. I would never ask for such a big favor for such a trivial dispute, but he didn't know that. He turned white and said, "Are you threatening me?"

"No, I am just going to do what I just said. There isn't anything illegal about it, is there?"

He immediately crumbled, "Listen, I'm just a little guy. If you're who you say you are, of course, I should let you have this account. I'll just call the Stardust poker room and check your ID. If it's okay, then you can have the account." I turned his risk-reward personal equation around and got what I wanted.

Here's another way to apply these principles. When you feel that an employee is acting against your interests because he is looking out for himself rather than his organization, ask for his name. For instance, you have probably been frustrated when you called a company's customer service department. You talked to someone who is supposed to help you, but saw he wasn't really trying, just wanted to get rid of you because your call was an inconvenience, and he felt he gained nothing by helping you. If you ask, "What's your name?" their personal equation is instantly reversed.

Let's say you asked for some information. To get the right information takes his time, and he gets no reward for being right. So it's easier and safer for him to say, "I don't know," or "Contact another department." Many people, especially employees of big organizations, want to be anonymous. They don't get rewarded for doing something well, but they can be hassled or punished for violating procedures.

When someone gives you his name, you take away his anonymity and expose him to new risks. If you make a complaint, his bosses may blame him. You don't even have to threaten to complain. By breaking his anonymity, you implicitly threaten that he can be exposed and punished. You have changed his personal risk-reward equation to your benefit.

During forty years of driving, I have gotten virtually no speeding tickets, even though I have been stopped dozen of times.

The reason is that I realized that the typical cop (like Todd Jones and almost everybody else) does not want to feel like a mere cog in a wheel.

One way for him to do this is to "play God." He wants the people he stops to hope they will be given a pass. He wants them to look at him with pleading eyes and wonder, "Do I have any chance of getting his mercy?"

I'm not saying that he consciously thinks quite so nastily, but unconsciously he enjoys seeing people's desperate desire to avoid the ticket. But to get the pleasure of possessing that power, he must occasionally use it. And it stands to reason that the people who get passes are the ones who are the most obsequious to him.[18]

With this in mind, I have always been super-obsequious and try to be one of the handful of people who benefit from his desire to play God. His need to give a pass is almost as strong as my desire to get one. I've been successful almost every time. Notice that in this case, I played into his willingness to do the opposite of what he was hired to do, unlike in the other two cases, but that's not my problem.

Al's Comments

I have great difficulty visualizing David being super-obsequious. It just doesn't fit my picture of him. But it shows that if he can profit from it, he will act unnaturally.

Organizational research clearly supports David's position. Most employees are not rewarded for performing well; their bosses think they are just doing their jobs. But if they don't follow the manual and something goes wrong, they can get criticized or punished. So they naturally learn that following the manual is

---

[18] I doubt that this technique would work for extreme violations. He probably wouldn't give passes to people going 30 miles an hour over the limit.

much safer than taking chances, even if the organization would benefit.[19]

Researchers often describe this tendency as "displacement of goals." The slang term is "CYA," which means "cover your ass." Even if you think that the organization will gain by violating the standard procedures, don't do it because the bosses can punish you if you fail or even if you succeed.

David's technique changes other people's risk-reward equation so that it favors him. It also made tiny contributions to Prentice Hall and First Interstate Bank, but they were just a side effect. In the case of the speeding ticket, it actually defeated the organization's purpose, but so what? It kept him from getting the ticket.

---

[19] The fear of taking risks has caused some spectacular mistakes. For example, more than a dozen large corporations turned down the inventors of Xerography and Polaroid Cameras. One inventor started his own company, and one went to a very small company. They made billions for themselves and others. I doubt that the people who rejected them were punished.

"Irrationality" May Be Okay If Recognized

When I was fourteen years old, my dad and I took a trip to Atlantic City. In those days there weren't any casinos, but it did have the beach, Board Walk, Steel Pier, and many other attractions including a burlesque show. Since I was the usual bundle of adolescent hormones and curiosity, I begged, "Dad, *please* take me in. I really want to see that show."

He smiled indulgently and said, "Oh, come on, David, it's just skin." I thought about it for a moment and realized, "He's right." But I still wanted to see that show.

Despite being generally opposed to being irrational, I don't always fight my irrational desires, and neither should you. Just analyze situations well enough that you know what the more rational decision is. Then feel free to chose the more irrational alternative if the feelings you get from it are worth it.

Of course, you must understand and accept the consequences of doing so. I put quotation marks around "irrational" in the title because I meant irrational by most people's standards, not necessarily by yours.

Recognizing your irrationality is the critically important first step. Most people don't recognize how irrationally they are acting. They may deny it, deliberately or unconsciously. They lie to themselves or intentionally avoid or ignore information about the consequences. There is a perfect word for what they are doing, "rationalizing." If they recognized their irrationality, they would probably feel obliged to be more sensible.

Understanding and accepting the consequences of yielding to your feelings is equally important. Make sure that it isn't costing you more than you can afford financially, socially, or psychologically.

If the costs and benefits are acceptable, do it without feeling guilty. Many people just can't do it. Even if they understand and accept the consequences, they feel they are weak or immoral if they yield to an irrational desire. They may still eat that second desert, sleep late, or take a drink, but they can't fully enjoy it.

Many years later I was thinking of taking up golf and thought it would be more fun if my wife joined me. When I raised the subject, she said, "Golf is a ridiculous game. Grown men just hit a ball, one time after another, trying to get it into a little hole. Then they keep on doing that same thing over and over." Again I realized she was right, but still wanted to do it. I also felt a little sorry for her and others who feel that way because they can't enjoy golf and perhaps other pleasurable activities.

One thing I really enjoy is playing Frisbee. Of course, my enjoyment is a bit odd. The Frisbee just goes back and forth, back and forth, with only small variations. I will never make a penny from it. But so what? It's fun, and it doesn't cost me anything but my time. More importantly, I don't let recognizing my irrationality keep me from enjoyable activities.

Although it's okay to be irrational about some unimportant issues, it's wrong for important ones. Let's contrast recreational and professional poker.

If you enjoy playing poker and lose only money you can financially and psychologically afford, it's just like spending money to see a show or take a vacation. It's okay to play poker badly as long as your enjoyment is more important to you than the money you lose.[20]

However, if you quit your job and try to become a poker pro without having the abilities and doing all the necessary work, you can waste your life. I've seen hundreds of failed wannabe pros. They struggle to make a marginal living when they could do much

---

[20] This subject is thoroughly discussed in "Some Bad Bets are 'Okay'" starting on page 235.

better in another occupation. They usually play reasonably well, but don't have all the abilities or just won't work hard enough.

The bottom line is that you're not a machine. You have emotions and drives, including some foolish ones. If the costs are not too great, you should occasionally yield to them even if it seems "irrational."

I described my own irrationality to help you become more accepting of your own. It's not worthwhile to do consistency-inconsistency and cost-benefit analyses for every issue. But you should certainly do them for important decisions. My goal is to help you to understand and cope with your own irrationality and its consequences.

If you are completely rational, you may even get depressed. "Some studies have shown that depressed people appear to have a more realistic perception of their importance, reputation, locus of control, and abilities. People without depression are more likely to have inflated self-images and look at the world through 'rose-colored glasses.'"[21]

However, under no circumstance should you refuse to search for the correct or logical answer. It's okay to make irrational decisions only when you know what the rational decision is.

Furthermore, it's never correct to be irrational about how you try to attain goals. It may be illogical to want to be a great Frisbee player, yet still be okay to seek that goal, but don't be irrational in the way you try to *attain* that goal.

This idea that it's okay to be irrational can also extend past trivial things like Frisbee and golf. For instance, the sub-prime mortgage crisis is partially solvable by forgiving some of the debt of irresponsible people. Such forgiveness will benefit many others because a healthier economy should result. In spite of this, many people are opposed to helping these irresponsible borrowers.

The bailouts of the banks and the Wall Street firms may be an even better example. Again, even though this bailout probably

---

[21] http://en.wikipedia.org/wiki/Depressive_realism.

helps the man on the street, many of them are against it. They are willing to take a hit just so those $#%&* on Wall Street don't get bailed out. From a purely economic standpoint this attitude is irrational, but if you feel better with a little less in your pocket so that those fat cats suffer, that's your right. Again, all I ask is that you make this "irrational choice" with full knowledge of what it will cost you.

However, take this concept only so far. If you take it into areas of extreme importance, you are kidding yourself. I have heard many cigarette smokers say something like: "I know that cigarettes are bad for me, that they might give me lung cancer and other deadly diseases. But everybody has to die eventually, and I enjoy smoking."

It may seem they are applying the principles of this chapter, but it's nonsense. I have never heard anyone who quit smoking for years say. "I'm sorry I quit. I feel healthier and will probably live longer, but it wasn't worth it because I enjoyed smoking."

Al's Comments

Many of my friends are poker professionals, and they usually play for substantial stakes. Because they know that they can't make much money from each other, they deliberately look for games with weak players. In fact, as our friend and publisher Mason Malmuth put it, "Once you reach a certain level of competence at poker, your most important decision by far is game selection."[22]

But my friends and many other pros occasionally play in games they can't beat just for the fun of it. Most of these games take place at homes or in social clubs. The stakes are usually trivial. If you saw the way they drink, play and giggle, you would never believe that poker is their profession.

---

[22] "Selecting The Best Game," in *Poker Essays,* p. 132

Making the Best Decision

When you must choose between two alternatives, don't always take the one that is more likely to produce better results. There are three different times that you should pick the other one. Two of them are based on EV. You should always compute and compare your alternatives' EV instead of just considering the probability of being "happy." The third time we'll get to later.

Pick the less likely alternative when there is a small chance of a giant reward, and the supposedly better alternative doesn't include a decent chance for a big payout. You should also choose the "inferior" choice when the "better" one includes the possibility of a catastrophe, but the apparently inferior one doesn't.

This is all common sense, and many people already take these extreme possibilities into account when making their decisions. They sometimes choose an alternative they know is less than 50 percent to succeed. However, average people think in EV terms only when there is a possibility for an extremely good or bad result. When the possibilities are not as extreme, most people incorrectly revert to the incorrect strategy of picking the decision more likely to turn out better. (See "The 30 Percent Syndrome," starting on page 174.)

Even when there is a chance for a giant reward, some people ignore EV and choose the alternative that is more likely to turn out better. For example, in Bob Stupak's slot tourney the four finalists agreed to take $60,000 each because in three cases out of four it was more than they would win. The second, third, and fourth prizes were $50,000, $20,000 and $10,000. However, since the first prize was $1,000,000 and they had exactly the same chances to win any prize, each of them had an EV of $270,000.

Here is another gambling example. When you play blackjack, the goal is to get as close to 21 as possible without going over. The dealer is required to take cards until he has 17 or higher.

Suppose you see the dealer's hole card, know he has a total of 17, and your total is 11. You can "double down." If you do, your bet is doubled, but you can take only one card. When you know the dealer has 17, should you double down with your 11?

Most people would say, "Yes." The upside of doubling down is that you will win twice as much if you catch one of seven cards (7, 8, 9, 10, J, Q, or K). Doubling down hurts you only if you catch one of five cards (A, 2, 3, 4, or 5). If you catch a six, it's a wash. About 58 percent of the time doubling down will make you happy. Only about 42 percent of the time will it make you sad.

But this analysis misses something. You will never gain more than one bet if you double down. But not doubling will sometimes gain three bets. If you catch a small card, you can still win by catching a second small card. When it happens (about 15% of the time), your decision not to double down turns a two bet loser into a one bet winner. That's a three bet swing. Add that swing to about a 27 percent chance of saving one bet (when you don't double down and lose) and your expected value is better if you just ask for a card.

Now let's look at the third reason to choose the "inferior" alternative. Do it when that choice lets you change your mind after getting more information, but the other one doesn't. For example, during the 2008 financial crisis, Congress initially voted down the $787 billion bailout bill. A major reason, whether they admitted it or not, was that a "No" vote could be changed, but a "Yes" vote couldn't.

The stock market plunged right after that vote. The public opinion polls also shifted from "opposed" to "in favor" of the bailout. These very visible events were enough to change the minds of some who had originally voted against the bill.

Another less controversial example that I previously mentioned in my book, *Getting The Best Of It,* involved painting a room in your house. Even if you think you would prefer a darker color to a lighter alternative, you should probably check out the light color first. If you're not happy with your choice, you can easily paint over the light color, but not (I assume) the dark one.

A Bird in the Hand
is Worth Several in the Bush

Most highly successful people can postpone gratification to achieve their goals. They study and work while others are having fun. Instead of spending their money, they save it, and they reinvest their profits They may also take chances that others wouldn't.

Taking chances is not the same as postponing gratification. Instead of just delaying gratification, you may get nothing or actually lose. Are people who delay gratification or take chances doing the right thing? That's partly a matter of opinion and partly math.

For example, suppose you could choose between receiving $1 million today or having a 40 percent chance of $20 million in 10 years. I submit that, for most people, it's a close decision, even though waiting gives you an expected value of $8 million. It's close for at least seven reasons.

1. **Marginal utility:** For everyone except very wealthy people, $8 million dollars is not eight times as valuable as $1 million. The exact multiplier depends on your net worth, income, and taste for extravagant living. But I believe that most people would hesitate to flip a coin getting $8 million to $1 million odds. So I think it's fair to say that most people would consider that $8 million as being no more than three times as much as $1 million.

2. **You can't spend EV:** An EV of $8 million is not really worth that much because it's not certain. As a professional gambler, I would usually ignore this discount since my eventual profits would be the sum of my EVs. But, when the

numbers involved are much larger than the amounts usually risked, the results of this gamble would swamp all others. So even I would not base my decision on pure EV.

This principle is doubly true if the probability of winning is small. For instance, if I were offered a 1 percent chance of $1 trillion, my EV would be $10 billion. But I would gladly take a guaranteed payment of a tiny fraction of $10 billion.

3. **Compound interest:** If you invested $1 million at 7 percent, you would have about $2 million in 10 years. This one fact turns your EV of $8 million into $4 million in today's dollars.

4. **Inflation:** In ten years $8 million won't buy what it buys today. Since inflation tends to be about the same as the interest rate, you are not going to benefit as much as you think when you finally get your money (if you do). That brings your $4 million down to about $2 million.

5. **You might die:** Waiting 10 years doesn't hurt you only because of the interest rate and inflation. It also hurts because you might not be alive. If you're young, this factor shouldn't greatly affect your decision. If you're 80, taking the $1 million is obviously a slam dunk (if you can't bequeath your rights).

6. **Missing out on fun:** Most people have more fun when they are young or at least they are able to have more fun. If the $1 million will provide an enjoyable life for 10 years instead of a dreary one, take it. This point is especially true if you think that you're too old to get as much enjoyment, regardless of your bankroll, ten years from now.

7. **Future Prospects:** If you are confident that you can make good use of this million and quickly turn it into several

million, it's probably the better choice. (But you had better not be kidding yourself.)

A 40 percent chance at $20 million that might end up being zero and is ground down by marginal utility, interest, inflation, and mortality, wouldn't be enough upside to get me to refuse the million given my age, bankroll, and future prospects.

On the other hand, if you change some parameters, I would gamble. Divide all the numbers by 10, or make it a 3 year wait, or change the 40 percent to 90 percent, and I'll give you a different answer.

Al's Comments

To apply David's lesson to yourself, you need to examine your own motives, situation, and priorities (as well as understand interest rates and inflation). In more formal terms, you need to understand your own utility functions. How much do you value immediate pleasures compared to later ones? How much longer can you reasonably expect to live? How happy are you with your current life? What would you do differently if you got the money now rather than later?

Those questions may annoy you, but it's important to ask and answer them. If you don't know what you really want, you probably won't make good decisions.

Some Gambling Silliness

We've been discussing some pretty heavy subjects, so let's lighten up for a moment. But, as always, there is a lesson to be learned.

One of the sillier examples of irrational thinking occurs when gamblers decide to reduce the size of their bet. Perhaps they've been betting $100 on blackjack hands or horse races. If they decide to reduce their bet, which way should they root?

Well, some people actually hope to lose that bet. You may ask, "Why? Wouldn't they rather win their $25 bet than lose it?"

No, they will feel better if they lose because then their decision to reduce their bet seems "smarter." They have outsmarted the horses or the cards.

A similar irrational reaction occurs when horse bettors are shut out because they get to the betting window after the race has started. You'll hear them actively rooting against the horse they would have bet on. If they are serious handicappers, shouldn't they still root for that horse to win? It would verify their expertise.

I understand that it's human nature to be irrational in cases like this. But since rationality is usually critically important, I think you should fight those feelings.

Disputes Between
Principles and Pragmatism

Some arguments are easily settled because the criteria are fairly objective. Who was the better baseball player, Lou Gehrig or Moose Skowron? Should you call or fold with queen-jack off-suit under the gun? Other arguments simply cannot be settled because the criteria are too subjective. Was Elizabeth Taylor prettier than Angela Jolie?

However, some disputes involving important issues fall between these two extremes. Specifically, I speak of controversial issues with a conflict between a pragmatic and a principled argument. For instance, is it okay to torture a terrorist to find out where the next attack will occur? Those who oppose torture will argue that the overriding factor should be the principle that "this country will never torture anyone. We are better than that." (They may also point out the "practical" facts that torture is often unreliable and that torturing people could result in our own men being tortured overseas. But they say these things only to bolster their main morality argument.)

The question is: What should be done when an argument involves these two asymmetric values? Well, first recognize that you're involved in that sort of dispute. Once you do, it's usually best to abandon the technique of merely arguing the pros and cons.

Good poker players are ruthlessly pragmatic, and our standards are generally unambiguous. When we argue about the best play, the winner will be the one who demonstrates that his play has the highest EV. But you can't use that technique or anything similar (at least not directly) when the conflict is between pragmatism and principle.

134

It's a waste of time to repeat the reasons for your position without acknowledging that they are in a different category than the reasons against it. In the torture case, one side keeps saying, "We have to torture to save lives," and the other side chants, "But we are better than that." They talk past each other and accomplish nothing.

Sometimes the only sensible alternative is to agree to disagree. Acknowledge that there is no way to come to a solution that everybody will accept. On the other hand, sometimes you can successfully use the concept described in "Money As Measurement" to create a fairly objective standard of comparison. Let's look at some examples.

Bailing Out Sub-Prime Borrowers

When we were writing this book, there was a major controversy about whether the government should rescue those irresponsible people who took out mortgages they couldn't afford. They foolishly gambled that house prices would go up forever. Many of them even lied on their mortgage applications about their incomes and assets. Bankers had always demanded verification of both, but because they could make a profit by packaging and selling mortgages to Fannie Mae, Freddie Mac, and others, some bankers did not check applications carefully.

The borrowers, bankers, and many others foolishly assumed that rising prices would cover all types of stupidity. When the boom ended and prices plummeted, the borrowers couldn't avoid losing their property, and some bankers couldn't avoid bankruptcy without a government bailout.

While it was generally conceded that keeping owners in their houses was a good thing for the country, there was a big backlash against bailouts. Some of it came from economists, but the strongest objections came from simple, hard-working Americans.

They insisted that it was unfair to help the irresponsible people, while they, the responsible ones, who chose to live within their means and live in less expensive houses, got no help at all.

How do you reconcile these two competing arguments? The practical argument is that the country benefits by keeping people in their houses and preventing the banking system from collapsing. The matter of principle is that it's unfair to reward irresponsible people, while doing nothing for the responsible ones.

Believe it or not, I think there is an answer, at least as far as a specific individual is concerned: Put a dollar amount on it. Let's say that you're one of the responsible people who objected to the bailout. If I walked into your home and announced that the bailout passed congress, but also stated that you won a small lottery prize of $X, What would X have to be for the combined news to put you in a good mood?

Say X was $2,000. Once we have established that value, we can look at your practical advantage of keeping these morons in their houses. If you can be convinced that there is more than $2,000 worth of benefit, you might now be in favor of the bailout. Conversely, if you think there is only $1,000 worth of benefit, you should remain opposed.

Giving
Amnesty To Illegal Aliens

This issue is similar to the bailout. Deporting all our illegal aliens would have some negative consequences. Although there would also be certain benefits, many people agree that the overall consequences would be negative. One solution is to give an amnesty to illegal aliens. Let them stay here in the same general way as legal aliens.

This solution offends many people. And it should because it rewards illegal behavior and punishes those who have stayed in their own country patiently waiting for the opportunity to immigrate legally. So again we have a conflict between pragmatic advantages and a matter of principle. And again the solution might be attainable if we put a monetary-type number on the principle's value.

Legalizing Prostitution

On this issue there are good pragmatic and important moral principles on both sides of the argument, but I'll discuss only the principled side. Many people would argue that we should keep it illegal, even if the law is not always enforced, simply to show our children that the government thinks it's wrong. We want to give it an official stamp of disapproval.

On the other hand, there is a principled argument for legalizing it: The government has no right to tell us what to do with our own bodies. With principles on both sides, applying my money as measurement technique would be more complicated than usual. But, in theory, it still can be done.

Legalizing Drugs

This is similar to legalizing prostitution, and there are serious proposals to do it. Many people think that there would be great advantages to legalizing "street" drugs. These advantages may be so great that even some fervently anti-drug, conservative politicians think it may be a good idea.

The argument against legalizing drugs is partly practical: It may increase drug use. However, because the evidence is ambiguous, that practical argument is not strong. On the other hand, when we include the matter of principle, the issue becomes close. Do we want to take away that official stamp of disapproval?

When analyzing these types of questions, we should clearly recognize which arguments are pragmatic and which ones are principled, and then try to find some measuring rod, whether it be money or something else, to equate the principle with the practical.

Conducting Embryonic Stem Cell Research

I will discuss one aspect of this controversy in "Gay And Sibling Marriage, Stem Cell Research, and Killing Iraqi Children," starting on page 211, but it also fits here. The practical reasons to conduct this research are to help sick people and save lives. The principled argument against it is that you should not kill humans. (Of course, if you don't consider embryos to be people, you have no conflict.)

Thus, the conflict mainly concerns anti-abortionists who believe embryos are humans. For them my technique may be useful even though they may dislike using money as the measurement. No matter what measuring stick you use, saving thousands of lives may be worth more to you than the pain of destroying a few hundred embryos. If so, you're in the camp of the many pro-lifers who reluctantly accept that the research should go on.

Then again, you may think that the principle of not harming innocent lives has essentially infinite value. If so, you will stick to your guns even with my technique. (Just make sure you are not inconsistent as I explain in the chapter about stem cell research and Iraqi children.)

Gun Control Laws

There are obvious practical reasons to make it easy for people to own a hand gun. But the practical reason against gun ownership clearly overrides those reasons: The more people who own guns, the more innocent people will be shot.

Owning a gun will sometimes keep you from being shot, stabbed, robbed, and so on. But, statistically speaking, that gun is much more likely to kill or maim someone accidentally or in a domestic dispute, than against a criminal. To justify opposition to gun controls, you must invoke the principle that people "have a right to bear arms."

Obviously, this principle is not trivial. It's even ensconced in our constitution. But it's a principled, not a practical argument. (It was a practical argument 200 years ago when the government was not so well armed.) Almost certainly fewer people would die if no one could legally own a gun.

I don't have a strong opinion on this issue but do think that my technique works well here. How much would you take to give up your right to own a gun? How much would you take to allow gun deaths to increase from 1 in 50,000 to 1 in 20,000, or whatever the figures may be? Of course, everybody would answer these questions differently. But translating the issue into numbers would at least give us some basis to reach an agreement.

Giving Condoms and Vaccinations Against STD to Young Girls

You can probably see where I'm going here. It would obviously reduce gonorrhea, syphilis, AIDS, and unwanted pregnancies. But there is a cost. Again, we are taking away our stamp of disapproval. Once the government or a parent offers protection that is needed only if the child is sexually active, many children will naturally think that such behavior is acceptable or close to it. I will leave it to you to try to figure out how my measurement technique could lead to a solution.

Ethnic Profiling

Suppose we know that redheads are more likely to invade houses or bring bombs onto airplanes. Does that mean cops should be allowed to stop redheads in their cars or subject them to stricter searches at the airport? If they could, there would be fewer home invasions and plane hijackings.

But there is a very strong reason not to allow these measures. They would make redheads feel like second class citizens. So again, let's look for a way to invoke my technique. The conclusion would depend on the exact statistics. If one in a million redheads were airplane bombers and one in two million non-redheads were, our conclusions would likely be different than if the number was 1 in 50 versus 1 in 1,000.

For this issue and most others, the people who insist that principles must not be compromised can win only because the probabilities are low. At some point, practical arguments will almost always trump principles. For example:

- Most anti-gun control people would accept gun controls if ten percent of gun owners were being shot by family members.

- Most anti-condom and vaccination people would accept both if twenty percent of teenage girls were getting pregnant or infected with STD.

- Most redheads would favor being discriminated against for searches if five percent of redheads were carrying bombs. If I were a redhead, I would not like being searched, but it would bother me less than being blown to bits.

One Last Thought

I am forced to leave you with an unpleasant thought. Matters of principle are usually overrated. In most of these examples, only the fact that the decision was fairly close gave the principled position enough power to swing people's conclusion. That's just the way it is. We don't advocate profiling because even the members of the suspect ethnic groups are very unlikely to be terrorists. We prohibit torture because we are rarely sure that it would prevent a disaster. We make embryonic stem cell research illegal because we are not certain that it will help or that we won't find alternatives.

But suppose one in five people of a certain skin or hair color were known to hide bombs in their body cavities, instead of one in a million? Do you really think that the principles that argue against profiling would win out? Or suppose that AIDS was so easily transmitted that you would always get it from unprotected sex. Do you really think that the anti-condom lobby would have a chance? How about if embryonic stem cells were the only way we could cure cancer?

President Bush quickly surrendered his conservative financial principles when he was told that retaining them would result in history's worst depression. He is no different from 99 percent of us. Principles are a good thing to have and in a few rare cases they should be stuck to regardless of the consequences. Most of the time though, principles are just one factor and are often not the most important one to consider when deciding what to do.

Al's Comments

I must begin by emphatically agreeing with David that "matters of principle are usually overrated." Far too many people convert substantively minor issues into "matters of principle." The "principle" involved is often little more than stubbornness. People insist that something is a "matter of principle" because they can't stand to lose an argument over a substantively trivial issue. The "principle" is really "I must win this argument regardless of the consequences." This sort of rigidity often occurs after someone takes a position without seriously thinking about it and then refuses to reconsider because he wants to save face.

You should resist the temptation to convert disputes into "matters of principle" unless the principle is extremely important to you. Otherwise, you make it much more difficult, perhaps even impossible, to reach a mutually satisfactory compromise. While teaching negotiating skills, I often said, "Whenever I hear someone say, 'It's a matter of principle,' I expect him to act stupidly."

Once issues are seen as "matters of principle," compromise becomes difficult or impossible. Nobody wants to compromise on principles which means that stating issues as matters of principle virtually guarantees rigidity. It works against a fundamental negotiating principle: Make it easy for both sides to compromise.

Converting issues from principles to dollars makes compromise immeasurably easier. Nobody wants to compromise principles, and any concession you make on your principles seems much bigger to you than the other party's reciprocal concession. Of course, he feels the same way. But, if you express things in dollars, both parties know how much movement has occurred. A $2 concession is worth exactly twice as much as a $1 concession. When you can see how much each side has moved, it's much easier to reach a compromise.

Thinking David's way is not intellectually difficult, but it can be extremely stressful. You have to overcome your natural resistance to putting principles into dollar terms. Then, whenever you see that you or other people are talking past each other, ask the sort of question that Michael Binger asked that beautiful poker player in "Money As Measurement," "Would you sleep with Mike Matusow to save the lives of thousands of starving African children?" Note that he did not ask if she would do it for $5 million to spend on for herself. He converted dollars into saving lives which she cared about.

Whenever you or other people are talking past each other, ask yourself, "Is this one of those times that using money as measurement would improve the discussion?" If it is, think of ways to express the issue in dollars that are meaningful to both sides.

The Morning After Pill

Sometimes you can't put a dollar amount on a matter of principle. But you can still use logic and science to come up with a compromise or solution. Dispassionate, logical analysis can sometimes be made of highly emotional and controversial issues without requiring people to change their core beliefs. For example, abortion and birth control are hotly debated, and most people are in one of three camps:

1. Both abortions and artificial birth control are immoral.

2. Birth control is okay, but abortion is not.

3. Abortion is regrettable, but not immoral.

Most people who think that abortion should be illegal believe that embryos have a "soul," placed there by God. Therefore, abortion is homicide or it's at least the prevention of a specific soul's living out its life.

Many people, usually Catholics, object to artificially preventing even non-specific souls from starting life and living it out. They are therefore against condoms, IUDS, birth control pills, etc. But that is, philosophically speaking, a different can of worms, and many people who are anti-abortion are not anti-birth control. Their stance is that a yet to be determined soul need not be protected. (If you believe that God waits until an embryo is created before deciding to place a soul in it, you essentially imply that "no soul is harmed" if a sperm is artificially stopped from reaching an egg.)

This chapter is directed *only* towards those in the second camp, namely those who think that birth control is okay, but abortion isn't. I contend that, if it's okay to use birth control to

144

prevent an egg from being fertilized, then it's also okay to destroy an egg a day or two after it has been fertilized because God has not yet put a specific soul in harm's way.

If He is withholding souls until He knows for sure which embryo to place them in, it stands to reason that He would also wait to see if an embryo splits and not make His decision until that split is no longer physically possible.

I say that because for almost two weeks the fertilized egg can split, creating identical twins, triplets, etc., and this split could, at least theoretically, occur artificially. Mice, sheep, and even monkeys have been born after the embryos were split artificially, and a sufficiently skilled surgeon could most likely create human twins.

The practical implication of this chain of reasoning is that many pro-lifers should be able to accept the "morning after" pill since it works only on an egg that has been fertilized quite recently.

People as Presents

I first moved to Vegas in the early seventies. Shortly thereafter I met Sherry and lived with her for the next eight years until a tragic accident ended her life. (The personal tragedy that I mentioned in the chapter about Caribbean Stud.) We lived in Vegas for awhile and then moved to Reno to take advantage of their single deck blackjack games and to give me some quiet time to work on my first book, *Hold 'em Poker*. (I actually wrote it in long hand.)

When Sherry's birthday came up almost a year after we moved, I wracked my brain trying to think of a great present. Since I was doing well and had been generous to her, there really wasn't anything she had her heart set on that I had not already bought her. The only thing that she didn't have was the opportunity to see her family whom she had left in Vegas.

She especially missed her brother, Steven, who was about 12. My first thought was to buy her an airplane ticket to go back home. But to get more dramatic impact, I asked her parents to let her brother fly to Reno as a surprise. They gladly agreed. On her birthday I told her to look in her closet for her present. She opened the door, and out popped her little brother. She often told me it was the best present she ever got.

Many years later I repeated that surprise with someone else. Her sister was in Texas and she was in Vegas. On her birthday we walked into our living room, and there was her sister.

Again, you can see that outside the box thinking is not just for gambling or math problems. Even if you find it difficult to think this way, you now have a very specific suggestion for a gift that will have a greater impact than virtually anything you can buy.

If you can't find a relative who would make a nice gift, give *yourself* as a present. My parents and I were once invited to a wedding, but I was too busy to go. After begging off, my parents drove 800 miles to attend that wedding. But then I got some unexpected free time and jumped on a plane and showed up right before the ceremony. It really tickled my parents, the bride, and the groom because they had not expected to see me.

In that case I actually had a change of heart, but you might want to set the situation up purposely. Even though you could attend, say that you can't. It would be the flip side of the revenge I discussed in "The Acceleration Effect." There I got revenge by giving a beautiful girl hope and then taking it away. But you can also purposely take away hope and then give them something they thought they wouldn't get.

That combination has much more psychological impact than simply saying, "Yes," in advance. Tell someone you can't accept an invitation to a wedding or party or picnic, especially one that's far away. Then show up. It's just a small idea to brighten up someone else's day, but one I thought was worth sharing.

Knowing the Rules and Jargon Doesn't Make You Smart

Many people have criticized me for sticking my nose into subjects that I haven't mastered. They insist that even with my high IQ, I should not assume that my ideas will be better than the experts, the ones who have apparently mastered the intricacies. Rather than defend myself, I will attack. It's not so much that my brain lets me overcome a lack of training and experience. Instead, it's my belief that many complex subjects invite semi-dummies.

Obviously, "dummies" is an exaggeration. But many endeavors are so complex that just understanding all the "rules" makes a person look smarter than he is. Economics, derivatives trading, medical research, football coaching, and conducting wars are all good examples. Since you need to know so much "stuff" to do these things, an outsider may think that anybody who uses the jargon correctly or has a lot of credentials and experience is an expert.

Unfortunately, knowing all the rules has little to do with ingenuity. It just means that you were a good student and were willing to slog through a lot of memorization. It's admirable, but it doesn't change the fact that few good students are particularly ingenious. And to come up with original ideas you often need brilliance, frequently of the mathematical sort.

Economics is an obvious example. The news shows often bring on so-called experts. Since they almost invariably disagree with each other, they obviously can't all be real experts. They are just people who know the rules, ones who know that high interest rates stop inflation, the intricacies of the stock market, and so on. But they are not smart enough to come up with new solutions, and they would probably gain from consulting people who know fewer technicalities but can think better.

Some of the best-performing investment managers already agree with me about derivatives trading and even more complex financial machinations. They are hiring mainly physicists and mathematicians rather than finance majors. It's fairly easy to teach rules to smart people, but nearly impossible to teach rule-memorizers how to become smart.

On the other hand, just knowing all the complexities of derivatives trading requires so much memorizing that the people who do it, even if they do it badly, can become indispensable. Their bosses don't know how to do it, and they can't quickly learn. That's the reason that A.I.G. and many other financial firms were so desperate to retain people who knew the rules, despite their incredibly bad track records, that they received enormous bonuses. Smart people don't lose hundreds of billions of dollars, but A.I.G. and other financial firms insisted that they had to pay enormous salaries and bonuses to attract and retain "the best and the brightest."

I fear that medical research is primarily populated by mediocre memorizers. Of course, I respect their dedication and thoroughness, and their discoveries have certainly improved our health and lives. Since there is a lot less money in research than in private practice or trading options, the fault may lie in the selfish geniuses who do not become researchers.

Medical researchers must master an enormous body of knowledge, but they may be unable to think of original approaches. Since their minds are so "cluttered," I think that the chances of curing cancer, AIDS, and so on would be greatly increased if the research teams included mathematicians, game theorists, and generals. They might not get involved in the day to day activities, but they could propose original approaches. Meanwhile, the researchers should learn how to think more creatively by spending time doing puzzles and mastering games. People have often said that war is too important to leave to the generals. Perhaps medical research is too important to leave to only the doctors, chemists, and biologists.

As far as coaching football is concerned, I and others have previously written about all the dumb decisions coaches make because they haven't bothered to study probability. This includes not going for a first down on fourth down when only small yardage is needed and only rarely trying a fake punt or a fake field goal.

Modern wars are so complex that only masters of strategic theory should conduct them. But because there is so much to know, most generals are only moderately adept at it. They are picked to a large degree for other attributes such as personal courage. It's an essential quality for lieutenants, captains, and majors, but since generals don't risk their own lives, it's nearly irrelevant for them.

But at least some generals have a better appreciation for math and science then the general public. They probably realize, for instance, that our success in WWII was largely due to the mathematicians who broke the German and Japanese codes, and, of course, the physicists and engineers who created radar and the atomic bomb. More recently, we kept our casualties down because our engineers developed the Abrams tank and unmanned reconnaissance airplanes. Plus, I've been told that some generals use game theory.

The bottom line is that you should never confuse being knowledgeable with being smart. Just because you think you know everything about a subject, don't dismiss the advice of really smart people who may not know that subject as well as you.

Al's Comments

Shortly after David drafted this chapter, he sent me a great *New York Times* article by Nicholas Kristof, "Learning How To Think."[23] It begins, "Ever wonder how financial experts could lead the world over the economic cliff? One explanation is that so-called experts turn out to be, in many situations, a stunningly poor source of expertise. There's evidence that what matters in making a sound forecast or decision isn't so much knowledge or experience as good judgment — or, to be more precise, the way a person's mind works."

That's exactly what this chapter and book are about. We want to help you to think clearly, and one element of clear thinking is healthy skepticism about "experts."

That skepticism is necessary because, as Mr. Kristof put it, "even very smart people allow themselves to be buffaloed by an apparent 'expert' on occasion." He described a study of 82,000 predictions by 284 experts.

"The predictions of experts were, on average, only a tiny bit better than random guesses — the equivalent of a chimpanzee throwing darts at a board...

"It made virtually no difference whether participants had doctorates, whether they were economists, political scientists, journalists or historians, whether they had policy experience or access to classified information, or whether they had logged many or few years of experience...

"Indeed, the only consistent predictor was fame — and it was an inverse relationship. The more famous experts did worse than unknown ones. That had to do with a fault in the media. Talent bookers for television shows and reporters tended to

---

[23] http://www.nytimes.com/2009/03/26/opinion/26Kristof.html?ref= opinion

call up experts who provided strong, coherent points of view, who saw things in blacks and whites…

This chapter relates directly to "Trust your instincts?" Your instincts may tell you to believe the famous expert on TV. Don't trust your instincts or the experts. *Learn how to think.*

When Your Goals
Don't Coincide with Theirs

If you are betting on people, investing in them, or employing them, try to ensure that their goals are the same as yours. If there are irreconcilable conflicts, you should usually reconsider working with them or at least take this difference into account before making decisions. To clarify my idea, I'll start with some gambling examples, and then relate it to business and investments.

One common example is betting on a sporting event when the favorite is giving up many points. For example, if you take the favorite in a basketball game and give sixteen points, your goal is different from the team's. They simply want to win, but you need to win by sixteen. These conflicting goals create a major problem when your team is well ahead with a few minutes to go, but not by the full sixteen points. They will usually protect their lead by playing slowly and cautiously to run down the clock. It's the right strategy for them, but the opposite of what you want.

Conversely, if you bet on a significant underdog, taking many points, you may be winning your bet with a few minutes to go because they are only a few points behind. But they don't care about the point spread. Since they just want to win, they may take wild chances and/or repeatedly foul. So the other team gets some easy points, turning your expected win into a loss.

I'm not saying that you should never bet on a basketball or football game with a big point spread. Sometimes, despite conflicting goals, you can still find a good bet. However, most fans should probably concentrate on games with small or nonexistent point spreads.

Here's a horse racing example. If you bet on a horse to show, you win if he comes in first, second, or third. You may have discovered a horse that, if he runs his standard race, has a very good chance to come in at least third. However, if the jockey or harness driver is uninterested in coming in third, he will ride his horse in such a way that it is likely to win or finish out of the money. Thus, a show bet may be worse than it seems.

Some poker players have the same attitude about tournaments. Let's say that you can get either 100-to-1 that Phil Ivey will win a tournament or 12-to-1 that he will make the final table. Because the rewards for winning are several times as large as for making the final table, Phil (as opposed to someone with a smaller bankroll) has little incentive to sneak onto the final table. If you bet that he makes the final table, he may play in a way that conflicts with your interests. In this example a pure win bet probably has a higher EV.

Conflicts come up all the time in poker-backing contracts. If you are seriously considering backing a poker player, make a deal that does not reward him for playing a strategy that he wouldn't use if it was his own money. For example, if he gets one-third of each winning session, but you take all the losses for losing sessions, he should gamble aggressively (if he is maximizing his own self-interest). After a month or two he could be way ahead, while you could be way behind. Better deals would involve hourly pay and a graduated percentage pay scale. The specifics are beyond the scope of this book.

Many years ago, when wanting to play high stakes blackjack, I proposed an unusual deal to a potential backer. It deliberately reduced my EV to show that I understood and adjusted to his concern that I would gamble excessively, hoping to get lucky. It's thoroughly discussed in "My Caesar's Palace Blackjack Proposition," starting on page 194.

Here is one more gambling example. In the old days some pit bosses would bar dice players who aggressively risked a small amount of money and placed bets with the smallest house edges. They would either lose a little or win thousands. Obviously, in the long run these people would lose. However, for the pit boss personally it was a can't-win situation. If he let them play, he would get no reward for the few hundred dollars they usually lost. But, on the rare occasions that one of them walked away with $5,000, the pit boss could get scrutinized or criticized.

So the pit boss' risk-reward equation conflicted with the casino owner's. Since the casino grinds out a small percentage of every bet, the owner wants nobody barred. Obviously, the owner should prevent this problem by telling the pit boss that he will never criticize or punish him for allowing an honest dice player to play within the betting limits.

Now let's relate that principle to more serious situations. If you are a top executive, investor, or owner of a company, make sure that you and the people who work for you have the same risk-reward equation. That is, don't let them have incentives to make decisions that reduce your EV, but increase theirs.

Suppose you find a stock that you consider a good investment simply because its market capitalization is slightly below its book value. If you bought every share and then sold off all the company's assets, you could theoretically have a slight profit. Many people think that you must have the best of it with such a stock purchase, but they are mistaken. (They would be right if the book value was *much* greater than the market cap because a corporate raider would almost certainly buy up all the stock just to liquidate the company.)

For example, some companies are not yet earning money, and their hopes ride on an innovative product that is not quite ready to be marketed. And, when it's marketed, it may not succeed. Those companies will continue to spend their assets and go down in value until they can market a profitable product. Many smaller pharmaceutical companies are in this category. However, this is to be expected and is not related my point.

A more relevant example would be a company that has no innovative products in the pipeline, yet continues to operate at a small loss because the executives care only about keeping the company afloat to get their paychecks. They may even pass up highly positive EV, but risky opportunities. They would rather muddle along, not quite breaking even, so they can draw their salaries for several years.

Obviously, if you are the owner or stockholder, their strategy is against your interests because their risk-reward equation conflicts with yours. They won't take necessary risks because they will not benefit as much as you do if they successfully innovate. But as long as the company survives, no matter how low the stock goes, they'll get their salaries.

One way out of this dilemma is to give key employees stock (rather than options). If you give stock to key employees, their risk-reward equation is similar to yours. If the stock goes up, they profit. If it goes down, they lose, and they will do their best to keep the stock from continuing downward.[24]

On the other hand, if they are given options, they have limited downside. So you may run into the flip side of the problem described earlier. Now they may have incentives to reduce your EV and increase theirs by being *too* risky. Once the stock goes below the strike price, they get nothing. So they may take foolish risks hoping to drive the stock back above the strike price. Since many employees are given options or bonuses based on short-term performance, their interests and the owners directly conflict. They have an incentive to take more risks than prudent owners would take. If they get 10 percent of the gain and none of the loss, they should flip a coin for a million dollars even if that coin is slightly weighted against them.

That's essentially what happened recently on Wall Street, but the coin wasn't slightly weighted. It was grossly unbalanced. The compensation plans encouraged executives and traders to take crazy risks because they got enormous rewards for good moves, and paid little or nothing for mistakes. In 2007 and 2008, the executives and traders at AIG, Bear Sterns, Lehman Brothers, and so on, got bonuses of several billion dollars. But the stockholders (and then the taxpayers) lost hundreds of billions of dollars.

---

[24] The stock should be restricted so that they can't sell it immediately.

Selling and Seduction

When I was young, I briefly sold encyclopedias door to door. It wasn't my kind of job, but the sales manager did teach me an important lesson that I sometimes use in other areas. He taught me that, after someone answered the door, to stick out my hand and say, "Hello, my name is David." When he took my hand, I should pull slightly, just enough to put him a little off balance.

His natural reaction would be to pull back a bit. And I would just let him pull me into his home. He probably did not want me in there, but once he pulled me in, he probably would not ask me to leave.

So what's the principle? When you pull people in one direction, their natural reaction is to pull in the opposite direction. When this pulling is not purely physical, it's called "reverse psychology," and it works in places where other techniques fail.

People don't like to be pulled or pushed around. They want to assert their independence. If you seem to want them to do something, they will often do the opposite just to show (perhaps unconsciously) that "you can't control me."

My favorite use of this principle involves women, specifically ones under thirty. Obviously, the age difference is hard to ignore. But if one of the first things I say is, "I think you are beautiful and amazing, but unfortunately, you're too young for me" (as opposed to "I'm too old for you'), it often works miracles.

Those Handicapped Parking Spaces, etc.

An excellent way to combine logical and creative thinking is to look for opportunities to eliminate waste and become more efficient. Good chess players often search for a "fork," a move that simultaneously attacks two of their opponent's pieces. A lowly knight can threaten the more powerful rook and queen, and only one of them can get away. Real life contains many similar opportunities.

When Bob Stupak was running for mayor of Las Vegas, he asked me to spend a few hours with city councilman Steve Miller to learn and then brief Bob about the issues. When we were discussing traffic, a serious problem in Las Vegas, I mentioned an idea.

At that time there were hardly any left turn lanes back east. At traffic lights you could turn left in front of traffic only by stepping on the gas as the light was turning green or just before it turned red. Otherwise, you had to wait for breaks in traffic. Since you were in one of the through lanes, other drivers could be stuck behind you.

Out west we had more room, so many intersections had a separate left turn lane which usually included an arrow signal. When that arrow was green, oncoming cars had a red light. At busy intersections this system greatly increased the number of cars that could turn left during any cycle. On the other hand, if the intersection was not busy, the arrow actually increased your waiting time. Without an arrow you turned left during your green light whenever there was no oncoming traffic.

I saw a way to improve this system. The busiest intersections benefited from having an arrow, and the ones with sparse traffic gained from not having one. But what about moderately busy intersections? Why not combine the best of both worlds? Light the arrow briefly, but still allow left turns when the arrow was unlit and the oncoming traffic has a green light. Put up a sign to that effect. Steve Miller loved this idea. About a year later this system was used all over Las Vegas. To this day I don't know whether it was a coincidence.

Let's look at some more examples of this kind of thinking. My favorite involves handicapped parking spaces. As you have probably noticed, they are everywhere, are the best spots, and are usually unoccupied even when the rest of the parking lot is full. It's a ridiculous waste of money, space, and time. The owner spends money to provide those spaces, and nearly everybody wastes time looking for a space, while those excellent spaces just sit empty.

One obvious solution would be to reduce the number of such spaces, but that would be needlessly mean. With fewer spaces handicapped people would occasionally be forced to park a distance away, just to save some time and steps for a few able bodied people. Still, it seems awfully wasteful to have all these convenient spaces sitting empty nearly all the time.

My solution would be to install extremely expensive parking meters (probably ones that take credit cards) at some of these spaces. Charge something exorbitant such as $1 a minute, with a $5 minimum. Keep the fines for misusing the spaces at their current high level. The minimum and per minute prices could be adjusted for the venue, time of day, and circumstances. In the busiest lots and times the prices could be even higher.

The price should be set so that that there would nearly always be a few vacant spaces, but some spaces would be earning money. Perhaps a few spaces would have no meter at all and remain only for the handicapped.

A large portion of the money collected would be used only to benefit the handicapped. For example, it could pay for free wheel chairs, free medications, or research.

If this idea was fine-tuned correctly, nearly everybody should be happy. If you're wealthy enough to pay the parking meter, you would have the opportunity to buy some convenience without feeling guilty because your money is going to a good cause. In fact, you and others might opt to pay the meter even if they're not in a hurry, just to combine convenience and charity.

On the other hand, handicapped people should not mind this idea either. First, they will almost always have spaces available to them. And during the rare times that all their spaces are taken, they will usually have to wait only a few minutes; hardly anyone would pay $1 a minute for long periods. Second, if a handicapped person has to wait a while or park in a regular space, he can take comfort from knowing that "his space" is earning money for his benefit.

But what about the healthy drivers who can't afford the expensive meter? They gain also. First, there will be a few more regular spaces available for them. Second, if they are nice people, they will be happy to see more money spent on a good cause. Perhaps a few people will resent being reminded that some people can pay for a convenience they can't afford, but they are not worth worrying about.

You can probably see how this type of scheme could be used in many other venues. Take those long, frustrating lines at airport security. Why not add an extra line for people who are willing to pay something like $50 to shorten their wait? Some of that money could be used to reduce airline fares a little or perhaps other conveniences such as moving walkways.

Carpool lanes provide another example. They are a bit trickier because in some cities even these lanes are sometimes clogged up. But when the regular lanes are busy, and the carpool lane isn't, a $50 or $100 fee could be charged to those single drivers who would be willing to pay. Please note that everybody gains since every driver who pays to go into the carpool lane is one less driver congesting the other lanes.

You may think that the logistics would be difficult, but we already have EZ-Pay lines at toll gates for bridges and toll roads. And Israel has a toll road with no toll gates. Cameras take pictures and you get a bill in the mail.

The general principle is that time is extremely valuable to some wealthy people. If they are willing to give us their money, why not take it? It's a win-win situation. Forcing them to waste time waiting in traffic or hunting for parking spaces when they would gladly pay serious money to save time is just a waste. It costs us all money and keeps our lines longer.

You can probably think of other examples that take advantage of the fact that some people would pay fairly exorbitant amounts to save time and frustration. If the average person who can't afford these perks knows that he is gaining something from such practices, he probably would not object.

The "flip side" of this principle could be applied to empty places that a business wants to fill. For example, movie theaters, DisneyLand, hotels, and baseball fields have tiny crowds at certain times. Why not dramatically lower the prices to handicapped or elderly people or those on food stamps? To prevent abuses they should be required to take mildly embarrassing actions such as showing some sort of identification card that they are handicapped or on welfare.

To reduce complaints from regular customers, these discounts should be offered only at times that business is extremely slow. The full-paying customers should not be crowded or forced to wait in line.

When I was in Russia before communism toppled, I took a Russian lady to an art museum. Since the line stretched around the block, we would have to wait two hours. I asked if she was willing to endure that line, hoping she would say, "No."

She said, "Lines like this are routine to me." She hesitated, clearly wondering whether to continue. Then she said, "If you want to get crazy, you could pay an exorbitant fee to go to the front of the line."

"How much?"

"About $7 each."

At that time $7 was the average Russian's wage for about two days' work. Of course, a few minutes later we were enjoying some great art. What's the lesson? Even though Russia was a communist country that frowned on decadent excesses, they had no problem applying a similar principle to the one I am espousing. They may not have had our leaders' capitalist mentality, but unlike some of our leaders, they obviously had some brains.

Courage or Expertise?

President Bush, President-elect Obama, the passengers on his airplane, and just about everyone else effusively praised Captain Sullenberger's courage for saving his passengers' lives. "Sully" had just taken off from LaGuardia when his airliner flew into a flock of geese. They destroyed both engines, leaving him without power or enough altitude to glide to any airport.

He made an immediate and brilliant decision. He abruptly turned the plane, glided over the George Washington Bridge, and made a nearly perfect landing in the Hudson River. All 155 people on board survived and he then walked through the plane twice to make sure that everyone had evacuated before leaving it.

While I am awed by his accomplishment, I think "courageous" is the wrong word to describe him. He is unquestionably a very brave man who kept his head and did his job magnificently. But he did not show as much courage as Captain Richard Phillips. When pirates took over Captain Phillips' ship, he traded himself as a hostage for his crew. And Sully was not as heroic as someone who runs into a burning building to rescue a child.

The rescuer deliberately places himself in danger. He can avoid all risks by just staying where he is. Sully did not have that option: His life was already at risk. He saved his own and 154 other lives by acting decisively and effectively. (Of course, choosing to be the last one to leave required courage.)

But the most admirable element of his feat was knowing exactly what to do and then doing it perfectly. He succeeded because he had prepared thoroughly for many years. He had studied virtually everything about his plane and the art of flying. He had even studied the psychology of airline crews during crises. While other pilots were drinking beer, chasing girls, or just relaxing, he was preparing himself for unexpected situations.

An engineer who knows him well said that he "has not just spent his life flying, but has dug very deeply into what makes these things work." Another pilot said, "When he flew ... he always prepared for unthinkable emergencies."[25]

Sully's courage has been emphasized because many people subconsciously don't like complimenting studiousness they don't have. In fact, they often have derogatory terms for people who study and work too hard such as "grinders" and "nerds."

If Sully had been a bit less courageous and didn't walk through the sinking plane twice, the only thing that might have changed is the magnitude of his accolades. But if he had studied the theory of aeronautics a bit less fervently, they would all be dead.

In fact, a short time later fifty people died near Buffalo, NY because the pilots of a Fedex plane made many errors.

"In its final report adopted today, the Safety Board said that the probable cause of the accident was the failure of the captain and first officer to establish and maintain a proper glidepath during the night visual approach to landing. Contributing to the accident was a combination of the captain's and first officer's fatigue and failure to adhere to company flight procedures [and] the captain's and flight engineer's failure to monitor the approach."[26]

The members of that flight crew may have had as much courage as Sully, but they weren't remotely as well prepared. Courage is a wonderful quality, but don't confuse it with hard work and meticulous preparation. You may not have extreme

---

[25] Both quotations are from stories on page 8A of the *Las Vegas Review Journal,* January 17, 2009.

[26] http://www.aviationattorneys.com/national-content.cfm/Article/6366/Fed-Ex-Aircraft-Crash-Caused-By-Crew.html

courage, but you can prepare for unexpected threats by thorough study and other preparation.

Al's Comments

When David and I discussed Captain Sullenberger, I immediately thought of something David had written. "With proper coaching, practice, and study [most people] can frequently surpass people who have much more talent but don't want to study and practice."[27]

That's what David and this book are about. You can't change your innate qualities such as intelligence and courage, but if you study, work, and analyze your own thinking, you can accomplish more than many highly talented, but less diligent people.

---

[27] *Poker, Gaming, & Life: Expanded Edition,* Henderson, NV. Two Plus Two Publishing LLC, Third edition, 2009, page 145.

Have the Stock
Markets Become Too Liquid?

Capitalism distinguishes itself from other systems by allowing you to make money with money. You need not actually do labor. Although this may seem unfair, it helps make capitalist societies powerful and prosperous. But many people misunderstand how stock markets contribute to this prosperity. The capitalist concept is to risk money to help businesses to get started or expand. In return for taking that risk, you get a chance to make a lot of money by having a piece of the ownership.

Our system allows innovators and entrepreneurs to go ahead with their projects before they could finance them with their own savings and when they don't have the collateral or experience to borrow. Investors are more willing to risk their money when they have a chance for great rewards rather than a fixed interest rate.

Please note that the investors who risk their money are providing an essential service. If they did not take the risks, most entrepreneurial projects would never get started. The same cannot be said for people who risk their money to profit in other ways. A professional sports bettor is in a much different category from someone who invests in a startup company or an initial public offering.

But what about the secondary investors, the people who buy and sell stocks that are already listed on the stock exchange? Are they selfish gamblers or are they also helping the economy? In the past, they were clearly providing a useful service, though not as useful as the original investors. Without a stock market and those secondary investors, the original investors would have more difficulty selling their pieces and would therefore be less apt to make their original, risky investments.

We certainly need a stock market to grease the wheels for these original investors. Taking it further, this market should not have large transaction costs, specifically commissions or large bid-asked spreads. If the transaction costs are too high, even long-term investors won't invest. Over the past few decades, both commissions and bid-asked spreads have been drastically reduced, making the markets much more liquid. However, it's not necessary that those transaction costs shrink to nearly nothing as they have in the last few years. That small extra saving is not necessary to accomplish the capitalist system's goals. The question is: Do the recent changes, that have made the spread between bid and asked prices as little as one penny, have any downside?

I can't prove it, but they might. Because the spread has become tiny, many people have become stock traders, hedgers, etc., which is bad for our society and economy. It's like having bookies, accept 101-to-100 or offering poker games with virtually no rake. Those trivial costs would encourage people who previously thought the games were unbeatable to reconsider and seriously get involved in short-term gambling.

I believe there are several reasons why making the stock market easier to beat might be bad for the country and may even be one of the reasons for the 2008 economic meltdown. At the very least, the financial market's extremely small charges encourage talented people to leave productive fields because they know that they can make even greater fortunes in what has essentially become a big casino.

Al's Comments

When David told me this idea, I got excited. It's an original idea that will offend people, and we both enjoy controversy. His position may seem heretical because many people, both expert and non-expert, regard liquidity as completely desirable. Therefore, they believe that there is no such thing as too much liquidity.

David has again thought "outside the box" of conventional wisdom.

Of course, we wanted to know whether anyone else had made his point. A google search for "stock market" + "too liquid" got almost 400 entries. A few other people believed that the stock markets could be too liquid, but for slightly different reasons than David's. They weren't concerned that talented people would leave productive occupations to trade stocks, but they did believe that excessive liquidity caused many investors to focus too much on the short term.

One analyst stated that Warrren Buffet, the most successful investor, "has aptly stated that he invests as if the markets will be closed for several years. His refusal to subject Berkshire Hathaway to stock splits reduces trading volume, keeps short-term investors away, and conversely attracts dedicated long-term investors."[28]

David is primarily concerned that encouraging people to become traders will cause talented people to leave productive jobs and do something that is essentially useless. He made a similar point in "Knowing The Rules Doesn't Make You Smart." Some of the smartest young people are now working for investment firms because they can earn much more than they can make as professors and researchers. He thinks that the economic meltdown may be good for science because some of those people will go back into research.

---

[28] Sham Gad, "The Downside of Stock Investing," http://www.fool.com/investing/value/2008/01/30/the-downside-of-stock-investing.aspx

The Pawnshop Principle

There's a famous saying, "You can never go broke making a little profit." Of course it's true, but some people go too far and extrapolate that principle into a reason to make bad decisions. They overemphasize how much they paid for something then add on a "reasonable" profit. I believe that poorly run pawnshops make this error.

That's why I chose this title. Fortunately, neither Al nor I have much experience with pawnshops. Therefore, our opinion about how they operate is mainly speculation. But these general concepts are valid regardless.

A pawnshop's selling price should be based primarily on how likely an item will sell fairly quickly at various prices. In fact, the seller would often make a better pricing decision if he did not know how much it cost. He should sell it as if it had been *given* to him.

(This principle applies more to pawnshops than retail stores because a pawnshop will usually have only one of each item, while a store will have many of them. The store's owner knows what items have sold for and how much his competition is charging for identical or similar ones.)

I think that pawnshops tend to sell many items too cheaply. They do it because they have so little invested in them. They also make the opposite mistake. If they paid or lent too much on an item, they will stubbornly try to sell it at an unreasonably high price. It they did more thinking about what items are worth as opposed to what they cost, they would increase their profits.

Bad poker players often make an analogous error when deciding whether to call a bet. They often base their decision on how much money they have personally invested in the pot. Good poker players know that it's a mistake. The correct criterion is, "What pot odds are you getting?"

169

There is usually a correlation between your investment and the total pot. Therefore, the players using this incorrect criterion — the amount they invested — will often accidentally make the right decision. But a little thinking will show that you should ignore the amount you have invested, and once you put a dollar into the pot, it isn't yours any more. It's the same as every other dollar. Thus the key issues are:

1.   How many dollars are in the pot?

2.   What does it cost to call the bet?

3.   What are the odds against your winning the pot?

A similar error is made by many people when they sell things, especially personal things. They usually have little or no idea of the market. So they overemphasize what they paid for it, then add a reasonable profit or subtract a tolerable loss.

The selling price should be close to what the winning bid for the item would be at an auction. Perhaps it should be a tad less since you aren't auctioning it, but it should not be a lot less. Notice that I did not mention the price you paid. If this optimum amount happens to be less then you paid, so be it. Conversely, if it's quite a bit more, don't let that fact deter you from trying for a giant profit.

Deducing
Concepts from Statistics

I like to notice patterns and try to figure out why they occur. It's the opposite of the way most analysts think, but it has yielded some good results. For instance, the semi-bluff[29] could have been deduced through calculations, but I didn't discover it that way. Shortly after hitting Las Vegas as a young man, I watched the best players and tried to figure out why they were winning. The semi-bluff was not named at the time. I coined that term a few years later, but it was already a well known tactic.

Good players often bet weak or drawing hands with more cards to come. They much prefer that the bet wins immediately, but can also improve to the best hand. When watching them make this play, I took a pencil and paper, did some calculations, and realized why it worked. That is, I came up with the general concept by deducing from my observations.

Here are two examples from medicine that may or may not be true. I'm mentioning them mainly to demonstrate the potential value of statistically-based deductions.

I have rarely heard about somebody having two different types of cancer simultaneously. Cancer often spreads, but that's not what I'm referring to. It's my belief that very few people get both pancreatic and prostrate or lung and breast cancer, etc. I observed this pattern many years ago, and it made me think that somehow cancer may prevent cancer.

---

[29] "A semi-bluff is a bet with a hand which, if called, does not figure to be best at the moment, but has a reasonable chance of outdrawing those hands that originally called it." Sklansky, David, *The Theory of Poker,* Henderson, NV, Two Plus Two Publishing, 1999, p. 91.

Years later I read that tumors emit a chemical that spreads throughout the body and prevents other tumors from getting sufficient blood. Treating cancerous tumors by cutting off their blood supply was first proposed by Dr. Judah Folkman in 1971. "Though his hypothesis was initially disregarded by most experts in the field, Folkman persisted with his research. After more than a decade, his theory became widely accepted."[30]

Hopefully, the implications of the idea that cancer can prevent cancer will be thoroughly investigated. In fact, researchers may already be investigating it. My goal is simply to show how a non-expert can come up with a scientific idea through simple statistical analysis.

The other situation is more interesting, both medically and mathematically. Unfortunately, I have not been able to pin down whether my facts are accurate. Still, I wanted to write about it because of its potential importance. Several years ago I read something in a question and answer column about the risk of getting AIDS when you have multiple partners or maybe just multiple encounters with the same partner. The columnist said that the risk went up multiplicatively rather than additively. If you have five times as many partners or five times as many encounters with one partner, your risk of getting AIDS is approximately twenty-five times as high.

I immediately realized that, if this was true, the AIDS virus often needs to hit you twice before it creates the disease. Perhaps the first contact creates a predisposition or vulnerability, and the second one creates the disease. Why do I say that? It's just a matter of knowing combinations.

1. If you have five partners, there are ten combinations of two.

2. If you have ten partners, there are forty-five combinations of two.

---

[30] http://en.wikipedia.org/wiki/Judah_Folkman#Work_on_angiogenesis

3. If you have fifteen partners, there are one hundred five combinations of two.

So by doubling the number of partners, you have approximately quadrupled the number of two-partner combinations. By tripling the number of partners, you have increased the number of combinations by 10.5 which is a bit more than three squared.

We all know that some people have gotten AIDS from just one contact with the virus, especially from blood transfusions. So any double hit idea would have exceptions. But if the advice column accurately depicted the facts, then somebody should investigate my idea. If AIDS normally requires two hits, this idea could make an important contribution to combating it.

Al's Comments

Neither of us has enough medical knowledge to evaluate cancer or AIDS research. David is just proposing possible research approaches based on very limited statistical data. As always, he is primarily concerned with the thinking process.

David doesn't claim that his ideas are right, just that they are worth investigating. If he is even a little bit right, the benefits could be enormous. For the moment, let's assume that it often takes two exposures to get AIDS. If researchers incorporated that fact into their work, it should help them to understand the disease's mechanisms, and that knowledge could lead to a cure.

The same principle applies to you. The less you constrain your thinking, and the more possibilities you are willing to consider, the more likely you are to solve your problems.

The 30 Percent Syndrome

Most people tend to dismiss the possibility of something once they think its chances of occurring are below about 30 percent. They go about their lives assuming it won't happen.[31] It's obviously a mistake. A related mistake is not distinguishing between unlikely events and even more unlikely ones such as putting a 25 percent shot in the same category as a 10 percent shot.

Professional poker players could not survive if we made these errors. We base most decisions on the comparison between the odds offered by the pot and the chance of winning it. If those odds are favorable, we regard the bet as positive EV and make it. Frequently, we assess our chances of winning as well below 50 percent, but we won't fold. In fact, if the ratio of the pot to the bet was 3-to-1 or higher and we had a 30 percent chance of winning, it would be a terrible mistake to fold. On the other hand, with a 10 percent chance, we should usually fold.

Because we constantly think in terms of EV, good poker players and other types of successful gamblers are nearly immune to the 30 percent syndrome. So are professional statisticians. But most other people are likely to fall into this trap of under-estimating 30 percent shots.

Actually, I believe that the major reason that most people make this mistake is not their lack of mathematical acumen, but their feelings. 30 percent is a large enough probability to give them hope, but they will still be disappointed more than twice as often as they are satisfied. If something has a very low probability,

---

[31] The flip side of the 30 percent syndrome is that people often assume that a 70 percent shot is a done deal. We discuss the effects of this mistake in "Favorites Parlay To Underdog," starting on page 187.

such as a lottery ticket, they don't expect to win and aren't surprised or seriously disappointed when they lose.

In addition, the tiny chance opportunities (such as lottery tickets) involve minimal investments. But, to win a significant amount in situations with a positive EV and a 30 percent chance of winning, you have to invest significant money or other resources such as time. Since people don't want to risk significant losses, they tend to pass up these positive EV situations.

They do it because being happy frequently is more important to them than EV. Because they don't think in EV terms, they think that they won't be happy often enough to make it worthwhile. We saw a spectacular example of this mistake in Bob Stupak's Slot Tourney. All four finalists had an EV of $270,000, but were willing to settle for $60,000 because three-quarters of the time they would be happy with their decision, and were not astute enough to realize this was a terrible criterion to use.

One of the best examples of this syndrome occurs frequently in the financial and stock market newsletters and TV shows. The pundits almost always recommend buying stocks that they believe are more likely to go up than down. And they recommend selling or not buying stocks that they believe are more likely to go down than up. But even if they are right about the likelihood of going up or down, a stock that is likely to go down can still be a good buy. If a $60 stock has a 70 percent chance of dropping to $55 and a 30 percent chance of moving up to $100, it has an EV of $68.50. Yet I have never heard any financial expert speak in those terms.

I don't know whether they are yielding to the 30 percent syndrome or just trying to keep up their batting average. That is they look better if most of their picks go up even if their clients would profit from buying stocks that have a less than fifty percent chance of going up substantially. But either way, it shows that they can't be trusted.

My first recommendation is: *Don't let your desire to be happy or your fear of being sad cause you to make poor decisions.* Teach yourself to think of money in the detached, long-term way that professional gamblers do: With few exceptions, the only thing that matters is EV. If you make enough positive EV bets of approximately the same size, you must win. If you make enough negative EV bets of approximately the same size, you must lose. Ignore the emotional ups and downs of your short-term results.

Another recommendation was stated in "The Acceleration Effect." *Have a lot of irons in the fire*. If you're working on 10 different projects, and you think each has a 1 in 4 chance of success, at least one of them will probably succeed. If that one success more than makes up for the failures, you're a big favorite to end up happy.[32]

But what should you do when you don't have multiple opportunities? You should still go for it as long as the EV is highly positive, the chances of success are not too small, and the downside risk is tolerable. If you have to fly across the country to interview for your dream job and know that getting it is a bit of a long shot, do it anyway. Fight that inclination to avoid an action just because it's more likely than not to make you feel bad. Try to treat your feelings like poker chips by investing whenever your EV is positive.

Interestingly, I believe that many people who do go for it, do so for the wrong reason. Instead of thinking that something is a 25 percent chance, but is still worth taking, their egos convince them that they're actually a favorite. For example, they will fly across the country because they erroneously think, "I'm so good that I'll probably get that job."

Similarly, many people also make the mistake described in "Favorites Parlay into Underdogs," starting on page 187, about the way multiple favorites parlay into underdogs. Their project may require many steps, each with a small chance of failure, and they don't realize that their overall chance to reach their goal is well

---

[32] However, if working on many projects at the same time means your work quality drops off significantly, it may be best to have "less irons in the fire."

below 50 percent. Had they realized it, they would have never started.

In these examples, people make two errors that cancel out each other:

1. They won't start the project unless they think it will probably succeed.

2. They overestimate their chances to succeed.

So they go ahead with it, just as I would have advised them to do.

Unenforceable Rules

Live poker games have a well known and very sensible rule, "One player to a hand." You can't get advice about how to play your hand because it would create an unfair advantage over the other players. Casinos sometimes let friends sit behind a player, but they can't give advice.

But what if you play poker on the Internet? Should it be against the rules to give or receive advice? And because nobody can see who you are, something even worse happens: An entirely different person, even a famous pro, can play using your name. So people think they are playing against you, but they are really playing against a pro. Both of these violations of the one player to a hand rule have been called "ghosting," and I believe some Internet poker sites allow it, and some don't.

When asked for my opinion about ghosting, my instant reaction was that it should be allowed. But I don't trust anyone's instant reaction, not even my own and needed to see whether my answer could be justified logically. After thinking about it, I realized that anti-ghosting rules belong in a more general category: rules or laws that seem reasonable, but still shouldn't be "on the books" partly because they are unenforceable. To be more precise, it's my opinion that this sort of rule should not exist whenever three criteria are met.

1. The rule must be truly unenforceable. That is, it's nearly impossible to catch violations.

2. The rule, though reasonable, should not involve important moral principles.

3. The rule relates to economic competitions, and rule-breakers would have a definite advantage over rule-followers.

You would probably agree that anti-ghosting rules meet all these criteria. So would a rule against athletes' taking an aspirin before an event if aspirin helped them and there was no way to detect it. My primary objection is the third criterion: Such a rule penalizes the rule-follower who will never cheat. I want him to be able to take that aspirin as well. We should get rid of rules that help cheaters and punish good citizens.

On the other hand, my opinion applies only when there is virtually no chance of catching a cheater and only if the issue involved is not a serious one. If there were an undetectable and dangerous illegal drug that helped athletic performance, it would violate my second criterion, and the rule should remain despite its inability to be enforced. If there are serious moral issues involved, it's important that society keep the rule to avoid sending the wrong message.

Even a Kid
Can Recognize Fallacies

"Most Math Is Just Good Thinking," starting on page 250, tells how Carl Gauss, a great mathematician, used child-like thinking to figure out how to sum an arithmetic progression. When he was about seven years old, he derived a technique that most fifteen year olds merely memorize without fully understanding it. But they would have no trouble understanding if it was explained to them in the simple way little Carl thought of it. Here are two similar examples from my own life.

When I was six years old, my parents and I went to New York City to visit my aunt and uncle. At dinner, Uncle Arnold told us he had started to go to the racetrack every day and was doing well with his system. Starting with the first race, he would bet $20 on the favorite. If it won, he would go home. If it lost, he would bet enough on the favorite in the second race so that, if it won, it would result in an overall profit of about $10. If he won, he would go home. If not, he would bet even more on the favorite in the third race. The idea was that eventually he would win a race, show an overall profit, and go home. Then he would go back the next day to start over.

Some of you will recognize that he had a terrible system. It was a variation of the Martingale System in which bets are increased in such a way that you need win only one bet to be ahead. Smart gamblers have known for centuries that the Martingale System is fallacious.

My uncle used this system to finish the day ahead, and up until that point, he had always done so. Such systems produce frequent small wins along with eventual catastrophic losses. Because your bets keep getting bigger, losing four or five in a row can force you to risk much more than you want (or have) on the next race. If you lose every race (which happens fairly often), you will lose more than you can win back in months. People playing the horses, craps, roulette, and other games with Martingale-type systems have lost large amounts of money. In fact, if they play long enough, they must inevitably lose.

Uncle Arnold had to lose ultimately because each bet had a negative EV, and no Martingale-type (or any other type) of betting system can turn a disadvantage into an advantage. Of course, I knew nothing about that when I was six, so could not advise him to give up his scheme. But even as a little kid, I could see that there was something else wrong with his system.

He would go home the moment he got ahead. Despite being only six, it didn't make sense to me. Why go all the way to the track and then return home after only a race or two? How was the third race or the fifth one any different from the first or second?

"Uncle Arnold," I said, "why would you go home after a winner and then come back again the next day? Why not pretend that the next race after your win is the beginning of the next day and go back to your $20 starting bet?"

In other words, even if his method was actually profitable, he was costing himself money by artificially ending his day before he had to. Needless to say, my father was very proud of me for spotting this irrefutable error in my uncle's strategy, and my uncle quickly saw his error as well. But even though a six year old could catch this error, millions of people make the same sort of mistake.

It is related to what Mason Malmuth calls "The Extremely Silly Subject of Money Management."[33] If you have the best of it, don't quit just to ensure a win. I saw that when I was six. Unfortunately for my uncle, I knew nothing about race track take outs. So even if he took my advice, he was doomed to fail.

About the same time I overheard some adults talking about how WWII ended the Great Depression. But something about the

[33] *Gambling Theory and Other Topics,* Henderson, NV, Two Plus Two Publishing, 2004, pp 36-40.

conversation bothered my young mind. Apparently building all those bombs and other stuff helped our economy. But if getting people to build things that were just going to be blown up helped the economy, then why didn't we do it in 1937 and drop the bombs in the ocean?

I came to the conclusion that there had to be more to this than simply the amount of money the government was pouring into the economy. Maybe the war made people work harder. Or maybe it encouraged people to invent things and become more innovative.

Nothing that has happened since has changed my mind. In fact, the Iraqi war reinforced my belief. It sure didn't help the economy despite all the money the government was spending. And I think one of the reasons is that it did not motivate people to work harder. It did not create the same sense of urgency as WWII.

Without knowing it, my young mind had deduced what is now called "the broken window fallacy," the idea that breaking a window is good for the economy because it puts people to work. But it's not true unless there are positive side effects. The broken window must make people work harder than usual or galvanize them to invent innovative products that help the economy, just as it did in WWII.

Lying to Yourself

Do you remember that British colonel in the movie "The Bridge on the River Kwai?" His Japanese captors forced him to build a bridge that he knew would help the Japanese to move soldiers and equipment that would kill British and allied troops. He was originally opposed to building it and hoped it would be destroyed. However, as the project moved forward, he became obsessed with building the best possible bridge to demonstrate his own and British superiority.

When his allies were ready to blow it up, he wanted to protect "his baby." It was easy to claim (and he probably believed) that he wanted it destroyed when he didn't think it could happen. But once its destruction became a serious possibility, he had to face the devastating truth about his feelings.

We don't need to go to the movies to see similar examples. Just take Jesse Jackson, a major black leader. He marched with Martin Luther King and devoted much of his life to achieving equality for black Americans. Yet he was embarrassed when an open microphone caught him bad mouthing Barack Obama before his election as our first black president.

That election should have been the culmination of his life's work, but he apparently had mixed emotions. How could he continue to fight as strongly against racism when Obama's election proved that much of the fight had been won? Of course, we still don't have full equality, but Obama's election had enormous real and symbolic impact on that issue.

Jackson's emotions later changed, or at least they appeared to change. But at least for a short period, I believe that Jesse Jackson was subject to the same syndrome as the British colonel. He didn't want to admit to himself that he was a little glad that no black man had been elected president since fighting against racism was his *raison d'etre*.

183

I'm not picking on Jesse Jackson. I think this syndrome is widespread among political people and anyone committed to a cause. For example, even if he doesn't realize it, Rush Limbaugh would probably not want to see a hard right conservative in The White House. Or to take an even more extreme example, I believe that Osama bin Laden would become depressed if America became a Muslim country.

Here are three examples that are closer to home. My buddy, who I'll call "Charlie," had always dreamed about being an entertainer. His greatest talent was as a mimic like Frank Gorshin or Rich Little. He impersonated several celebrities quite well and practiced his routine for thousands of hours. But he never actually got to perform on stage. He entertained his friends at parties while hoping to make it to the big time.

Or was he? Charlie spent most of his life in the gambling world, sometimes working and sometimes playing small stakes poker. He never achieved much success. But he always clung to his mimicking ability as something that kept him from being just another face in the crowd. He frequently lamented not knowing the right people to break into "the business."

When Charlie, Bob Stupak and I were talking about his ambition, Bob said, "You can work in my lounge. Prepare your act, and tell me when you want to start."

He thought he was doing Charlie a favor, but wasn't. Charlie turned white. My friend suddenly had to admit that he was not quite good enough. It was easy to deny reality as long as there was no opportunity. But when Bob made that offer, he could no longer preserve his delusion.

Many years ago, a girl I really cared about started drinking too much. Before we met, she had a drinking problem, but seemed to have it under control when we were together. After not seeing each other for a while, it looked like the problem was back. She claimed it wasn't. She admitted that she liked to drink, but said that her drinking was totally under her control. She could take it or leave it.

She had very little money. To clarify her position, I asked her hypothetically, "If I offered to give you $100 a day if you don't drink, would you take it?"

Thinking I wasn't serious, she quickly replied, "Of course. I'd love that deal."

"Okay. You've got it."

She immediately started crying. When I asked why, she said, "I never thought you would actually do that. But I believe you and it's a deal, and the money will be great. I cried because the moment you offered to pay me, my first reaction was dread, not happiness. You made me realize I actually am an alcoholic."

She stayed on the wagon for only two weeks.

By the way, when my son's drinking troubled me, I tried the same ploy. I'm happy to say that though it cost me more money, I was the one who ended the deal. He would have cheerfully taken my money forever.

The example of this syndrome that I most frequently see involves poker players with a flamboyant and highly volatile game that often brings them a reputation they don't deserve. They are usually not great players, but often make great plays. Eventually, these players go broke, and when they do, their results are often blamed on poor "money management." "I didn't have a big enough bankroll," or "I spent too much on living expenses."

In other words, these players claimed that their only leaks were financial and emotional and emphasized not knowing when to quit. They didn't mean they should quit because their opponents were too tough for them. Instead, they blamed their inability to quit when bad luck was killing them, and were unable to accept the fact that they weren't good enough.

This is another example of rationalizing. If they played better than their opposition, artificial quitting times would do nothing to improve their results. And since some of them knew it, a second excuse was given: Going on tilt. "I had so many bad beats I went on tilt and blew my bankroll." Again, they were just rationalizing.

Exactly how you can use these ideas is not clear. It may actually be better to lie to yourself if the truth will hurt and there is no way you can change it. "Mary would have married me, not Bob, if I wasn't forced to leave our home town to get my degree." On the other hand, if confronting the real truth shakes you up and makes you change yourself, it may be worth the pain.

Al's Comments

Despite David's commitment to being honest with yourself, he said, "It may actually be better to lie to yourself if the truth will hurt and there is no way you can change it." I agree because everybody has a limited capacity to cope with the truth, and learning too much truth too quickly can be harmful. We need some lies to protect our egos.

For example, was Charlie better off losing the pleasant delusion that, if he just got a break, he could make it big as an impersonator? I doubt it. That delusion did him almost no harm, while allowing him to escape from his life's mundane realities. Once he knew the truth, he lost his pleasant escape.

On the other hand, learning and accepting the truth could have changed those losing poker players into winners. They could choose a different profession, take lessons, or just play in smaller, softer games.

That alcoholic girl would lose very little and gain immensely by accepting the truth about her drinking. David helped her to see that she was an alcoholic. He planted the seed which we hope will ultimately get her into treatment.

David repeatedly encourages you to analyze the way your emotions and other irrational factors affect your thoughts and actions. But don't look too hard at harmless fantasies. If you enjoy fantasizing about running away to live on a desert island or winning the lottery, and you don't quit your job or spend too much on lottery tickets, enjoy yourself without feeling guilty. However, if you see that you're harming yourself or others by thinking or acting in certain ways, do whatever it takes to learn the truth.

Favorites
Parlay into Underdogs

Many people screw up their lives because they aren't aware of something that every smart baseball bettor knows: If reaching a goal requires meeting all of several sub-goals, it's much harder to achieve than it may appear. If you parlay six baseball games and are a 2-to-1 favorite in each game, you will win your bet only 64 out of 729 times. You're more than a ten to one underdog, but it doesn't feel like you should be.

(This "parlay effect" is one of the reasons I think that John Wooden is underrated as a college basketball coach even with all his accolades. His super-long winning streaks were even more unbelievable than people realized. They devalued them somewhat because he usually had the best talent. But even if the bookies had him as a 5-to-1 favorite for each game, the odds against winning 88 consecutive regular season games and 38 consecutive NCAA tournament games were enormous. Those streaks might have been extraordinary luck. But it's much more likely that they were caused by Wooden's ability to get players to play over their already tall heads.)

Winning eight consecutive 70 percent shots is tougher than a streak of four even money shots. (More generally a streak of x even money shots is easier than 2x 70 percent shots. DUCY?) So why is the parlay effect important to your non-gambling decisions? If your goal requires that many things all go right — starting a successful business, winning a tennis tournament, becoming a movie star, bringing in a project on time and within budget, landing on the moon, etc. — you must guard against overconfidence.

If there are many roadblocks and you're about 70 percent to get past each one, your chances of ultimate success are low. As I

188 Part Two: More Exploits, Ideas, and Advice

discuss in "The 30 percent Syndrome," people tend to assume that anything above 70 percent is pretty much a done deal. That's a bad mistake in all cases, but it's much worse when parlays are involved.

If you are striving for something that requires many consecutive successes, you may want to reconsider. Or at least have other irons in the fire. (See "The Acceleration Effect" starting on page 92.) Even if the chances for each individual success are high, you may be better off focusing on goals that require fewer intermediary steps, even if those steps are a bit less likely to be achieved. Alternatively, you might aim for a goal which gives you more wiggle room, one that allows an occasional failure.

Placebos
and Peeping Toms

I remember reading that Bill Gates described intelligence as the ability to find connections between things that seem unrelated. I tend to agree, but don't know whether you must inherit this ability or can develop it. But I do know that many breakthroughs in science, engineering, business, and so on have been made because somebody used this talent for connecting two seemingly disparate situations.

An amusing example of this type of thinking entered my mind a few years ago. I realized that prescribing sugar pills under the guise of being real medicine has something in common with looking through your neighbor's window while she is undressing. DUCY?

Although sugar pills have no pharmacological value, they often work! It's the well known "placebo effect," which is so powerful that the FDA requires that all drugs be tested against it. Two equivalent groups of patients get either the placebo or the drug. If the drug does not help significantly more than the placebo, it will not be approved.

If the patient receiving a placebo thinks he is getting a real drug, he often feels better or has other improvements. However, if he knows he is getting a fake, it doesn't work. Thus, when a doctor gives a patient a placebo (or a drug that he knows is not effective such as an antibiotic for a viral infection), he frequently helps the patient. On the other hand, suppose the doctor is charging serious money for prescribing that placebo or useless drug. We'll get back to that subject in a minute.

There is something odd about the crime of voyeurism. Whom does it hurt? Obviously the victim is the person being watched. But as long as the peeping tom does nothing but watch, and it

190 Part Two: More Exploits, Ideas, and Advice

never leads to anything else, nothing truly bad happens to the victim unless she finds out about it.

If you're a detective and arrest the peeping tom as he is staring through a telescope, you're not doing the victim a favor (again assuming there is no greater danger lurking) by informing her of what was happening.

Obviously, almost all other crimes are not like this. Any victim would appreciate finding out that you detected and stopped somebody from mugging him or embezzling from his bank account. But, there is at least one other crime that has this weird aspect.[34] Suppose a detective discovered that a doctor was prescribing placebos and overcharging his patients for them. This detective is in the same situation as the one who caught the peeping tom. If he arrests the doctor, the victims will find out that they have been getting a fake drug, and the placebo effect will disappear, making them worse off.

Shortly after drafting this chapter, I was walking through Caesar's Palace. Congress had just passed the $787 billion economic stimulus bill, but the president had not yet signed it. I saw that the very expensive shops were packed and since Las Vegas business had been terrible, it was quite surprising.

As always, I tried to figure out what was happening. The stimulus bill wasn't even a law yet, and it would certainly take months to have any direct economic effects. But people were obviously spending money as if the economy had improved.

Then I saw a connection to this chapter. To a considerable extent, the success of the economic stimulus package depends upon the placebo effect. If people believe it will work, they will become more confident, spend money, and stimulate the economy. Perhaps that's one reason the President and Congress rushed it through without much concern for the details.

---

[34] A third example might be stealing a Babe Ruth home run ball and replacing it with a nearly identical ball.

I didn't write this chapter to make you better informed about these two crimes or the effects of the economic stimulus legislation. You are unlikely to commit or be a victim of either crime, and more knowledgeable people have discussed the strengths and weaknesses of that legislation. Rather, it was to give you an example of how I'm always trying to find connections and analogies where others aren't looking. If you can develop a similar way of looking at things, it can help you solve other, perhaps more important problems.

How to Parallel Park

Many of you know that I pride myself on giving not just good advice, but also the reasoning underlying that advice. I do it so that, instead of taking my words on faith, you can figure things out for yourself. Doing so is especially important when the situation changes slightly. Without knowing the underlying theory, you won't know whether to change your answer or strategy from what I've recommended.

My father taught me the same way. He did not just tell me something but rather almost always explained it, usually in great detail, because he wanted me to learn how to think for myself. But there have been a few exceptions. Every once in a while he would teach me a tactic or strategy without explaining why it worked.

Just before I was to take my driver's license road test, he taught me an incredibly simple and accurate parking method. (I don't know whether or not he invented it, but I've never seen it anywhere else.) Parallel parking may not be that important, but millions of people don't do it well. And, of course, the ones who can't do it well are likely to fail their driving test. If you're one of those people, just do what my father taught me:

1. Pull up about a foot away from the car in front of your parking space.

2. Back up, keeping your wheels straight.

3. When the back of the car next to you is at the middle of your car, stop.

4. While stopped, turn the steering the wheel as far right as it will go (assuming that the curb is to your right).

5. Resume backing up, keeping the steering wheel fully turned. You will go into the parking space at a steeper angle than most drivers do.

6. When you are close to the curb, stop. The definition of "close" depends upon your car. Make a few practice runs to determine how close you need to be.

7. While the car is stopped, turn the steering wheel all the way to the left.

8. Resume backing up.

9. If you have chosen the right place to change course, you'll be in almost perfect position without any further adjustments.

10. If you get good at this, you might not need to do anything else. When you need to do something else, it will be simply moving a tad forward and, perhaps, straightening up a bit.

I have no idea why this method works so well and my father never explained it to me. Perhaps it won't work for an occasional car with an unusual turning radius. But I have never encountered an exception and just tested it with my brand new Jaguar. Despite its tight turning radius, it worked perfectly.

This chapter may be a bit off the beaten path, but some people are so frustrated about parallel parking that they would gladly pay $50 or even $100 to learn how to do it easily and virtually perfectly. If you're one of them, this chapter alone is worth more than what you paid for this book.

My Caesar's Palace Blackjack Proposition

"When Your Goals Don't Coincide With Theirs" analyzed the problems that can occur when you and your employees or partners have different risk-reward equations. Not too many people even think about this problem, and even fewer fully understand it. But when I first hit Las Vegas, I encountered someone, let's call him "Harry," who did fully understand it.

At that time my best game was blackjack, but it takes a lot of money to play it professionally. Even if you play extremely well, your edge is small meaning that you need a big bankroll to assure survival. Otherwise, a run of bad luck will break you, and these runs occur frequently. Since I didn't have enough money, I needed a backer.

It's hard to get a backer because he takes all the risks, but splits the profits. If the player wins, he usually gets about half. If he loses, the backer takes the entire loss. So it's usually a great deal for the player, but a bad one for the backer.

Harry was a professional backer. He really knew what he was doing and made a lot of money by backing only the best players. Unfortunately, it was hard to prove that I was good enough to meet his standards. He didn't know me, nor did he know much about blackjack. He mainly staked poker players.

Many players tried to join his "stable." Las Vegas is full of poker and blackjack players and just plain hustlers who insist, "I'm sure to beat that game." Most of them are lying or exaggerating because they have nothing to lose and a lot to gain. Harry usually turned them down.

The game at Caesar's Palace was highly beatable if you knew what you were doing. I knew much more than most players because, at that time, not much had been written about blackjack.

Many casinos had much more liberal rules than they do today, and the ones at Caesar's were the best of all. They used only one deck, allowed doubling down after splitting, surrendering, and the dealer had to stand on soft seventeen. Plus they dealt three-quarters of the deck. Those rules gave good players a small edge right off the top! With a 4-to-1 bet spread any competent card-counter would have about a 2 percent edge.[35]

However, since so many people had tried to hustle him, Harry would not believe my claim that I could beat the game. So my problem was: How could I convince Harry to back me?

Remember, because he did not know blackjack, words alone would not prove I was an expert. But they could prove that I believed in my expertise and Harry knew that it was probably true if I believed it. So what deal would convince him that I really believed it?

I came up with the an unusual proposal. He would risk $5,000. With that money I would bet either $100 or $200 on every hand, but would get nothing of the first $3,000 won. Above that, I'd get half. I couldn't quit (unless Caesar's barred me). He could quit any time he was ahead.

With this deal I had almost no chance to win any money for myself if I wasn't really an expert. Reducing the bet spread cut my edge from 2 percent to about 1 percent, making it much tougher to win. So, winning proved my expertise.

I would have had a bigger edge, and a much greater chance to win $3,000 if my big bets were $400 and my small ones $100. But that proposal might make Harry think that I was just hoping to get lucky. However, to win $3,000 while betting only $100 or

---

[35] Card counters determine when the deck favors them, and they then increase their bets. "Bet spread" is the ratio of the largest to the smallest bet that a player can make, and the larger it is, the greater advantage the player has. Casinos watch the way players vary their bets and generally bar card counters. See *Sklansky Talks Blackjack,* Henderson, NV Two Plus Two Publishing, 1999 and 2004.

$200 was extremely unlikely if I couldn't actually beat that game. This smaller bet spread also reduced the amount that Harry had to invest.

He took the deal. Unfortunately, I was barred after winning about $10,000.

I included this anecdote not to teach you about blackjack or how to formulate a gambling proposition for a backer. Rather, I wanted to show how to get around the problem of conflicting risk-reward equations. More generally, I wanted to demonstrate the importance of understanding and adjusting to the other person's motives and thoughts. It's a critical task during any negotiation.

Using Probability
When Punishing Criminals[36]

When dealing with crimes and punishments, probability is not used nearly as much as it should be. I think we should use probabilities when (for instance):

1. The death penalty is involved.

2. The criminal is unlikely to be caught.

3. Luck (i.e., probability) determines the outcome or a criminal act.

The Death Penalty

No matter how carefully we act, we will occasionally convict an innocent person. If we try to make this miscarriage of justice almost impossible, nearly every guilty person would be acquitted.

However, when the death penalty is involved, the equation changes. For less heinous crimes the error of convicting an innocent person must be accepted as a possibility because the alternative is setting too many criminals free. But in death penalty cases the error of sparing someone who deserves to die is relatively unimportant as long he gets life in prison. Therefore, even a slight doubt of guilt should be enough to keep a person from being executed. (For the purpose of this essay, I assume that

---

[36] For more on this subject see pages 296-307 of my book, *Poker, Gaming, & Life: Expanded Edition,* Henderson, NV, Two Plus Two Publishing, 2009.

some executions are justifiable. I have no position on whether all capital punishment should be abolished.)

That statement should not be controversial. Even the most fervent capital punishment advocates should be willing to forego executions to prevent the slight possibility of killing an innocent person as long as those who may deserve to die spend the rest of their lives in prison.

My specific suggestion is that, when a guilty verdict is handed down in a capital case, the jury must also say that they are convinced beyond a *shadow* of a doubt. Without those extra words, the death penalty should be taken off the table.

I believe the primary reason that this obvious suggestion has not already been implemented is not that people are uncomfortable with sparing some criminals who deserve to die. Rather it's that they would be forced to confront the fact that some convicted defendants (namely those who were convicted without the extra words) just might be innocent.

A Criminal Who is Unlikely To Be Caught

The criminal justice system also ignores probabilities when a criminal has a good chance of not being caught. I propose that certain white collar economic crimes should have a punishment related to this probability. More specifically, judges should make sure that an economic crime is never positive EV. For example, a crime would have a positive EV if:

- People committing that crime have historically had a 10 percent chance of being caught

- The punishment is one year in jail

- The perpetrator would be willing to spend a year in jail for seven times the amount stolen.

As another example, suppose the perpetrator would do a year in jail for $3 million, he would be making the correct play (mathematically speaking) to commit that crime to "earn" $300,000 and only have a 10 percent chance of going to jail for a year or less. So the judge should sentence him to at least two years.

Outcomes Determined By Luck

Luck should not play a large part of the punishment for a crime. If a man shoots at you and misses, he should be punished almost exactly the same as if he was lucky enough to hit you. If a drunk driver kills somebody, he should not be punished much differently from a drunk driver who is lucky enough not to kill somebody. I think that the punishment for homicide while driving drunk should be lessened and the punishment for purely driving drunk should be increased. I will leave it to the reader to come up with other examples.

Al's Comments

Again we see David's commitment to logical, mathematically-based thinking. On the subject of crime and punishment, most people respond more to feelings than logic.

Please remember that David did not take a position on whether the death penalty should be abolished. He deliberately avoided that controversy because he wants his proposals to be assessed logically and unemotionally. Nor did he talk about whether criminals are bad or good people, whether we should emphasize punishment or rehabilitation, or any of the other issues that arouse such strong emotions.

All he is trying to do is encourage readers to acknowledge probabilities in a rational way. Unfortunately, I believe that far too many readers will react emotionally.

So what should you do? That's easy. Set aside your feelings. Then logically and dispassionately ask yourself, "Will David's recommendations improve or harm the criminal justice system?"

Stock Trading
and Poker Playing

A few years ago I was featured in an article in *Barron's Magazine*.[37] The subject was what investors could learn from professional poker players. But I was not pleased with the article because the author got something very wrong. He claimed that investors should take a page from poker players who don't hesitate to exit from losing situations. But often they shouldn't.

A professional poker player knows that losing may be evidence that the game is tougher than he thought. And, if he comes to that conclusion, he will not be swayed by the desire to get even, and he will quit. There will be plenty of easier games where he can get even.

But it's not correct to say that an investor is in an analogous position when his stock price has dropped. The poker player who doesn't quit must continue to play in the same game, but the stock buyer is now involved in a different "game" because his stock has become cheaper.

While it's just as correct for an investor as a poker player to ignore the fact that he's in the red if quitting is presently the more rational strategy, it's much more likely that losing investors should actually stay the course since the stock's decline may mean it's now a good buy.

---

[37] Santoli, Michael, "Two of a Kind? With a Poker Face, Wall Street Sees Similarities Between a Card Game and It's Own Game. *"Barron's* June 28, 2004.

Jump-Starting a Friend's Car

My buddy, Henry (not his real name), is a bit absentminded. About twice a year he leaves his headlights on all night and wakes up with a dead battery. Sometimes he has called me to come over and jump-start his car. No problem, that's what friends are for. I know he would do it for me.

However, as the years have passed, my financial status greatly improved, while Henry's hasn't. I also learned the technique described in "Money As Measurement" and started applying it to run of the mill chores. Those chores should be equated with the amount of money it would cost to have someone else do them. (Keep in mind that I say, "run of the mill." It's an important factor in this story.)

When Henry called me to jump-start his car, I realized that it would bother me much less to pay $50 to have a service do it. If there were no alternative, I would definitely have done it myself. But since this service was available, I told Henry, "I'm busy right now. Just call The Car Doctor and pay for it. I'll reimburse you."

Henry was offended and refused.

I tried to get Henry to understand that using a service solved both our problems efficiently. "Henry, I'm your friend and should help you. But I'm relatively rich and want to solve your problem in the way that minimizes the disruption of my life."

Perhaps unsurprisingly, Henry was annoyed and insulted by this offer and explanation. Despite knowing I'd reimburse him, his gut reaction was that my solution was unfeeling and arrogant. Fortunately, Henry is a good poker player who understands how destructive emotional thinking can be. Since he values dispassionate analysis, I was able to convince him that my logic was irrefutable.

First, I got him to admit that the personal touch he wanted was unimportant. This was just a run of the mill chore that he did not want to ask me to do. It wasn't as if he had asked me to drive him to the airport when he was flying off for a vacation. If I had said that I would rather pay for his cab, being bothered would be more reasonable since personally seeing him off would have been part of that request. But in this situation my personal presence was irrelevant.

I asked, "Would it be okay if I sent over my son?"

"Sure."

"How about if I sent over my personal assistant?"

He thought a bit and said, "Okay."

"Then let's just assume I'm hiring the Car Doctor as my personal assistant for this specific task."

He didn't like my way of putting it. If I was paying a personal assistant by the week and sent him, it would have been okay. But using a service for just this task felt different.

Henry also disliked the fact that he had to pay and then get reimbursed. Since he would not personally be willing to pay $50, he felt uncomfortable about laying it out and then getting it back from me. Changing tactics, I said, "Henry, if you won't do it this way, you wouldn't be acting as my friend."

Remember that he knew I absolutely would have gone over if there had been no alternative, he didn't want to inconvenience me, and he knew that $50 was irrelevant to me. So he agreed.

Perhaps some people will think that my choice rubbed in the fact that I was doing a lot better financially than he was. But we were good friends, and he knew I was not trying to put him down.

The bottom line is that my solution was actually better for both of us. I got to avoid a chore, and he got to avoid imposing on me, except for an irrelevant $50. I considered it my obligation to get his car started and his obligation to help me to do it in my preferred way.

Al's Comments

Henry's first reaction was not at all unusual. Many people would be offended or at least have mixed feelings. We would be grateful for the offer of help, but resent the type of help. We would want David to come over personally, and we might even feel insulted by his offer. A few people would have such strong feelings that they would not accept the help or only grudgingly accept it, but continue to feel resentful.

Henry's reaction was actually less irrational than the one that some sensitive people would have. Their sensitivity would make them more emotional and less receptive to logical arguments. A few would even think or say, "If that's the way you feel, I'll get someone else to help me, you #@$^$."

These feelings would be especially strong for anyone who is sensitive about money. The fact that $50 was peanuts to David, but much more than Henry would pay could be seen as an insult. Fortunately, Henry knew David well enough to know that he was not being insulting. Even more important, Henry values logic and has the good poker player's desire to control emotional reactions. Every good player has seen emotional players make terrible mistakes.

So David's logic worked here, but would not work with many people. When we were discussing this story, David said, "I was pushing the envelope, forcing Henry to examine his feelings."

Then I asked, "What would you have done if Henry were more sensitive about money, more easily hurt, and less logical?"

"I would have used a completely different approach. I emphasize logic only with people who understand and respect it."

Our primary goal is not to help you to influence other people. It's to improve your thinking, and you can't think well when you're emotional. Unfortunately, everybody has a few subjects that trigger strong, irrational feelings.

We constantly emphasize the need to think logically because emotions can have such disastrous effects. When you suspect that your emotions may be interfering with your thinking, take four steps.

1. **Analyze your own thoughts and feelings.** Ask yourself, "Am I thinking logically?" It's not easy to answer this question because you don't want to believe you're being illogical. You must fight that desire and look critically at yourself. If you see that you're being illogical, take the next three steps.

2. **Recognize your own "triggers."** What kinds of situations and behaviors cause you to react emotionally? If you analyze your thinking often enough, you will see that you are much more likely to react emotionally in certain kinds of situations.

3. **Analyze the exact ways that your emotions interfere with your logic.** Do you want to fight or flee? Do you overestimate the importance of some factors and ignore others? What other illogical reactions do you have? Why do you have them?

4. **Take whatever actions will make you less emotional.** It may be walking away from the situation, or sitting at a computer writing down ways to cope, or talking to a friend. But one way or another you must reduce those emotions so that you can think logically.

A Tip About Debating

Many people have told me that my profession should have been that of an attorney because I'm pretty good at proving my points. Twoplustwo.com's forums have sharpened those skills and given me many opportunities to demonstrate them. But I wouldn't be a good lawyer. They have to argue for the side they are given. But, as a logician, I argue only for the side that makes sense to me.

However, even when I am clearly correct, some adversaries fight tooth and nail to discredit my arguments. They usually have a personal interest in my being wrong. Sometimes, it's a financial interest; more often it's a psychological one.

Since they don't have truth on their side, they grasp at straws, and I sometimes make the mistake of giving them those straws. I say too much and they twist my words, and use them against me. While arguing for correct positions, many people make the same mistake. They embellish their points to make them more interesting, forceful, or easier to understand.

From experience, I have learned that when you are debating, you must avoid the inclination to say or write things that are not absolutely necessary to your point if those things are at all debatable. My specific recommendations are:

1. Don't exaggerate.[38]

2. Use only examples or analogies that perfectly fit your point.

---

[38] Scientists rarely exaggerate, at least not when discussing their specialty. First, exaggerations hurt their credibility. Second, in scientific discussions, both sides are trying to determine the truth, and distortions work against that purpose. Lawyers have exactly the opposite objective: They deliberately distort the truth to win the argument.

Otherwise, your opponents will seize on your inaccuracies or inconsistencies to discredit your main thesis.

You may think that their tactic is dishonest since your exaggeration, inaccurate analogy, or inappropriate example doesn't mean your thesis is untrue. But their goal is not to determine the truth. They want to score points, put you down, and convince others that you're wrong. So why give your adversaries a chance to muddy the waters?

Al's Comments

David and I were discussing a recent example of his thesis, the great health care debate of 2009. Instead of arguing points rationally, some of those in favor of what has come to be called "Obamacare," demonized the opposition by invoking the term "Nazis" when describing them. On the other side, some of those who opposed the President used the term "death panels" when describing end of life counseling and medical rationing.

But both tactics actually harmed the cause of the people who used them. They were so outlandish that those who were accused actually welcomed these descriptions. It helped them to discredit their detractors. Meanwhile, it sidetracked those who wanted to have an intelligent debate.

Punish the
Police, Not Society

In the battle between major criminals and the public, the authorities are required to play by the rules, while the criminals break them. And if the police or prosecutors break those rules, it often causes them to lose the battle. Despite their obvious guilt, the criminals are frequently set free.

Most lawyers, especially the ones who make lots of money defending criminals, act as if it's just the way the game is played. But it's not a game. Not just because of the serious nature of the battle, but also because there are others who are affected by the outcome, namely you and me. Whenever obviously guilty criminals go free, they and others become more likely to commit other crimes. That fact should change things. Since the current rules work against the public's best interests, I believe that the punishment for breaking some rules should be changed.

Hardly anyone disagrees with the rule that police can't beat a confession out of someone (or anything else along those lines). But what about the rules and repercussions regarding nonviolently, but improperly obtained evidence? Searches without a search warrant or with a warrant containing a small technical flaw, wiretaps without a judge's approval, failure to read Miranda rights, or other violations of that nature. Are they good rules? If they are broken, should the evidence be thrown out of court?

I say they are generally good rules, but we must remember that they are on the books to protect the *innocent*, not to help major criminals escape the punishment they deserve. The tradeoff is probably worth it to most people. Freeing an occasional criminal on a technicality is a small price to pay to protect *us* from police misconduct. But can we reduce this price?

I believe that the public would be better served if the rules were changed so that, for serious crimes and dangerous criminals, illegally obtained evidence should be allowed in court. The obvious question, of course, is how can we keep this proposal from bumping up against the public's desire to be relatively safe from police harassment?

The answer is to continue to penalize the police for gathering evidence illegally. But the penalty should not be to set free major criminals (even though I would support releasing minor criminals). Letting serious criminals walk penalizes everybody, including law-abiding citizens. Rather, the law enforcement officers who broke the rules should be punished.

The exact penalty should depend on the circumstances. Perhaps a hefty fine that goes to the innocent victim of the illegal search. In flagrant cases, perhaps even jail time. And this justice should probably be dispensed by civilians. Certainly such a system would discourage illegal searches and fishing expeditions and other types of police misconduct at least as much as the present system does. With one exception.

If my idea was implemented, police in a few cases may contemplate using measures that would now be no good. For horrific crimes they would use these measures despite knowing that they are "illegal" and can get them into serious trouble. Heroic cops would ignore that risk in extreme cases (partly for the good of everyone and partly because they know that, just like for any other crime, mitigating circumstances will be considered when their misconducted is evaluated).

Certainly, if they break in "illegally" on a child molester in the middle of a crime spree, no judge or jury would convict them (and, under my proposed rules, the evidence would stand). Even if they made a mistake with an innocent person that was obviously done in an effort to get this child molester, I would expect the cop to emerge almost unscathed.

Obviously the details of my idea would require a lot of effort to get out the kinks. But I think it would work.

Al's Comments

In "Using Probability to Punish Criminals" David makes the irrefutable point that increasing a crime's EV increases the likelihood that this crime will occur. No matter why you like or dislike the current rules about throwing out tainted evidence, there is no doubt that these rules increase both the EV and the number of crimes.

That point brings us to "Disputes Between Principles And Pragmatism." David argued there that "Matters of principle are usually overrated. In most of these examples only the fact that the decision was fairly close gave the matter of principle the power to swing your conclusion. If a high enough percentage of redheads blew up airplanes, even the redheads would not object to being profiled." When we were discussing this chapter, he put it even more bluntly: "If the probability of a terrible result gets high enough, pragmatism that will lower that probability *always* trumps principles (that don't)." Therefore, I think that the probability and pervasive fear of becoming a crime victim have become so high that many people, perhaps most, would welcome a change in these rules.

Gay and Sibling Marriage, Stem Cell Research, and Killing Iraqi Children

As already discussed, rationalizing is an utterly ubiquitous thinking flaw. We reach emotionally-based conclusions or take foolish actions and then invent rational reasons to justify them. Everybody does it, but truly rational people work hard to guard against this natural tendency.

For example, scientists have developed double-blind experiments and peer-reviewed journals to minimize the effects of their emotions. I constantly examine my own thinking to see whether my emotions have influenced my thoughts. When I see it happening, my conclusions are revised. Unfortunately, people without mathematical or scientific training, the ones who are most likely to rationalize, are also unlikely to examine their own thinking processes. So they rationalize all the time, usually without realizing it.

The problem is that, if you are trying to rationalize a conclusion that you reached without much thought, your arguments will not really prove your conclusion. I recently came across two good examples.

When President-elect Barack Obama chose Rick Warren to give the invocation at his inauguration, the gay community was outraged. They vehemently argued that Warren was anti-gay because he had publicly opposed gay marriage. While defending himself, Warren claimed that he was not anti-gay. He was against any non-traditional marriage and used the example of a marriage between adult siblings.

Congressman Barney Frank (who is openly homosexual) said that Warren had likened homosexuality to incest. Upon hearing

Frank's remarks, I realized that he was on thin ice. Remember that Warren was talking only about the marriage of adult siblings. Of course, such marriages have genetic risks, but I doubt that they were Frank's main concern. Instead, he was simply stating an emotional conclusion.

To eliminate the genetic risks, let's consider only adult siblings who cannot have children with each other. (Ironically, one example of an infertile couple would be same sex siblings.) What argument could Frank make against such marriages that couldn't also be used against gay marriages? If the issue were presented to him in those terms, Frank might admit that he was justifying a conclusion he made without thinking.

The second example is about people who think that embryonic stem cell research is wrong, but that bombing Iraqi houses with children in them for the purpose of killing terrorists is right. If we stipulate that embryos are children, we must conclude that either both acts are right or both acts are wrong.

In fact, many people accept this symmetry. Some pro-lifers reluctantly accept collateral damage in bombings as well as stem cell research even though they are against abortion and think that embryos are human. Other pro-lifers conclude that their values force them to oppose both. Since their positions are consistent, I have no quarrel with either group.

On our website at www.twoplustwo.com, there was a debate involving people who thought that stem cell research was wrong, but bombing military targets with children in the house was okay. I will argue against only those people.

They felt so strongly that they strained to find a logical rationalization. They argued that stem cell research *requires* the embryo's "death," but bombings don't require the children's deaths, even though they nearly always die. Since their deaths were not intended, they claim a moral distinction.

This argument disgusted me. They were not just splitting hairs, but were very obviously rationalizing. I proposed a thought experiment to prove my point. Suppose the president knows that there are two equal value terrorist targets in two different Iraqi houses. The first house contains five children and one terrorist. The second house has ten children and an equally dangerous terrorist.

Because there is only one plane and one bomb, the president orders the pilot to bomb the house with the five children. Since everything else is equal, he wants to reduce the innocents' death toll by five. But while the pilot is enroute, the president is told a new and odd piece of intelligence. The house with the five children is built in such a way that, if those children weren't there, the terrorist would survive. The children's deaths (for some architectural reason that we need not know) will be what *causes* that terrorist's death. If the plane is diverted to the other house, the bombing will certainly kill the terrorist and ten children, but it will be for normal reasons.

Does anybody seriously think that the plane should be diverted or that any rational president would divert it? If we accept the rationalization about stem cells, he should.

By the way, I haven't seen anyone propose this argument. I believe that there are at least two reasons. First, perhaps nobody has thought of it. Second, even if someone thought of it, most supporters of stem cell research also support abortion rights, and they are looking out for their own interests rather then trying to argue logically. My argument stipulates that killing the embryos is justifiable homicide. Most of the people who support stem cell research won't stipulate that abortion is homicide. So despite it being a great argument, they won't use it because they are worried about their own agenda. And that point brings us right back to rationalizing and arguing emotionally rather than logically.

Al's Comments

I am much less optimistic than David about Barney Frank's admitting his error. He's a politician, and politicians will do almost anything to avoid admitting mistakes, especially emotionally-based ones. But Frank's rationalizing is not the issue. Yours is. Everybody rationalizes, but you can reduce the frequency and counter-productive effects of rationalization by taking two steps.

1. **Constantly examine your own thinking.** You may be tired of hearing me beat that drum, but it's absolutely indispensable towards thinking more clearly. Whenever you may be rationalizing, ask yourself, "Why did I take that position?"

    Don't accept your first answer. Look hard at your reasons, especially your motives and emotions. Ask follow-up questions such as: "Do I have any motives or feelings that would affect my thinking?" "Are my feelings making me ignore or distort the evidence?" "Did I analyze the situation objectively before reaching that conclusion or did I come up with good reasons afterwards?"

2. **Do what virtually all scientists do.** Even though we are naturally more detached and objective than most people, and have been trained to distrust our gut feelings, we still rely heavily on procedures and external controls to reduce the effects of our biases. Virtually all research reports include a methodology section so that readers can see how conclusions were reached, and all serious research is reported in peer-reviewed journals so that spurious results are not published.

Smart businesspeople and professionals have friends or colleagues who tell them the truth, even when they don't want to hear it. For example, Robert Townsend, the former chairman at Avis, once wrote that he ran his ideas past critical people: "My batting average at Avis was no better than .333. Two out of three decisions I made were wrong. But my mistakes were discussed openly, and most of them were corrected with a little help from my friends."[39]

Good doctors frequently get a second opinion about a diagnosis and treatment plan before drawing any firm conclusions. They are also taught from their first days in medical school not to reach a diagnosis too quickly because once they do so, they will place more weight on evidence that agrees with it and minimize or ignore contradictory evidence.

If you follow the lead of David, scientists, and doctors, you will avoid expensive, embarrassing mistakes. In simplest terms, *don't trust your first reaction.* Check it carefully before making decisions.

---

[39] *Up The Organization: How to Stop The Organization from Stifling People and Strangling Profits,* NY, Knopf, 1970, p. 115

They Would Pass
a Lie Detector. So What?

They sincerely think they are telling the truth, but aren't. For example, people who ask to borrow money often believe that they will repay the loan promptly. They expect to get a job, collect debts from other people, win a lawsuit, or whatever.

I think it's one reason that the rich avoid less wealthy people. They expect, perhaps unconsciously, to be asked for money or other favors by people who intend to repay them, but never do. This problem is particularly common among poker players and other gamblers. I frequently get asked, "David, will you back me in that game? It's a weak table, and I know I can beat them."

This person is usually not lying. He believes he is better than they are and may even be right. However, as I have often said, most people do not play nearly as well as they think. So even though my potential horse sincerely believes he's a favorite in this game, he may really be a big underdog. And, even if he's a favorite, he's almost certainly not that big a favorite, and small favorites are not worth backing.

Perhaps the most frequent example of a sincerely believed falsehood is: "I will love you forever." We have all heard it and believed it, but look what happened.

If you express your doubts, people may be offended by your "distrust." People naturally personalize the situation because communicating, even indirectly, that you don't believe someone is personally insulting.

So what should you do? I honestly don't know.

But I do know what you shouldn't do. Don't act like you think he's purposely lying. And don't make him feel that you think he's an idiot for not realizing his promises won't hold up. Here are three strategies to use:

216

1.   When dealing with an intelligent person, explain why he may be deceiving himself.

2.   When dealing with someone who is too dumb to get the point, or someone you don't care that much about him, give a plausible excuse that won't hurt his feelings such as "I never lend money to anyone."

3.   When dealing with someone who isn't easily placated but isn't asking for that much, you can get rid of him by fulfilling the request.

Al's Comments

The lesson here is simple: Don't mistake sincerity for realism.

Common Business Math Mistakes

We saw earlier that Bob Stupak did not think correctly about his Diamond Ring Promotion. Here are four similar errors.

Allocating Slot Machines

Casino executives naturally want to earn as much as possible from every square foot of casino floor space. Until recently, an important decision for them concerned the number of nickel, quarter, and dollar machines to put in. (Many new machines allow customers to choose their denomination.) Because dollar machines have higher average daily winnings than quarter ones, executives often thought that they should replace as many quarter machines as possible with dollar ones. This change seemed like a no-brainer. Or was it?

Their reasoning was flawed. Replacing quarter machines with $1 machines might be a serious mistake even though they might earn more by replacing some $1 machines with quarter ones. The critical concept is incremental income.

Let's say that a casino had 200 quarter machines that earned a total daily average of $20,000 and 100 $1 machines that averaged $12,000 per day. Thus, each quarter machine averaged $100 per day versus $120 for the $1 machines.

But let's dig deeper. First, notice that a single $1 slot machine played continuously would win almost four times as much as a single quarter machine played continuously. (I say "almost" because the house edge on a $1 machine is usually a bit smaller than on a quarter machine.) Since the results in this hypothetical example had the $1 machines winning only 20 percent more than the quarter machines, the $1 machines were obviously not nearly as busy.

If half of the $1 machines were removed, the patrons who played those machines would still find plenty available. If you reduced the number of $1 machines to 50, you might still win about $10,000, which is $200 per day per machine. In other words, the second 50 machines might have added only $2,000 total or $40 per machine.

Now let's look at the quarter machines. Since they are busier, removing them would probably have a significant impact. I won't bore you with any more math, but even the worst quarter machines are probably making more than $40 per day. If you took them out to add yet more $1 machines, your income would probably go down. In fact, you might increase revenues by replacing $1 machines with quarter machines.

Should We
Have A Poker Room?

Many casinos executives resist putting in poker rooms because they seem to use floor space inefficiently. Slot machines earn much more per square foot than live poker tables. Executives of casinos with poker rooms usually regard them as a necessary evil. They need to attract customers by offering all types of games. But that rationale may be unnecessary. A poker room may be a worthwhile source of incremental revenue.

Executives who think otherwise may be making the same mistake that some of them make about slot machines. You cannot necessarily say that, since slot machines make $50 per day per square foot and poker rooms make $30 per day per square foot you reduce revenues by taking out slots to put in card tables. Unless your casino is extremely crowded, almost all your slot customers will simply squeeze into a slightly smaller space, and your poker revenue is primarily extra income that you would not have received otherwise. Put another way, the incremental income of those last square feet cannot be calculated by using the average income per square foot for the whole casino.

I should add that this error also occurs frequently when executives decide whether to add an unusual table game such as my *All In Hold 'Em*. They sometimes reject new games because they don't win quite as much as the average blackjack table. Hopefully, you now see their mistake.

Sports Bettors

I have known a few great sports handicappers. One of them wins about 58 percent of his bets, which is an excellent percentage. Despite his success, some people say, "He's a good handicapper, but a bad gambler." They argue that you should be very happy to make bets that will win 55 percent of the time. Therefore, this guy is obviously too conservative. But is he?

The critics are probably confused. His results don't imply that he is passing up games with a 55 percent chance of winning. Perhaps many of his bets are over 60 percent. If half his bets are on 55 percent shots, and half are on 61 percent shots, his overall result will be 58 percent.

Bank Officers

Because banks have lost so much money recently, bank officers are rarely criticized for being too conservative. But these criticisms were once fairly common. Suppose his boss tells him to loan money as long as he feels there is a 95 percent chance of being paid back. As years go by, his boss notices that 97 percent of the loans have been paid back. Since the bank makes money on 95 percent shots, he scolds his subordinate. But the boss is wrong.

The boss is making the same type of math mistake we just discussed. He is taking the average. But some of the loans that make up that average are above the loan officer's average risk, and some are below it. Some loans probably have only a 95 percent chance of being paid. But since some are close to 100 percent, his overall average could be 97 percent. Conversely, if his overall average was exactly 95 percent, he is almost certainly making loans that are less likely than that to be paid back, which costs the bank money.

Obviously, these kinds of errors can occur in many places, and you should guard against them. In other words, don't get confused by averages.

Casino
Catastrophe Insurance

Bob Stupak never got around to implementing a few of my ideas. One of my favorites should both please gamblers and make more money for casinos. Since it's too late to patent it, I'll offer it as a gift to my casino owner friends.

As usual, my promotion combines math and psychology. I was looking to guarantee customers a minimum amount of playing time and a chance to win much more money, while simultaneously increasing the casino's average profits. Insurance against catastrophic losses would encourage customers to make more and larger bets.

Suppose you're a casino owner and have a customer who likes to make the even money roulette bets. He has a $100,000 credit line and makes bets up to $500. The theoretical earn on each of those bets is about $27 (with a double zero wheel). Over a weekend he might make 1,000 such bets, and your profit will be around $27,000. Of course, you would prefer that he bet $1,000 per spin, enabling you to have an expected win of $54,000.

He is worried that, if he makes those $1,000 bets, he will lose his whole $100,000 credit line before the weekend is over. But you, as a casino owner, can *guarantee* that he won't run out of money. You tell him, "You're guaranteed a thousand $1,000 bets, but can't lose over $100,000."

"What?"

"If you make a thousand or fewer bets and your losses exceed $100,000, everything over $100,000 is forgiven."

"Wow."

Since this person can't lose any more than $100,000, he can increase his bets without fearing he will have to stop. If his losses exceed $100,000, he can keep playing without risking another

222

penny. He can win some or even all that money back. It looks like you're being extremely generous, but your downside is actually negligible. DUCY?

If he makes a thousand even money roulette bets, he should win about 473 of them. Your guarantee will cost you money only if he wins fewer than 450 bets. I won't bore you with the math, but it won't happen very often. And, even when it happens, he will usually just miss 450. You will rarely have to forgive anything, and you will almost never forgive much. In return, you get twice as much total action. So your EV almost doubles.

The scheme would work with different formats for various games. The exact numbers would depend on how long the player wanted to play and the house's edge. Slot machines can easily use this method. In fact, there is now a patented slot machine that does it (and I have heard of a video poker machine with a similar feature).

I believe that the slot machine's patent is legal even though I had discussed this idea with Lyle Berman (CEO of Lakes Gaming), Mark Yoseloff (ex-CEO of Shuffle Master), and Steve Weiss (Ex-CEO of Casino Data Systems) long before they got their patent. My idea had not reached the public domain which is the criterion for disallowing a patent.

The slot machine offers a fixed number of pulls with a maximum loss. For instance, you might get one hundred $1 pulls and a $30 maximum loss. At the end of a hundred pulls, if you are losing more then $30, you are forgiven the excess. Catastrophic losses are rare, and this system eliminates the fear of them. So some players will bet more money for a longer period of time.

Baccarat provides another example. Some casinos are already offering rebates to high rolling baccarat players. Typically, when a high roller wants to make big bets for several hours, they offer him a flat percentage refund (perhaps 10 or 15 percent) on anything he loses. However, if they offered a much higher percentage, but only on everything above a certain threshold amount, both the casino and the customer would be happier. High rollers don't care much about a small percentage refund when they take a small loss, but they would love to get back 50 percent or more on everything above a fairly large loss.

Since casinos cherish high rollers, keeping them happy is essential. When you can keep them happy while simultaneously increasing your EV, you're really doing well. Since both the casino and the customer are happier with some variation of my idea, it's clearly the way to go.

Sports betting probably provides one of the neatest ways to apply my concept. For instance, you could allow people to bet on ten football or basketball games, but be obligated for a maximum of only one-half the total amount that would normally be risked.

The point spread in football and basketball games makes both sides even bets, so you put up $110 to win $100. That extra $10 is the bookies' commission, which is often called "juice," "vigorish," or "vig." Normally, if you bet ten games and win all ten, you would make $1,000. If you lose all ten, you would lose $1,100. If you bet $110 on each of five games, your total risk would be $550, and your maximum possible win would be $500.

With my scheme you could bet ten games, win a maximum of $1,000, but any loss beyond $550 would be forgiven. If you were betting with a casino bookie, you would just give him $550. If you won, you would be paid your winnings plus your $550. For example, if you won all ten games, you would be paid $1,000 plus your $550. If you won nine games you would be paid $790 plus your $550.

Sounds great, doesn't it? You may even wonder how the bookies could afford to do it. It's another time that thinking creatively about probabilities can help you to understand issues and make better decisions.

The bookie's downside is quite small. He is penalized only when you win fewer then three games. This scheme costs him:

- $550 if you win no games

- $340 if you win only one game

- $130 if you win two games

Since the promotion will rarely cost the bookie much, his total earn compared to your betting five games actually increases. Let's look at the math. If you would normally bet 10 games at $110 each, the bookie would expect to earn $50 since he gets $5 per bet. With these rebates his profit goes down, but not nearly as much as you might think. Since the $550 forgiveness occurs only about $\frac{1}{1,000}$ of the times that someone bets on ten games, it costs him an average of $0.55. The $340 forgiveness occurs about $\frac{1}{100}$ of the time; that's $3.40. The $130 forgiveness occurs about $4\frac{1}{2}$ percent of the time, or about $6. All together this promotion costs the bookie a total EV of about $10. That's a pretty amazing figure; it means that this promotion merely reduces his EV for the ten games from $50 to $40.

To show how truly amazing this promotion is, put yourself in the shoes of a player who walks in with $550, planning to bet $110 on only five games or to bet $55 on ten games. The bookie says, "Sir, I'll let you bet $110 on ten games so that you can win $1,000."

Naturally, you reply, "I've got only $550."

The bookie than shocks you by saying, "Don't worry about it. That's the most I'll take from you. If you lose more than $550, I'll forgive the rest."

If you agree to this "generous" offer, he has raised his EV from $25 to $40. The bookie's "generosity" has increased his profits by $15. But you're happy because you've doubled your upside without changing your downside.

I believe that someday many bookies will use this astonishing little wrinkle. The more general principle is that casinos and sports books should develop rebate plans that are very generous as long as the larger costs rarely occur.

Even if you're not interested in casino economics, you should realize that my scheme is crudely analogous to buying an insurance policy with a very high deductible. The insurance company accepts the risk of a substantial loss, and you pay a small premium to protect yourself against that loss. I believe such insurance is pretty much a win-win situation, and it's one of the few variations of standard insurance that I have no problems with.

Al's Comments

When David first told me this idea, I thought, "It's got to be a scam. It just sounds too good to be true." When he mentioned the insurance analogy, it became clear because I have often bought high deductible policies. Since the insurance company has to make a profit, and the administrative costs are a high percentage of small claims, it's silly to insure against risks you can afford to accept.

I wish the people who are arguing so bitterly about revising our health care system would read this chapter and understand the meaning of the word "insurance." Until recently it has always meant protection against unpredictable, serious losses. No rational insurance system protects people against events such as routine doctors' visits. The costs of processing the paperwork for small expenses are absurdly high.

Just look around any doctor's office and count the number of people pushing paper back and forth. It doesn't matter who pays their salaries or the salaries of the people at insurance companies and government agencies. Ultimately, all the costs are paid by you and me. We can pay it in taxes or insurance premiums, but we will certainly pay it.

We now waste large amounts of money every year on unnecessary paperwork. Many of the schemes promoted to "improve" our system will greatly increase that waste and our costs. Reducing waste would benefit everyone, but it won't be done until people stop insisting on unnecessary "insurance."

A Little More
Thinking Outside the Box

About ten years ago I was lucky enough to make the acquaintance of a gorgeous young lady named Shay. We have kept in touch throughout the years, and she is now probably the most beautiful surgical technician in Las Vegas. Not surprisingly, I liked spending time with her and would sometimes bend over backwards to make sure she felt the same way about me.

One day we were at the Las Vegas International Airport to pick up one of her friends. We saw three women about her age wearing attractive cowboy hats. They were identical and had almost certainly been bought at a Las Vegas shop. Shay fell in love with those hats. Upon seeing how she felt, I said, "Well, let's find out where they got them, and I'll buy you one." Of course, she really appreciated my promise and was looking forward to getting one.

When I asked these women where they got their hats, they couldn't help me. Either they couldn't remember the store, or they may have told me the store was sold out. Shay was disappointed because she thought I couldn't keep my promise. But she was wrong. I let my mind think outside the box and asked, "Who will sell me her hat?"

They looked at me like I was crazy. Shay covered her face and said, "Oh, my God, I can't believe you said that!"

I said, "Why?" Then I asked the women, "How much did those hats cost you?"

One woman said, "About 60 bucks."

I instantly replied, "I'm paying $100 to whoever wants to sell me one."

It was enough to get one of them to say, "Well, sure."

Shay happily walked away, wearing the hat she wanted. She looked at me, shook her head, and said, "David, you're crazy. I can't believe you did that." But deep down she was tickled pink and impressed that I wasn't constrained by normal rules, and as previously stated, neither you nor I should be constrained by unimportant rules.

As far as I was concerned, this situation was similar to buying out the $1 to $4 players that I discussed earlier in "A Little Creative Thinking." I think this incident occurred first, but it doesn't really mater. The important thing is to recognize when and how to think outside the box.

It didn't take Shay long to feel okay with my "craziness." As the years went by, she would occasionally tug on my sleeve and say, "David, I need that hat or that belt." Or even one time, "those shoes." I was usually able to pull it off.

However, thinking outside the box is not without risk. I discovered one of them when Shay and I were on a movie ticket line. As usual, many men and women stared at Shay, a beautiful olive-skinned girl. And of course, I enjoyed the envy that many guys showed. Our conversation turned toward physical fitness which led me to say, "I'm in better shape than you think. Beneath this layer of fat are pretty solid abs. I've even let people punch me in the stomach to prove it."

Besides being beautiful, Shay is a great athlete. She wanted to call my bluff and punch me, right there in the movie line. I thought it was a bit silly, but since she insisted, I let her do it. She wound up and hit me with all her might. It stung, but didn't really hurt me. I was feeling proud of myself, even preening a bit. Then this young, athletic looking black kid comes up and says, "Can I do that?"

Well, obviously, I wouldn't let him hit me. And, of course, it annoyed me that he was using my little demonstration to hone in on my girl.

But I had an idea to establish the upper hand. He was wearing an outlandish necklace, filled with stones that looked like diamonds, but obviously couldn't be. Shay was staring at it. Remembering my past successes, I said to this kid, "No, you can't hit me in the stomach. But I would like to buy that necklace for her. What would you charge me?"

I was willing to pay two or three hundred dollars to put him down. He shocked me by saying, "Well, I paid $750,000 for it."

Of course, I didn't believe him, so I replied, "Yeah, sure you did!"

Then Shay said something I'll never forget. "David, do you know that you're talking to Floyd Mayweather?"

My Abusive
High School Teacher

Something was wrong with my ninth grade art teacher. He liked to hurt his students. One of his favorite tricks was to push his finger between a kid's collar bone and neck. Almost everyone in his classes received this treatment or something similar.

Because he was a good teacher and his antics occurred infrequently, no one complained at first. His cruelty didn't appear dangerous, and no one was hurt. Besides, nobody wanted to look like a sissy or a snitch. Still, his actions were against the rules and probably illegal, and some parents found out and complained.

The authorities reprimanded him and put a stop to his shenanigans, but couldn't decide whether to fire him. (Nowadays, they would have fired him instantly, but the authorities then did not know how dangerous abusive teachers can be.) So they decided to leave it up to us. They appointed Carol, a classmate, to conduct a private meeting with us without any adults attending. We would vote to decide his fate. It didn't look good for him because earlier conversations clearly indicated that almost every student wanted him fired.

But Carol made a mistake when conducting the vote. She started by saying, "Please raise your hand if you want him fired." The kids looked around the room to see what the others were doing. Almost no one raised his hand. She immediately announced, "Well, I guess we'll let him stay."

The reason I remembered and brought up this story is totally unrelated to the subject of abusive teachers or whether students should decide their fate. It's that I immediately recognized that she hadn't thought things through. DUCY?

Remember, she almost certainly knew that we wanted to fire him. Setting aside the fact that she should have conducted a secret ballot, why didn't she first ask, "Who wants him to stay?" The way she asked the question almost guaranteed the opposite result from our true preference. Since the kids realized that going on record as opposing him risked retaliation, they played it safe by not raising their hands.

"Why didn't Carol realize that?" More generally, why didn't anyone except me realize that her way of asking the question basically "fixed" the vote?

I'm pretty sure that Carol did not purposefully influence the outcome. She just wasn't thinking ahead, nor do most ninth graders. But you are not in ninth grade anymore, and you will undoubtedly find yourself in situations that require you to understand what is going through other people's minds, including their desire to avoid getting into trouble. So hopefully you won't make the same mistake that Carol made.

Al's Comments

This simple story has several lessons. They aren't original, but they are often ignored. Before acting, ask a few questions:

1. How do other people see the situation?

2. How do I want them to think, feel, and act?

3. What should I do to get the desired reactions?

It's not rocket science. In fact, answering these questions just requires to do what Carol didn't do: Think before acting.

You're probably not as bright as David. So we have to put in more hours studying math, logic, and so on. You can't change your genes or your previous experiences, but you can compensate for your limitations through hard work. It won't be easy or pleasant, but you can become much better at reading people, predicting how they will react, and planning, then executing the steps that get the results you want.

Sympathy
Trumps Empathy

People can say or do what they want for any reason. They need not worry about being irrational or contradicting their own general ideas, morals, or precepts.

Unless they expect other people to agree with them. Once they hope that happens or they try to persuade others of their position's rightness, they should be willing to take the test of logical consistency. You can hold positions for visceral reasons, but if they are inconsistent with your other stated positions, don't expect intelligent people to agree with you.

A case that personally bugs me involves the willingness to help strangers in need, but only when you personally come upon them. I fully understand that this is a widespread and understandable proclivity. But what bothers me is that people will claim that this characteristic is admirable. They expect admiration, not just for their desire to help, but for being more inclined to help when they personally witness the distress.

I am not comparing helping a new neighbor with aiding African children. Other issues are involved there that might muddy the waters. I'm comparing apples to apples. Let's assume that:

1. All the people needing help are strangers, and they all have the same relationship to you.

2. They will not receive help if you don't give it to them.

Even in that case almost everybody will contribute much more when they are staring the distress in the face. They would be even more inclined to do so if the distressed person can personally interact with them.

For example, many people would contribute money or time to save a child whose father was carrying his medicine, but was stranded and begged for help to get that medicine to him. However, far fewer would make this sacrifice to save two children they read about in the paper, even if they were sure they would die otherwise.

That's all well and good. People are like that. They have no obligation to save anybody, and some won't do it. So those who would save the child whose father they met are more admirable than those who would save no one. But they are less admirable than the guy who would save two children whose father was never met. Period.

If you would save one rather than the two, you're reacting to selfish impulses. You get more pleasure from seeing how your charity helps, or you feel less guilt about not helping when you don't see the results. And whereas you deserve plaudits for helping at all, it's ridiculous to give you extra credit for being selfish. If you don't need added incentives to help, you're more admirable. The first person should, in fact, have some approval subtracted because without the added incentives he wouldn't help.

In real life most people have this backwards. They look down on someone who won't contribute to help that desperate father who was lucky enough to encounter them, but have a much smaller problem about not making an equal contribution to the local children's hospital.

Suppose you encountered that desperate father when you were driving a truck full of medicine to save other children's lives. Even if you had never met those other children, you certainly should not divert that medicine.

Let's make it more personal. You stop when you see an auto accident. Two people are unconscious, and one is conscious. You have enough medicine to save the lives of the two unconscious people or the life of the conscious one (for some reason, he needs more medicine than they do). If you save the other two, the conscious one will beg you to save him, "How can you do this to me?"

You know that, if you let him die, his words will ring in your ears for a long, long time. What would you do?

Now let's turn the tables. You somehow know that you will be one of the three people in an accident. You have a two-thirds chance of being unconscious. Which type of person do you want to arrive at the accident? Doctors and paramedics are trained to be impersonal, to do whatever saves the most lives — in this case the two unconscious victims. Do you want someone with that impersonal attitude, which means that you have a two-thirds chance of survival? Or would you prefer to half your survival chances with the one who will save you only if you are conscious?

You may want to fall back on a comment like: "Of course you're right, David, theoretically at least. It's just that people who can look at things that way, especially if they aren't doctors or whatever, seem kind of creepy to me." If you feel that way, I won't argue with you. Just don't claim that the "feeling" person is somehow superior to the impersonal, "creepy" one.

That's what this book is about, taking effective action, not reacting emotionally. We want to help you to take the actions which have the best consequences, not the ones that feel or look good.

Some
Bad Bets are "Okay"

If you've read my other books, you may be shocked by that statement. I have written so often about the importance of maximizing long-term EV that many people use the term, "Sklansky Bucks" as shorthand for the theoretical dollars you win or lose by making positive or negative EV bets regardless of your actual results.

But maximizing your EV is a means, not an end. My other books' primary purpose was to help readers to maximize their long-term profits. If your primary goal is to have fun or to have a shot at a big win, some types of negative EV gambling may be okay.

Many factors determine whether negative EV gambling is reasonable or unreasonable, and these factors' importance depends upon the individual. Some people prefer games of skill, while others don't. Some enjoy betting long shots because a chance for a big win is more important to them than winning smaller amounts more frequently. Others have exactly the opposite preference. When making your decision, ask yourself these questions:

1. Is the pleasure you gain from gambling more valuable to you than the money it costs you?

2. Do you recognize and accept that you will lose money in the long run?

3. Can you afford to lose that money?

4. How important is skill to you? Generally, but not always, the more skill influences your results, the more pleasure you gain from winning or even just playing. Unfortunately, you might also get more pain from losing at skill games.

5. How much is the amount risked compared to the amount you hope to win?

6. Do you prefer frequent small wins or occasional large ones?

7. How great is the house edge?

8. Is that house edge clearly known or hidden?

Before using these questions to evaluate various forms of gambling, let me briefly digress. In 1999 I testified before The National Gambling Impact Study Commission. The U.S. Congress established this commission to conduct "a comprehensive study of the social and economic impacts of gambling in the United States."

After testifying, I chatted with one of the commission's nine members. He was a big shot on the pro-gambling side. I asked him, "What do you think would happen to the Las Vegas casino industry if probability and statistics became a required high school course?"

To my surprise, he said, "It would be a catastrophe for us."

Of course he was right, but it was surprising to hear this. Perhaps the commission member knew that if he said anything else, I would realize he was lying. The undeniable truth is that the casino industry would not be remotely as successful if people were more intelligent and knowledgeable about probabilities and statistics. Or we could put it another way: Casinos depend on their customers' ignorance.

The cigarette industry also exploits its customers, but it does so differently. Cigarettes cause more harm than gambling, but cigarette manufacturers are less reliant on people's ignorance. Virtually all smokers today know what their risks are, and they have freely decided to take those risks. On the other hand, many casino patrons do not know the risks. If they knew all the facts, they would either stop gambling or at least gamble differently.

Personally, I have little sympathy for dumb gamblers. Plenty of information is available, and people who don't obtain and use this information and then lose lots of money deserve what they get. However, I still see it as ironic that Las Vegas and the whole state of Nevada depend so heavily on stupidity.

Las Vegas and Nevada depend on tax dollars to educate their citizens, and most Nevada politicians claim that education is a top priority. Yet the money to educate our citizens comes primarily from people they need to keep uneducated. If they were better educated, they would lose much less money and the tax revenues would plummet.

As I'm writing this, we are in the midst of a huge nationwide economic crisis. Las Vegas and other Nevada towns are doing even worse than most other places. In addition to nationwide problems, there is the fact that gambling is not a necessity. When people have to cut expenses, it's one of the first things some of them will drop. Also players are becoming more educated and are not as apt to return to stupid behaviors even when the economy improves.

Getting back to my original substance, what exactly is my take on various gambling games? I just comment briefly here. For more information, see pages 169-227 of *Getting The Best Of It.*

Obviously, I have no problem with games that allow a skillful player to have an edge. After all, that's how I made my living for years. An expert can get an edge in many games, with poker being the foremost example. It offers the greatest possibility for profit, and learning how to play poker helps you in myriad ways. In fact, Al Schoonmaker and I wrote an essay called "Poker Is Good For You" that you can find in the appendix.

Other games that allow experts to get an edge are blackjack, sports betting, and horse racing. Even if you're not an expert, sports and horse betting can give you lots of pleasure for your money. You can spend many enjoyable hours studying the teams or the horses and arguing with your friends before making a bet.

If you bet on a game, watching it is much more exciting. And most games take hours. Horse races are over quickly, but there is no feeling quite like rooting for your horse as it races down the home stretch. And, after the race or game is over, you can talk to your friends about your good or bad handicapping. So I have no problem with blackjack, horse racing, and sports betting.

I'll go even further and say that many casino games that cannot be beaten are still reasonable and that playing them does not make you dumb (unless you risk money you can't afford to lose or erroneously think you have an edge). When you play a casino game with a disadvantage, you get entertainment and a chance to win significant money for the negative EV (Sklansky Bucks) you "spend."

If you go into a casino with $100 that is not particularly relevant to you knowing that you have a chance to win thousands, that feeling of anticipation is worth something. So is the fact that the game may be entertaining or even interesting and skill-dependent enough to provide mental exercise.

Because of these benefits, I believe it's fine to play many casino gambling games even though you're playing against an edge. You could play craps (making only the small disadvantage bets), or roulette on a single zero wheel, or one of the skill games like blackjack without having quite enough expertise to beat it.

Poker machines are also acceptable even though there is usually a slight house edge. Most of them give you a pretty good gamble (between 96 percent and 99 percent), and they are fun to play. There's some thought involved, it's a relaxing game, and you have a reasonable chance of hitting a pretty big jackpot. The royal flush jackpot is about a 40,000-to-1 shot; if you play many hours, you have a small, but not impossible, chance to hit it.

Many casinos that cater to Las Vegas residents are filled with good payback poker machines. They are not as luxurious, and their real estate is less expensive than the ones on The Strip, which allow them to survive on machines that win as little as $10 an hour (for the casino) when played continuously. The Strip's casinos have fewer poker machines, and they typically have a payback schedule with about double the hourly win rate of the locals' casinos. Still these machines are not bad.

However, slot machines are bad. Unlike poker machines, they need no skill. You just pull the handle or press the button, and their hourly win rate is exorbitant because the wheels spin so quickly. Even a 95 percent return machine will win a significant amount of money per hour. The expected win rate is almost certainly far higher then the average customer realizes.

So we have a machine that offers you very little entertainment value since it's a mindless game, and it takes lots of your money. The only possible redeeming feature would be the large jackpots, but they are incredibly difficult to hit, much more so than they appear.

Not too long ago a slot machine had 20 symbols on each of three reels, and the jackpot symbol appeared once on each reel. Then the jackpot occurred once in 8,000 times.

$$8,000 = (20)(20)(20)$$

The only way to allow for bigger jackpots was to use 4 or 5 reels, turning the probabilities from 8,000-to-1 to 160,000- or 3,200,000-to-1. However, when they added reels, the customer realized what he was up against or at least he had an inkling of it.

Nowadays, slot machines do not display each symbol at the same frequency. A computer uses a random number generator to decide which symbol to display. On a 3 reel slot machine, the jackpot symbol may come up only once in 200 times. The jackpot itself would therefore be about a one in 8 million shot.

$$8,000,000 = (200)(200)(200)$$

Some customers realize that things have changed, some are only vaguely aware, and some are clueless. They're pouring all this money into a machine thinking they have some slight, but reasonable chance to hit this large jackpot. But it may be hit only once every 5 years.

To further deceive customers (in states where it's not outlawed), machines display jackpot symbols much more frequently in the window than they appear on the "Pay Line." It looks as though the wheel just went a little too far or not quite far enough. But the computer decided in advance where it would end up. This bit of deception perpetuates the feeling, especially among inexperienced players, that it's easier to win a jackpot than it really is. Of course, some jackpots are so big that people usually realize that the odds against hitting them must be extremely large. But they still would probably be shocked if they knew the real odds.

I've often wondered what would happen if there were a Truth in Gambling Law like the Truth in Lending Law. What would happen if slot machines were required to display the probability of hitting the big jackpot? I believe that many people would stop playing them.

If that's true, doesn't it mean that the casinos are counting on the machines' deceptiveness? Personally, I have no sympathy for people who don't investigate what they're doing. But if you're more liberal politically, you might want to consider this issue.

Still, slot machines are not my least favorite game. That spot is reserved for baccarat. This choice may surprise you because the house edge on baccarat seems to be small, about 1.2 percent. However, that 1.2 percent is actually significant on even money bets. If you want to make a big score, the parlay effect will work against you. For example, if your goal is to multiply your starting bankroll by 35, you actually have a better chance by betting on a single number on a double zero roulette wheel than you do parlaying your $100 into $3,500 playing baccarat. The roulette wheel's edge is more than four times larger than the house's edge in baccarat, but you have to win so many bets that the cumulative effect of the house's edge would grind you down. If you just want to make even money bets (and know what you're doing), you're better off playing craps or blackjack. In those games the edge against smart players is under 1 percent.

Perhaps my biggest problem with baccarat is the little card they give customers to mark off the patterns of wins and losses; win, win, win, loss, win, loss, etc. to give players' information they will use to decide which way to bet. These cards encourage stupidity. You cannot get an edge or even reduce your negative edge in virtually any gambling game by observing the patterns of wins and losses. Mathematicians, smart people, and casino owners know it, but the casinos still encourage such nonsense.

Another problem with baccarat is that it's mindless and skill-less, requiring no significant decisions whatsoever (except it's slightly better to bet on the bank than on the player). Finally, baccarat tends to cater to very wealthy people who don't mind throwing away thousands or even millions in a foolish attempt to win money. I think that even politically conservative people should frown on such a waste of money, especially during our current economic crisis,when millions of people have lost their jobs, homes, savings, and pensions. Of course, people have a right to do whatever they please with their money, but that right does not make their behavior any less disgusting.

Let me close with an amusing fact that demonstrates the relationship between intelligence and gambling. During Comdex, a huge convention of computer people, the casinos are almost empty. Although many of the conventioneers are rich, they won't give their money to the casinos. But it's not because they are cheap. Just ask the strip club owners. The Comdexers will spend lots of money when they are getting value for it, and during Comdex, those places are packed.

Al's Comments

Although requiring high school students to study probability and statistics would be catastrophic for the casino industry, some people would still gamble stupidly. Knowledge alone will not prevent everyone from denying reality.

Since you may yield to irrational forces, compare your answers to David's eight questions with your gambling habits. You may find conflicts between them. For example, you may claim to prefer games of skill, but spend a lot of time playing slots or craps. Or take a common conflict: Some losing poker players refuse to work on their games because they claim to play for fun, but whine constantly. If losing makes them miserable, why don't they either work on their games or quit playing?

The worst conflict is probably about question three: Can you afford to lose the money? If you can't afford it, any negative EV gambling is destructive and should be stopped immediately.

Whenever you see a conflict between your answers and your actions, ask yourself, "Why am I acting this way?" Once you understand the forces driving your actions, you are less likely to act destructively.

Making
Inferences from Subtle Cues

Because my books emphasize math and probabilities, some people think I ignore psychology, both at the poker tables and in real life. After reading this far, you should realize that they are wrong. Here are a couple of stories about picking up and using subtle behavioral cues to make profitable decisions.

During the 2009 NCAA basketball tournament, President Obama picked North Carolina to win the championship. Upon hearing this, Duke's coach, Mike Krzyzewski, said, "As much as I respect what he's doing, really, the economy is something that he should focus on, probably more than the brackets."

Krzyzewski's comment was out of line. He might think it, but it was rude for a basketball coach to publicly criticize the president about such a normal remark. So I wondered why he said it and decided that he must be under a lot of stress to forget his manners that way. The most likely answer was that he was worried about his team's chances.

Duke had barely won its first tournament game against Texas, 74-69. In a few days Duke would face Villanova, a much tougher team. Duke was a $2\frac{1}{2}$ point favorite. I bet \$3,000 on Villanova and they beat Duke 77-54. That's a gigantic loss for a favorite, and it confirmed that Krzyzewski believed that Duke was in trouble.

(Incidentally, North Carolina beat Villanova 83-69 and then trounced MSU in the final game, 89-72. When he finishes his current gig, perhaps President Obama will become a sports handicapper.)

Here is a financial story. I was once quite friendly with a wealthy businessman. After several years of not seeing each other, we accidentally met at The Bellagio, sat down, drank coffee, and caught up on our personal news. He said he had sold his business and was concentrating on the stock market.

When he got up to leave, he walked about ten feet, stopped, hesitated as if wondering, "What should I do?" came back, and leaned down to whisper the name of a stock. That's all he said. Then he quickly walked away.

Because he's smart and successful, I would have bought some of that stock no matter how he had delivered the tip. But his wondering whether he should tell me suggested that he may have had some reason for not disclosing this information. Perhaps he was thinking, "Should I let David in on this opportunity? But, if I don't, I'll feel guilty." So I bought many more shares than normal. They shot up almost immediately, quintupling my money.

When this story was told on the Business, Finance, and Investing Forum at www.twoplustwo.com, some people lambasted me. "How could you base a significant financial decision on such weird information?" They made fun of my emphasizing the fact that he took several steps and then turned around.

They had a point (although many other 2+2ers disagreed with them). But it was not only that he wondered whether to tell me. It was also that also knew he was a winner. Without confidence in him, I would not have bought any shares. But that confidence, plus a little extra information, made me bet with both hands.

Al's Comments

These stories are consistent with my own experiences with David. We naturally talk about poker and like most other readers, I originally thought he focused almost exclusively on poker's mathematics. I soon found that he could teach me a lot about my own specialty, poker psychology. In poker, as in finance, he combines psychological and other types of analysis.

He's not like a few brilliantly intuitive players. They have been successive, yet they sometimes ignore the odds and rely only on their feel. David does a great deal of factual analysis, but if he can improve his decisions by picking up and using psychological cues, he does it. I urge you to follow his example.

Damon Runyon and "The Fundamental Theorem of Investing"

Damon Runyon wrote many enjoyable stories, including one that became the musical, "Guys and Dolls." Sky Masterson, a professional gambler, said his father gave him some very valuable advice. "One of these days in your travels, you are going to come across a guy with a nice, brand new deck of cards, and this guy is going to offer to bet you that he can make the jack of spades jump out of the deck and squirt cider in your ear. But, son, do not take this bet, for if you do, as sure as you are standing there, you are going to end up with an ear full of cider."

You may think I'm stretching it, but that quotation captures the essence of an important, but rarely applied principle for buying or selling stocks, bonds, and real estate, betting on sports, or making almost any kind of investment decision. This principle is especially important when there is a large market for the item in question.

If you think you have a good reason to buy a security or something similar, slow down and ask yourself, "Why are they willing to sell it to me at that price?" Of course, the converse is true if you want to sell, and someone is eager to buy it from you. I call it "The Fundamental Theorem of Investing."

> Before making any investment, you must be able to explain why the other party is willing to take the other side of the deal … if you cannot come up with a good explanation, your buy, sell, or bet is almost certainly not as good as you think.[40]

---

[40] *Card Player,* August 16, 2002, pp. 34-36. All these quotations come from that article.

If you have inside information, then the obvious reason is that he does not have that information. However, if you're buying based on a good balance sheet, excellent management, or any of the other widely known factors, and someone is willing to take the other side, you may be getting the worst of it.

The logic of this theorem is compelling, yet most people never even think of the other party's reasons. All of their attention is focused on themselves, their economics, their analysis, their reasons for buying or selling. If they thought about the other party's motives and perceptions, they might realize that they are making a disastrous mistake.

The principle is very clear. You should always determine as accurately as you can why the other party is willing to sell, buy, or do other business with you. Unless you have more and better information than he (or the market) has, or you are confident that his reasons are wrong, you should seriously consider changing your mind.

If you don't understand why he wants to do business with you, "all the statistics, income statements, balance sheet data, or analysts' recommendations mean little. There is still some reason they are taking your bet, and if you don't know it, you don't like it."

Al's Comments

People want to believe that they are smarter, more knowledgeable, and so on than they really are. Since virtually everyone wants to preserve that belief, you must constantly guard against it. Before making any important decision, look carefully at the information you have and the way you have analyzed it. If you don't understand the other party's perceptions and motives, *stop and find out what they are.*

Friendly Figure Skaters

As you have already seen, I often try to figure out why people do whatever they do. Perhaps my most general conclusion about people is that, with a few exceptions, nearly everybody mainly looks out for themselves, even if it appears otherwise. Of course, they may also have unselfish motives, but I believe that their primary goal is usually selfish.

My lady friend's recent experience supports that opinion. She recently took up a new hobby, figure skating. She plunged headlong into it and used the Internet to seek out other figure skaters. She found quite a few, and many of them were very good. They weren't champions or Olympic hopefuls, but had competed successfully in regional events. Even though they were experts and my friend was a beginner, they bent over backwards to encourage and teach her.

She said they were much nicer and friendlier than the people with whom she shared previous hobbies. That surprised me because experts at anything are usually not that friendly to beginners. Rather than just wonder, I tried to figure out what was going on.

I concluded that one reason for their friendliness was that, despite their expertise, they were relatively obscure. Because it looks simple on television, and they were not world class skaters, relatively few people could appreciate their talent and hard work. Other people didn't understood the intricacies well enough to appreciate how good they were.

I believe that these expert skaters were so encouraging and helpful mainly because they wanted my friend to gain enough knowledge and experience to fully appreciate how good they were. I'm not saying that this motive was conscious, or that they did not also have other motives. But people who are very good at something want other people to appreciate their skills, and it usually doesn't happen. For most endeavors, the only people who appreciate your expertise are at least mildly competent at whatever you do.

After writing this chapter, I got involved in a similar situation. Our website, www.twoplustwo.com, added a Chess Forum. Almost everyone who posts there is an excellent player, but not a world champion. Since I've just dabbled at the game, any of them could easily beat me.

Despite lacking experience, I have a few interesting thoughts about chess. Some of my posts were obviously somewhat naive or even dumb. Yet all the posters treated me extremely well and answered my questions respectfully.

You may think that they acted that way because of my reputation and role at the website, but the poker forums' posters aren't remotely as nice to me. In fact, they are often harshly critical. But the chess experts treated me the way that the advanced figure skaters treated my friend. It's paradoxical that they treat me more respectfully where I'm relatively unskilled than where I'm an authority.

Don't get me wrong. I don't mean to say these figure skaters, chess players, or whatever, are not nice people. I just believe that experts (but not world class ones) have a subconscious desire to nurture beginners so that they will appreciate the experts' talents.

I think you can use this insight to your benefit. If you want to develop your skills, particularly relatively rare ones, you may get some free advice and maybe even free lessons from experts or near-experts. Look for someone who is good, but not famous, and then butter him up and ask for help. Putting it on a little thicker then you actually feel can't hurt.

Al's Comments

When David first told me about the expert skaters, I did not even think about why they were so helpful. Neither of us skates, but David always wants to understand why people think and act the way they do. I'm a bit embarrassed by my lack of interest since I'm a psychologist, while he is essentially a mathematician. But his mind never stops analyzing, even when the subject is far from his primary intellectual interests.

You may think, "So what? Why think about their motives?" The answer is that the more skilled you become at understanding people's motives, the more effective you will be in a wide variety of situations. Developing this skill takes practice, just like any other skill. So, if you want to learn how to read your boss, friends, and competitors' minds, practice whenever you can.

Math is Often
Just Good Thinking

Being good at math does not simply mean knowing a lot of formulas and when to apply them. Rather it means understanding and applying logic and out of the box thinking to solve problems. This point is essential, but even mathematicians occasionally lose sight of it. Because they have studied and memorized so many formulas and equations, they sometimes don't ask themselves, "How can I answer that question most efficiently?"

Since I never took advanced math courses, I couldn't always do problems in the ways that the mathematicians prescribe. But, since my father taught me math logic at an early age and emphasized the need to think flexibly, I often found easier ways.

Carl Gauss, who many people think was the greatest mathematician ever, showed that childlike ability to do things simply. For instance, back in the 1780s, when he was about 7, his teacher wanted to keep the class busy so she could take a break. She instructed them to add up all the numbers from 1 to 100.

Unfortunately for her, little Carl almost immediately shouted out, "5,050!" She was shocked. She had gotten the same answer by using a formula for summing an arithmetic progression, but he almost certainly did not know that formula.

Since he didn't know the formula, he had to think outside the box. He instantly realized that, if he counted from the ends toward the middle, there would be 50 pairs of numbers, (100+1, 99+2, down to 50+51) and each added to 101. Thus, he multiplied 50 times 51 and got 5,050.

I've done problems with similar methods, especially when they involve gambling or probability (the only kind of math questions I have personally needed to answer). Here are some examples:

1. **A Simplistic Gambling Game:** We flip coins and the winner of the coin flip gets a dollar from the other player. You start with $3, I start with $2, and we play until one of us is broke. It will take at least two flips for you to break me and at least three flips for me to break you, but the game will probably last longer. The question is: What is the probability that I will win this freeze out?

    The typical mathematician will set up a few equations to solve this problem, but there's no reason to do all that work. The answer can be found through simple logic (if it is applied astutely). First, notice that, if we were to play this game a million times, we would come out approximately even. Why? Because we are flipping a fair coin and passing dollars back and forth. The coin and dollar bills have no idea that we are separating the flips into freeze outs.

    Since we must break about even in the long run, I must win two out of five freeze outs because I win $3 when I win, but lose only $2 when I lose. Two-fifths is the fraction of my winning freeze outs that will result in our breaking even.

    Such reasoning will also give you a much more general result. If two people are playing any gambling game where neither has an edge, and they play until one busts the other, each player's chances are the ratio of their original bankrolls. If I started with $8 dollars and you started with $5, I will win eight out of thirteen times. You don't need any complicated formulas or equations.

2. **Another Coin Flipping Game:** You and I flip a coin back and forth, and I go first. The first person to hit a head wins. It's over when someone hits a head. Obviously, I have an advantage since I can win instantly and you can't. What are my total chances of winning?

    Again, the mathematician might produce a formula: My chance to win immediately is $\frac{1}{2}$. I also win if we both get tails and then I get a head, which will happen $\frac{1}{8}$ of the time. I also win on the third round if we started with four tails in a row. Tail, tail, tail, tail followed by head would be one in thirty-two shot. We could sum this series,

$$\frac{1}{2} + \frac{1}{8} + \frac{1}{32} + \frac{1}{128} + \cdots$$

and so on. It's not that difficult. If you know your formulas, you can add these fractions and get an answer of $\frac{2}{3}$.

But there is a simpler way which is also more logically obvious. On the first round my chance of winning is $\frac{1}{2}$, and yours is $\frac{1}{4}$. Furthermore, no matter which round decides the contest, my chance for that round is exactly double yours because I win with a head, and you need a tail followed by a head. Since I am a 2-to-1 favorite on every round, I will win two-thirds of the time.

This method works for many similar problems. Let's say the question was: "What are my chances of winning if we both throw one die, and the winner is the first person to throw a 1? On the first round my chance of winning is $\frac{1}{6}$, and yours is $\left(\frac{5}{6}\right)\left(\frac{1}{6}\right)$, which is $\frac{5}{36}$. Let's convert our numbers to a common denominator: My chance of winning is $\frac{6}{36}$, and yours is $\frac{5}{36}$. Since that ratio remains constant no matter which round ends the game, I am a 6-to-5 favorite. I will win six out of eleven times.

3. **The Bellagio's Special $1,000 Chip:** The Bellagio Casino gives me a special $1,000 chip. It works just like any other chip except that:

    •   It can't be cashed.

- I must bet the entire $1,000. I can't change it to smaller chips.

- I can bet only on a double zero roulette wheel layout.

If I win a bet, I receive $1,000 and keep my chip to bet again. If I lose, they take the chip. On a double zero roulette wheel every bet, no matter whether it's on a color, a single number, or a group of numbers, has a disadvantage of a little over 5 percent. (We won't consider one exception because it's even worse.) Which type of bet has the highest EV?

1. A bet on a single number that will almost always lose and pays the highest odds, 35-to-1.

2. A bet on a group of numbers that will lose most of the time and pays off proportionate to that size. (The smaller the group, the higher the odds. If the group includes one-third of the red and black numbers, the odds are 2-to-1. If it includes one-ninth of the red and black numbers, the odds are 8-to-1.)

3. A bet on red-black or odd-even that will lose slightly more than half the time and pays even money.

Here again simple logic can give you the answer, even though that answer might be counter-intuitive. Many people would not bet on a single number because they would almost always lose immediately. Instead, they would make an even money bet because they want to win something, and they also want to have a good chance to make more than one bet. But from an EV perspective, they have it backwards: The longer they play, the more the casino's EV increases.

You should therefore bet on a single number to give the casino the smallest edge. Every time you bet a $1,000 chip, you "give" the casino a bit more then $50. If you play red or black, there's almost a 50/50 chance that you will be giving the casino much more then $50 because you will have to bet again. However, if you bet on a single number you will almost always lose, which is actually a good thing from the EV standpoint.

If you bet on a single number, your expected result will be to go home with about $950. You will lose 37 out of 38 times, but, if you win, you will get 35,000 real dollars and your original $1,000 chip (which you again bet on a single number).

Bet on red-black, and you will often bet two or more times, which will make your expected take home pay less than $900. But you don't have to do the math because all you need is simple logic.

4. **The Crap-Shooting Brothers:** This one is similar to the last problem and to one I discussed in my book, *Poker Gaming and Life*. Two brothers religiously play craps every day. The first one bets $10 on the pass line three times in a row and then quits. The second brother does the same thing unless he wins all three of his bets. Then he bets a fourth $10. If he wins that bet, he moves it up to $15. If he wins that bet, he moves it up to $20, and continues to increase his bets in increments of $5. Who will do better after 20 years?

Mathematicians would easily solve this problem, but many professional gamblers would not. They may think that the second brother will do better because he increases his bets only when he is winning — "The dice are hot." — but they would be utterly wrong. The clear-cut answer is that the first brother will do better because he is betting less total money with the same percentage disadvantage.

5. **The Chinese Children:** I don't know if it's still true, but I heard that for a while China allowed couples to have only

one boy and that, after having him, they could have no more children. Let's say that there are 100 million couples of child-bearing age in China, and they all obey that edict. (To keep the math simple, assume that boys and girls are born with equal probability, even though boys are born slightly more often.) How many children will be born?

Fifty million couples will have only one child because it's a boy. Twenty-five million couples will have two children because they have a girl followed by a boy. Twelve million, five hundred thousand couples will have two girls followed by a boy. You may notice that this is the series

$$\frac{1}{2} + \frac{2}{4} + \frac{3}{8} + \frac{4}{16} + \cdots + \frac{n}{2^n}$$

If you know some advanced math, you can use a formula to sum these fractions.

Since advanced math is not part of my arsenal, I can't do it that way. But it's obvious that 100 million boys will be born because every couple will not stop until they have a boy. And, if 100 million boys will be born, then 100 million girls will also be born. No scheme gets around our assumption that boy and girls are equally likely to be born. So the answer is 200 million.

Had you used advanced math to sum these fractions, you would get 2. But I didn't need to do it that way. I could solve the math problem by thinking of Chinese children! Likewise, I could solve many similar math problems by thinking of Chinese children with various edicts regarding them.

6. **Another Bellagio Special Chip:** Let's use that Bellagio $1,000 chip to answer the same type of problem as that of the Chinese children. Again the chip will be played until it loses, but now we'll assume that we play a casino game with no house edge such as roulette without any zeros. (Actually, you

don't have to use a special chip. You could use a normal $1,000 chip as long as you promise not to quit until you lose it.)

Because the game has no edge, no betting scheme can result in anything other than an EV of dead even. When you finally quit, on average you will walk away with your original bankroll of $1,000. We'll get back to that in a moment.

Suppose you choose to bet on red or black or some other even money proposition. Half the time you will walk away with nothing. One quarter of the time you will win your first bet, lose your second one, and walk away with $1,000. One eighth of the time you will walk away with $2,000, when you win your first two bets and then lose. One sixteenth of the time you will walk away with $3,000, when you win your first three bets and then lose. Your expected value is:

$$\frac{\$1,000}{4} + \frac{\$2,000}{8} + \frac{\$3,000}{16} + \cdots + \frac{1,000n}{2^{n+1}}$$

Since we know your expected value is to break even, that series must add up to $1,000.

You shouldn't be surprised because this series of fractions is exactly one-half of the one in the Chinese children's problem, which added to two. Once again, we can solve a math problem by turning it into a gambling problem.

You can actually fool around with a gambling problem and get the answer to many sums of series. For instance, suppose you chose to bet your $1,000 chip on a 2-to-1 underdog. On our zero-free roulette wheel, you would bet on a column of numbers. You would walk away with:

1. $2,000 two-ninths of the time, when you won your first bet and lost your second bet.

2. 4, 000 two-27ths of the time. (Your chances of winning your first two bets and then losing your third bet are $\left(\frac{1}{3}\right)\left(\frac{1}{3}\right)\left(\frac{1}{3}\right)$.

3. $6,000 two-81sts of the time.

   In this case we have a series of:

$$\frac{2}{9} + \frac{4}{27} + \frac{6}{81} + \cdots$$

These would be the expected values of the different possibilities and again they must add to one. I will leave it you to come up with other examples.

This is actually how the smartest mathematician's think about many math problems. But you don't have to be that smart. You just have to be willing to open up your mind, think logically, and break out of that formulaic box.

Al's Comments

Most people don't look for simple or creative solutions or try to apply math to everyday life because they never learned how to think about math. They may try to solve problems the way they were taught in school, get frustrated, and give up.

Even people who are reasonably good at math often have problems applying it because the teachers and books make it too complicated. They teach it as an academic subject, not as a tool for solving real life problems. That's one reason for this book. We want to help you find new and better ways to solve your problems, not just while gambling, but everywhere.

My Home Invasion

Although it's occasionally okay to be a bit irrational or emotional, you must accept that doing so usually hurts you. It's almost always true in business or poker, and it can be the difference between life and death in other situations — for instance, being robbed in your home at gunpoint. That's what happened to me just as we were completing this manuscript.

By using several tools that logic and poker have taught me, I emerged relatively unscathed. Without keeping calm, getting into the robbers' heads, and manipulating their thoughts and feelings, I could have been seriously injured or even killed. (In fact, home invaders had recently killed at least one Las Vegan.)

I'll let Al make most of the comments about my actions, and I'll just relate exactly what happened. I was sleeping in a small upstairs bedroom when the door was thrown open and someone holding a flashlight and what looked like a gun startled me awake. I quickly realized it was a home invasion, and my first thought was of my girlfriend sleeping in the downstairs master bedroom.

He shouted, "Don't look at me!" He couldn't have said nicer words because I immediately realized that he didn't plan to kill me. If your plan is to kill somebody, there is no reason to care whether he sees you. Within the first ten seconds I switched into poker mode.

I had been dealt a terrible hand and needed to minimize my risks and losses. Like all good poker players, I had to get inside my opponents' heads, determine how they saw the situation, and manipulate their thoughts and feelings to make the situation as least damaging as possible.

It helped immensely that I had repeatedly thought of what to do in such a situation. Since high stakes poker players sometime carry lots of cash, an armed robbery was always a possibility. So

I had run the scenario through my mind well before it came up, just like poker hands I thought about but had not actually played.

The most important thing was to convince the invaders that they need not worry about anything, not that the robbery would be disrupted, that I would resist, or that they would get caught. They had to be kept calm so they wouldn't do anything foolish.

I also had to stay calm to think clearly. Since emotions would interfere with my thinking, I needed to act like a poker professional. (Anyone who can't control his emotions shouldn't play high-stakes poker.) Staying calm would also keep down the tension and if it escalated or the robbers felt threatened, they might flip out and start shooting.

I realized that the crook talking to me was not drunk or on drugs since he was thinking about my recognizing or identifying him, and his manner and voice were well-controlled. (The other robber or robbers never said a word to me.) The talker was a professional, just doing his job. When he said, "Don't look at me!" my first words were, "I have no intention of looking at you. I don't want to see you."

The robber immediately grabbed my phones. Then he asked, "Where's your money?"

"In my pants, over there."

"Reach into your pocket, and give it to me, but don't turn your head toward me."

I walked over to my pants and gave him my poker bankroll which was between $5,000 and $10,000. I don't usually carry that much, but during the World Series of Poker, I sometimes have a lot of extra cash in my pocket.

He told me to walk into the TV room. As we walked there with my back to him, he hit my head with his gun. (At least I thought it was a gun, but now am not so sure.) He either thought I was turning my head or he just wanted to show me that he was not fooling around. It was the only time he mildly hurt me.

When we got to the TV room, he told me to lie face down on the couch and again not try to look at him. I complied and said, "This will be the smoothest robbery you have ever done."

At this point, a few things were going through my mind. Number one, of course, was what was happening to my girlfriend? The second thing was again that his concern for being caught made it likely he would not go out of his way to hurt or kill me because he just wanted to get my money without any trouble. Since hurting or killing me would make the cops work harder to catch him and result in more severe punishment if he were caught, allowing me to survive unscathed was +EV for him.

This situation reminded me of other endeavors in which your main concern should be minimizing the downside while letting the upside take care of itself. For example, in seven-card stud high-low-split, you play low cards trying to lock up the low side and let the high side take care of itself. All doctors take the Hippocratic Oath, which begins, "First, do no harm." Obviously, in many business situations just minimizing your downside will increase your overall EV. In a funny kind of way, the crooks were doing the same thing.

But then he increased my anxiety by saying, "I hope that nothing signaled the cops to come, because if they do, we're all dead. You're dead, and I'm dead," Saying, "We're all dead," made his threat more credible. If he had simply said, "You're dead," I would have taken it a bit less seriously. But if the cops surprised us and surrounded the house, having us all die was a more reasonable and frightening scenario.

When he made this comment, I worried that one of my neighbors would see his vehicle, become suspicious, and call the police. I wasn't sure whether to tell him since he might think my intention was to scare him into leaving, and that could make him mad. But he had already made his main score, my poker bankroll, and whatever else he could find in the house was less valuable.

So my decision was to tell him why I feared the cops could show up. But I tempered his concern with these words, "We are

not dead if they come because you're simply my cousin, George."
He seemed to like that. He continued to rummage around with his partner while I was still lying face down on the couch, wondering what would happen next.

Then he asked, "Hey, what do you do for a living?" He was probably surprised to find several thousand dollars in my pocket. I'd guess that most of his victims have much less cash (but more jewelry).

"I'm a professional poker player."

"Wow, you just play games for a living?"

I was glad he was impressed, but still had to walk a fine line. If I bragged about my wealth, he might think I was disrespecting him, get angry and hit, kidnap, or even kill me to prove that he was the big shot and not me.

So I carefully thought right then and throughout the robbery about choosing the right words. I stated that this loss was not that big a deal to me and realized it was my fault (because of my carelessness).

My words must have been chosen well because they reacted the way I wanted them to. They were clearly impressed by the money I made playing poker but did not feel that they were being put down. The robbers may have been jealous, but they did not mind acknowledging that my income was more than theirs. On the contrary, we had a "mutually respectful" conversation that even included a little good-natured teasing.

He actually asked, "Could you use a couple of bodyguards?"

It was music to my ears. It essentially told me that we would survive. Dead men don't hire bodyguards. I didn't answer the way some people suggested, "Certainly not you guys." It could have offended them, and no sensible person wants to offend an armed thief. Instead my answer was," Yes, as a matter of fact, I really could. I have an occasional problem in the poker world, and you guys obviously know what you're doing. So sure, when this is all over, find me, and we'll talk."

I don't know whether he was seriously looking for a job, but it was certainly an unexpected question. And, believe it or not, in someways it might make sense to consider using him. For a bodyguard, I'd want someone tough and threatening, but well-controlled just like him.

Thus, I was feeling a little better. The robbers showed some awe about my profession and had nothing against me personally. They probably didn't know who I was, nor did they want to hurt me. Robbery was just their job, and there was no power trip.

Some robbers often make their victims feel small and helpless and may even get a kick from putting down their victims, and people who feel small and helpless are unlikely to cause trouble. But these guys, or at least this one guy, did not withhold his admiration. All in all, my banter seemed to have reduced the tension.

Even the way he treated my cats demonstrated his self-control and professionalism. While lying face down on the couch, they jumped onto my back. He could have showed how tough he was by hurting them, but he just ignored the cats. Perhaps he understood that hurting pets can make people react irrationally.

But then he threw a little curve ball. "What kind of car is in your garage?"

"It's a 2009 Jaguar."

He then said, and I am not kidding, "Do you mind if we take it for a spin?"

Seeing that he was comfortable enough to tease me relaxed me further. To preserve the atmosphere, my reply was, "I guess not since you're the one with the gun." But it sickened me because I did not have theft insurance. (It had always seemed like a bad bet, and I was kicking myself.) After a few more minutes they tied my feet and hands in front of me (not behind me) with a zip tie. Still, I did not look at them and have no idea what they look like.

After tying me up, my accoster said, "We'll be in the house for awhile, so don't try to leave, don't try to get up, don't try to escape."

I finally asked,"What did you do to my girlfriend?"

I will never forget the answer, "We never woke her. When she gets up, she'll untie you. And your car will be found quickly and unharmed." (which it was).

"Wow!" I thought to myself, "These guys are really professionals. They don't want to cause any unnecessary problems." Fortunately, I obeyed their instructions (for a while) because 10 minutes later they came back to ask me how to start the car. Jaguars have special keys and anti-theft procedures. After hearing how to start it, they left again. This time I waited 20 minutes, wriggled my way out of that room, yelled to my girlfriend to wake up, had her untie me, and called the police.

When the cops came, there was almost no sign of a robbery. The crooks showed their professionalism by the way they left my house. Despite losing a lot of cash, my briefcase, two laptops, a TV, and some other items, I would have trouble proving that there had even been a robbery. The house looked essentially the same.

The crooks were surprisingly "courteous." Perhaps that's an incongruous word, but it fits. They did not harm either of us or our cats, did not wake up my girlfriend, didn't even tie me up until just before they left, and reassured me that my car would be undamaged and found quickly. The bottom line was:

1. My girlfriend was not hurt or even frightened.

2. I was not hurt seriously.

3. My car was quickly recovered.

4. My loss was smaller than a bad day at the poker table. In fact, it may have even been a financial gain since it gave me good material for this book.

On the other hand, they did take my wallet which contained some irreplaceable pictures and I would appreciate it if the robbers happen to read this, that they find a way to get them back to me. And of course, we need to have an employment interview.

After the cops left, I was interviewed by various newscasters. You can see one of the newscasts at http://www.kvbc.com/Global/story.asp?S=10598306. You can also read my own and other people's comments about this entire situation in the "News, Views, and Gossip Forum" at www.twoplustwo.com.[41]

After hearing that I told the robbers not to worry about anything, one interviewer said, "Critics will say that you acted like a 'Welcome Wagon for Crooks.' They will tell their friends, 'This guy is more than cooperative. Just knock on his door, and he'll give you whatever you ask for.'"

I replied, "No, it would not be a good idea to rob me because my security has been greatly improved. However, if robbers ever get through the security, I would again cooperate. I don't want them to be so nervous that they hurt me or anyone else and should know that there is no reason to do so."

Another interviewer asked, "What mistakes did you make?"

"I was too complacent about home security.

"What will you do differently?"

To avoid telling thieves what to expect, I just said, "I don't want to say, but we're much safer."

Again, as I told the police, the robbers were thoroughly professional. Everything they did was deliberate and controlled. They acted like top poker players, taking the actions which increased their upside and reduced both their chances of being caught and the penalties if they were caught.

First, they chose a very upscale, gated community, and as Willie Sutton once stated when asked "Why do you rob banks?:" "Because that's where the money is."

---

[41]   http://forumserver.twoplustwo.com/29/news-views-gossip/david-sklanskys-home-robbed-518473/

Second, they showed their professionalism by reducing the costs of being caught. If the prosecutor can make a strong case that they used guns, a jury is more likely to convict them, and they will receive longer prison sentences. But because it was so dark and he ordered me not to look at him, I can't swear that they used guns.

Third, being "kind" to me further reduced their downside. One cop said, "They can get fifty years for this." But I replied, "No, they don't deserve that much. They did not seriously hurt anyone and even let my girlfriend sleep." The cop looked at me like I was nuts.

Ironically, I had previously written that the convicted kidnappers of a prominent casino owner's daughter were punished too severely. Kidnappers often kill the victim, but these particular kidnappers should have received lighter sentences "because *she didn't die*... All laws should have built into them some significant incentive for the criminals to spare lives."[42]

But their kindness did cause them to make one critical mistake. When my car was recovered, there were a few things missing — the gate clicker and things of that nature. But there was also a box in the trunk with several of my books. And they let them be.

Al's Comments

My respect for David was never higher than right after this incident. I was once robbed at gunpoint and it put me completely off balance for days, and many years later, it still affects me. When I first saw him, only a few hours had passed and his extreme composure was astonishing. Then he told me he had started thinking and acting rationally a few seconds after believing

---

[42] "Some Short Thoughts" in *Poker, Gaming, & Life: Expanded Edition*, Henderson, NV, Two Plus Two Publishing LLC, pages 288-289.

that a gun was pointed at him and did exactly what he recommends in this book and in other places. He really practiced what he preaches.

First and most important, David suppressed his natural emotional reactions, accepted a painful reality, carefully observed the way the crooks were acting, objectively evaluated his options, and chose the ones with the highest EV.

He lost a lot of money, but immediately accepted that loss. As a good poker player, David recognized that money lost in a session or put into a pot no longer belonged to him. His decisions should be based, not on the situation which existed two minutes ago, but on the one that was happening now. He accepted his losses and concentrated on the much more important priority, protecting his girlfriend and himself.

David also immediately realized that he had to keep down the tension and that the robbers were not amateurs, drunks, or drug addicts. His words and manner clearly said, "I'm a reasonable guy, and you're professionals. So let's act reasonably." And they all did.

Many people would have whined or begged, which could have irritated the crooks and make them act irrationally causing much more damage and perhaps even death. But David essentially showed them respect, and they reciprocated it.

Instead of saying or thinking, "I'll get even with you," David completely disregarded the revenge motive. Foolish poker players often play to get back at somebody who takes their money. Good poker players shrug it off because money is absolutely fungible. One dollar or one chip is worth exactly as much as another one. So all you should care about is the amount you win or lose, not whose chips they are.

He also explicitly applied his Acceleration Effect by focusing on the positive elements of a terrible situation. Neither David nor his girlfriend were seriously hurt, he got his car back undamaged, and the expensive necklace that they thought had been stolen was found. David also got a refund of his $1,500 entry fee for a World

Series of Poker tournament even though his receipt was in the briefcase they stole. The publicity from the television interview and news stories will sell some of his poker books, and we even got some valuable material for this book. And after it was over, David used the televised interview and our forums at www.twoplustwo.com to send a message to the criminals: "I'm not out for revenge." instead of stating "I'd like to get my hands on those #$%@&.

One reason for his sensible reactions is that David had prepared thoroughly in advance. As he put it, "I had run the scenario through my mind well before it came up, just like poker hands I thought about but had not actually played." Preparation is one of his most important principles, and far too many people don't prepare well.

David also applied another one of his major principles: Admit and learn from your mistakes. As you'll see in a moment, he accepted that his attitude towards security had been too complacent, partly because he over-estimated the value of living in a gated, but unguarded community. So once David understood this, security locks and a sophisticated alarm system (plus other precautions he doesn't want to divulge) were installed at his house.

David also applied one of this book's major principles: Put things in perspective. In "Money as Measurement" and other chapters, you are encouraged to assign objective values to various possibilities, and then focus on the more important ones. David immediately recognized that the money they were stealing was much less important than his girlfriend's and his own survival. So he wrote it off, pushed away his emotions, and focused on preventing the robbers from hurting either of them. Many people can't do this and get hurt or killed by trying to protect their belongings.

David, his son, and I even got a few laughs out of this incident. He chuckled when telling us about the questions the crooks asked about becoming bodyguards and taking his car "for a spin." He got almost as angry about the way the Jaguar dealer and burglar alarm installer ripped him off as he was about the robbery. The dealer charged him $650 to recode his anti-theft key, and the alarm installer demanded an additional $1,200 for an "extra" that should have been part of the quoted price. David told them, "You're as bad as the crooks."

I asked him, "Why did you pay so much for the recoding? They had already proved that they didn't want your car."

He laughed and said, "Al, you'd never make it as a criminal."

"Why?"

"You don't think right. The robbers chose not to keep my car because they had not originally planned to steal it. Since they could not quickly and safely sell it, the car was just dumped to reduce their chances of being caught. Once they have the keys to a $60,000 car, arrangements can be made to sell it. Then they can easily follow me to a store or casino and grab it while I'm inside."

This banter with the crooks, myself, and others, and his ability to laugh about some aspect of the robbery showed a strong sense of humor. David recognized and laughed at events and remarks that would enrage many people. This is also an important asset not only for a poker player but for life in general. We lose money in so many bizarre ways and at times have other negative events, that we should laugh more often. Those of us who can't laugh are not only destined to lose additional money at the poker table by being unable to control our emotions, but also are destined to make life mistakes in other ways.

As you can see, David has applied the principles of winning poker to an extraordinarily wide range of situations and ideas. Here David applied these principles to a rare and extremely stressful robbery and is almost certainly the only person who ever thought about seven-card stud, high-low-split while being robbed at gunpoint.

Small Unguarded, Gated Communities

When the home invader said, "If the cops show up, we are all dead," I believed him and worried that the cops would come even though I couldn't and wouldn't alert them. But it was possible that a neighbor might see a strange vehicle parked in front of my house at night and call the cops. So I told the invader my concern and added, "If they do show up, you're my cousin, George."

He replied, "I hear you," but didn't seem too concerned, and even was talking in a foreign language on a cell phone shortly thereafter. Later, that phone call and the fact that they took my car and left it only a mile away, made me realize what must have really happened. Instead of parking in front of my house, they parked outside the community's walls, perhaps even a few blocks away.

The robber was almost certainly talking to the driver/lookout. He was outside the walls in a place that let him see if the cops approached the gate, and since it was the only way to enter the community, this person could warn the crooks and give them plenty of time to run out (with my money) and climb over the wall. Otherwise, they could load up my car in my garage and transfer the stuff a short distance down the road. Thus the "We are all dead" statement was almost certainly a bluff. As long as I didn't look at him, he wouldn't kill me.

But this tactic can work only in communities with one gate but no guard. I thought the gate would make me safer, but now realize that such communities are more dangerous than ones without gates or with both a gate and a guard.

Without walls and a gate, the cops can come from any direction or from several different directions. They can get to the crime scene faster and cut off the escape routes. The cops might

269

even grab the crooks before they get to their car, and even if they reach their car, the cops might see them drive away and chase them.

However, in an unguarded community with just one gate, the cops can enter only one way, and a lookout can warn the criminals well before the cops enter the community, giving them time to escape.

In a guarded and gated community, the guard might notice crooks climbing over a wall or a suspicious vehicle parked nearby and even be trained to look for this sort of thing. He can apprehend the crooks by himself, call the cops, open the gate so that the cops get in more quickly, or help the cops find the crooks. Thus it's likely that such communities are as safe or safer than ungated ones.

Developers and realtors may dislike my saying this, but I now realize that a small community with only one unguarded, gated entrance is actually the best pickings for a criminal. So the only reasonable conclusion is: *Do not live in such a place.*

Sticking to My Guns

For many of you, one of the most interesting aspects of this robbery should be my personal attitude toward the crooks. As mentioned in "My Home Invasion," one cop said, "They can get fifty years for this." I argued that they did not deserve that long a sentence. Except for the initial bop on my head, they went out of their way not to hurt anybody, and several years ago I wrote that criminals who can hurt their victims and choose not to do so should be treated much more leniently than those who harm their victims.

This isn't being said to reward nice behavior. Rather, I want to protect innocent future victims. My original writing involved the kidnaping of the daughter of Steve Wynn, owner of Wynn Las Vegas, because it's my opinion that the kidnappers were punished a bit more severely than they deserved. Most kidnappers hurt or kill their victims, sometimes for sadistic reasons, sometimes to lower their risks, but she was not hurt at all. Hence, I want kidnappers and other criminals to have as much incentive as possible not to hurt their victims.

When my position appeared in my book *Poker, Gaming, & Life*, some people said, "That's easy for you to say when you're not the victim." But I argued that my personal experiences had nothing to do with it. This home invasion gives me a chance to prove to everyone, myself included, that a personal experience won't change my mind.

This point is important to me. If you believe something to be true, and if its importance is based on logic, a personal experience should not change your mind. For example, I gave a very hard time to one of our regular posters on our forums at www.twoplustwo.com for doing just that. He is normally a very thoughtful poster, but he once made me angry by stating he had changed from pro- to anti-capital punishment after seeing Saddam

Hussein's televised execution — actually, the moments right before it.

How could he change his opinion about such an important issue, especially if this opinion was held deeply, because of seeing pictures of a dead body. The way the execution was botched is irrelevant. If you have strong opinions about something, you need to get seriously different facts before changing your mind.

I have also posted on our forums that I have some sympathy for people who are in bad situations through no fault of their own, but develop ingenious, non-violent methods of stealing. For example, if some African computer whiz hacks into the system of an American billionaire (especially one who did nothing socially useful to get his money) to steal several thousand dollars, it's my opinion that he's not doing anything terribly wrong. Many 2+2 posters said, "You wouldn't feel that way if you were the guy who was robbed."

But they are wrong. I'm aware that my wealth is somewhat undeserved. My work as a player and writer about gambling has contributed little to society.[43] I also know some people would be competent at high-paying jobs, but never have a chance to get them. They live in the wrong country, were raised by the wrong parents, or live on the wrong side of the tracks. And when guys who were possibly in a similar situation robbed me, my attitude did not change.

These robbers semi-seriously asked me for a job, and joked about taking my car for a spin. The bottom line is that I don't hate them. Let's not argue about whether this is the way it should be. The fact is that I don't.

Since they never showed their faces, I'll never know who they were. But perhaps they are reading this and will take from it what they will.

---

[43] One reason for writing this different type of book is to make a more significant social contribution.

Don't get me wrong. I'm not suggesting that they were within their rights to rob me or that they don't deserve punishment. Furthermore, I have these surprising feelings only because they bent over backwards to be nice. Other robbers invaded the home of a couple who had adopted several special needs children and needlessly killed the parents. They should be castrated without anesthesia, and I would enjoy watching it.

But that's off the subject. The point to make here is that if you have thoroughly analyzed an issue and have come to a firm conclusion about it, don't let a mere incident, emotional as it may be, change your mind.

Evaluating
Other People's Expertise

Although this book should help answer many of your questions without assistance, most people can't apply all of these logical and creative tools. But if you can't use certain tools, it's still important to recognize their power and get help from people who can use them.

So what should you do when a problem occurs that you can't solve, but think that someone else can? How do you choose which person to trust for the right answer?

Choosing the right expert may make an immense difference in your life. The right one will help you to make good decisions. The wrong one might even cause catastrophic mistakes.

Let's get specific. If two so-called experts disagree, what's the best way to choose between them when they both know more or think better than you do? Here are five criteria that can greatly improve your choice.

1. **Who has more knowledge of this subject?** Obviously, if everything else is equal and two people disagree, take the advice of the more knowledgeable person. For example, if you don't know whether to sacrifice bunt with a man on first, take the advice of the one who knows more about baseball.

   On the other hand, "Knowing The Rules And The Jargon Doesn't Make You Smart" pointed out that lots of people know the rules of baseball, economics, and so on, but don't think well. Obviously, you should not readily accept their advice. That point brings us to...

2. **Who is smarter?** And yes, by smarter, I basically mean who is better at math, or at least, who could be better at math if he

wanted to be. It's a somewhat restricted definition, but it's close enough. When really knowledgeable people say, "We need our best and brightest to get us to Mars" (or cure cancer, or accomplish something else), they should mean those who are smartest and most creative at math and logic.

If you cannot recognize fallacious arguments, your conclusions will always be suspect. For example, baseball fans think sacrifice bunts should be done much more often than mathematicians do, and those fans have been proven wrong. I'm not saying that a smart guy with only a little experience should always be trusted over a somewhat less intelligent person with much greater experience, but his high IQ does help bridge that experience gap.

3. **Who is least biased?** If a surgeon says to operate and a regular physician says not to, tend to believe the regular physician even if he is slightly less knowledgeable and slightly less intelligent. His advice is more likely to be unbiased, especially if that particular surgeon is the one who will earn the fee.

    Conversely, you can put great stock in opinions that contradict an expert's personal interest. Sadly, I had to apply this concept after taking my ailing, old cat to the vet who said that my cat's multiple ailments could be treated, but that he would suffer throughout those expensive treatments. For humane reasons his advice was to put my cat to sleep. Since this recommendation would cost the vet hundreds of dollars, I accepted it.

    A bias may be psychological rather than financial. If you ask somebody whether your child should go to a less prestigious university so that he can be closer to home, his answer may depend (deliberately or subconsciously) on which college he chose for himself or his children.

4. **How much would he bet on his answer?** In some ways, this could be a more important criterion then the first three, as long as this expert is reasonably competent. He may not be as smart as a guy disagreeing with him or know the subject quite as well, and he may even be biased toward his answer. But if he is willing to risk large amounts of money or prestige when there is no need to do so, while the other guy isn't willing to take similar action, I'll probably go with the first guy.

5. **Who places a higher value on being right?** Perhaps the strongest reason to rely on someone is his commitment to being correct. A few people base their self-esteem on being right, and they are horrified at the prospect of being publicly wrong. If they are not sure of their position, they will either keep quiet, or talk in probability terms — "I'm 75 percent sure…". If a genuine expert is so proud of not being wrong that any other personal biases take a back seat to it, you need not fear ulterior motives.

    Of course, even someone like this should not be trusted if he disagreed with someone who was significantly more knowledgeable and intelligent. But what if the opposite were true? What if you could find somebody who had the psychological horror of being wrong and at the same time was smarter than just about anybody? Might such a person exist?

Appendix
Poker is Good For You[44]

Many people have argued that poker should be considered differently from gambling in general. This argument has been made in discussions of legalization and related topics, and it's usually that poker is a skill game while other gambling games are much less dependent upon skill.

We agree. But we also believe that this argument has not gone far enough in explaining many of poker's unique characteristics since poker does not just require skill, it demands and develops many skills and personal qualities which are essential for making all types of decisions. These include choosing a career, investing money, performing a job, and buying a house.[45] Some of these characteristics are addressed below.

Characteristic No. 1: Poker is a great teacher. Research clearly proves that people tend to repeat rewarded actions and to discontinue punished ones. Poker teaches by rewarding desirable actions such as thinking logically and understanding other people and by punishing undesirable ones such as ignoring the odds and acting impulsively.[46] Other learning principles also apply to poker.

---

[44] This article originally appeared in the September 2007 issue of the *Two Plus Two Online Poker Strategy Magazine* and it has been edited from the original publication.

[45] We assume, of course, that you will not become obsessed with poker or play for higher stakes than you can afford.

[46] These rewards and punishments may not be instantaneous. It can take a while for things to average out.

Characteristic No. 2: Learning depends upon feedback.
Rewards and punishments are valuable feedback. The faster and clearer the feedback is, the more rapidly you will learn. Unfortunately, for learning many desirable qualities the feedback cycle is slow or unclear. For example, if you make a mistake with an important customer, you may never know why you lost his business. At the poker table, the feedback will often come quicker.

Until fairly recently, most people learned how to play poker primarily from trial and error. Over the past few decades a rapidly expanding body of books, videotapes, DVDs, classes, and coaches has helped many players speed up the learning curve, but there is no substitute for experience. You have to make good and bad plays and get rewarded and punished to learn poker's most important lessons.

Characteristic No. 3: The more frequently you get feedback, the faster you will learn. Most important real life decisions are made infrequently, and some of them, such as choosing a career, may be made only once. Poker players make and get feedback on hundreds of decisions every session which greatly accelerates the learning process.

Characteristic No. 4: Lessons learned in one situation often generalize to other situations. If poker's lessons applied only to how to play games, we would not have written this article. But its lessons apply to virtually every aspect of life. For example, if you are impatient, illogical, or can't analyze risks and rewards, expect to lose at poker, and you should make many mistakes in business and personal relationships. If poker teaches you how to control your emotions, you will be much more effective almost everywhere.

Characteristic No. 5: Young people generally learn more quickly than older ones. Poker's enemies often insist that they are protecting young people from developing bad habits, but they are really preventing them from learning good ones. Young people *love* to gamble, sometimes for money, but often for much more "things" such as grades, pregnancy, and even their lives.

They get a kick from taking chances, and some of their gambles are just plain stupid. A few on occasion will even risk dying or becoming crippled by crazy stunts on roller skates, bicycles, and snowboards. It's as impossible to prevent young people from "gambling" (in its broadest sense) as it is to prevent them from experimenting sexually.

Life is intrinsically risky, and learning how to handle those risks is an important part of growing up. Poker teaches you to think of risks and rewards before acting. If it taught nothing else, poker would prevent some young people from making terrible mistakes. More generally, most of poker's lessons will help young people to make critically important decisions in a more logical and rational manner.

Characteristic No. 6: Poker improves your study habits. Because we want to be respected, nearly everyone will naturally develop high status qualities and neglect low status ones. Unfortunately, status among Americans, especially young ones, is based primarily on physical attractiveness and athletic ability. The highest status people, the ones others envy and want to date, are physically attractive and good at games such as football and basketball. Of course, the good looking athletic children will probably end up working for the more studious ones, but they may not learn that lesson until it's too late.

Because of this, many young people resist studying math, psychology, logic, risk-reward analysis, probability theory, and many other subjects they will need as adults because these subjects seem unrelated to their lives. But poker quickly teaches them the value of these subjects. The "nerds" who study poker frequently also study subjects such as math, logic, and psychology. They even beat smarter people who are too lazy or complacent to study, and winning increases their status and confidence. Poker doesn't just develop study habits and other important qualities; it also increases the value people place on them.

Characteristic No. 7: Poker develops your math skills. Many people perform poorly at math and don't even want to get better. They essentially say, "Who needs it?" When they play poker, they quickly learn that they need it. The winners understand and apply it, while the losers either don't try or can't perform the necessary calculations.

Characteristic No. 8: Poker develops your logical thinking. Instead of thinking logically, too many of us make poor assumptions, rely on intuition, or jump to emotionally-based conclusions. But poker teaches you to respect and apply logic because it's a series of puzzles. Since you don't know the other players' cards, you need logic to help figure out what they might have, and then more logic to decide how to use that information well. The same general approach that works in poker will help you to make much more important decisions.

Characteristic No. 9: Poker develops your concentration. The first step toward solving poker or real life problems is acquiring the right information. Without it, costly mistakes are more likely. Poker develops information-gathering qualities, especially concentration. Virtually every good poker player has missed signals, including some obvious ones, made mistakes, and then berated himself, "How could I be so stupid?" We can't think of a more effective way to develop concentration.

Characteristic No. 10: Poker develops your patience. Poker develops patience in the most powerful possible way. If you wait patiently for the right situation, your EV against the impatient people who play too many hands should be positive. In fact, for many players, one of the first lessons of poker should be to "Be patient."

Characteristic No. 11: Poker develops your discipline. Many people lack discipline. They yield to their impulses, and on occasion will yield to destructive ones. Poker develops discipline by rewarding it highly. Virtually all winning players are extremely disciplined.

Their discipline affects many things they do. This could include folding hands they are tempted to play, resisting the urge to challenge tough players, avoiding distractions, even pleasant ones like chatting with friends or sexually attractive strangers, criticizing bad players, and controling their emotions. *They have the self-control to do the necessary, but unpleasant things that most people won't do.*

Television has created a ridiculously inaccurate image of poker. After seeing famous players screaming and trash-talking, viewers naturally assume that such antics are normal. They are utterly mistaken. Television directors show these outbursts for "dramatic value," and a few players act stupidly to get on TV. You will see more outbursts in a half hour of television than in a month in a card room.

Characteristic No. 12: Poker teaches you to focus on the long term. Impatience is not the only cause for short-sightedness. Learning research proves that immediate rewards have much greater impact on people than delayed ones. For example, poker players quickly learn that a bad play can have good results and vice versa. But they also learn that making decisions with positive, long-term expectation (EV) is the key to success. If you make enough negative EV plays, expect to lose. If you make enough positive EV plays, winning is much more likely.

Characteristic No. 13: Poker teaches you that forgoing a profit equals taking a loss (and vice versa). Economists call lost profits "opportunity costs," and they have written extensively about them. Unfortunately, most people haven't read their works, and if they did, they probably wouldn't agree. They would frequently prefer to pass up a chance to make a dollar than risk losing one. They therefore miss many profitable opportunities.

Poker teaches you that lost profits are objectively the same as losses. For example, if the pot offers 8-to1, and the odds against making a winning hand are 5-to-1, you should call the bet. Not calling is the same as throwing away money by making a bad call when the odds are against you.

Characteristic No. 14: Poker develops your realism. Most of us will, at times, deny unpleasant realities about our self, other people, and many other subjects. We frequently believe what we want to believe. But poker develops realism in the cruelest, but most effective way. If you deny reality about yourself, the opposition, the cards, the odds, or almost anything else, your expectation should be negative.

Hundreds of times a night you must assess a complicated situation: your own and the other players' cards, what the others are going to do, the probability that various cards will come on later rounds, your position, and many other factors, especially your own and the other players' skill and playing style. If you are realistic, your EV should be positive. If you deny reality, your EV should be less than zero.

Characteristic No. 15: Poker teaches you how to adjust to changing situations. Most people don't ask themselves, "How is this situation different?" They just do whatever they have always done. Poker demands adjustments because the situation is always changing. One card can convert a worthless hand such as a four flush into an unbeatable one. The player holding the flush and all the opponents should adjust immediately. The player with the winning hand should do whatever will produce the most profit, and the others should cut their losses.

Other things are changing as well. One hand after being in the small blind, the worst position, you have the button, the best position. Every time someone quits and is replaced by a different type of player, the game changes. Every time someone makes a surprising play by folding, checking, betting, or raising, you should re-evaluate the situation and adjust to the new information.

Characteristic No. 16: Poker teaches you to adjust to diverse people. Most people, especially younger ones, have little experience with diverse people. They live in relatively homogenous towns and neighborhoods, and usually relate to people who are fairly similar to themselves.

In online and casino poker games, you have to play with whoever sits down. You must compete against very different kinds of people — aggressive and passive, friendly and nasty, educated and uneducated, quiet and talkative, intelligent and stupid, emotionally controlled and uncontrolled, and so on.

You therefore learn how to understand and adjust to people who think and act differently. The faster and better you do it, the better your results are expected to be. Since you will certainly meet diverse people in more important situations, learning how to relate to them is extremely valuable.

Characteristic No. 17: Poker teaches you to avoid racial, sexual, and other prejudices. Prejudice is always wrong, but it's especially destructive at the poker table. It causes you to underestimate your opposition and make expensive errors. To play well, you should be "gender-blind, color-blind, and just-about-everything else-blind, because in the end, winning is based on merit."[47]

Poker provides an extremely "level playing field." In no other popular competition is everyone treated so equally. You can't play golf against Tiger Woods, but you can sit down at any poker table. You can play against anyone from a novice to a world class player, and you will all be treated as equals. If you get the cards

---

[47] Barbara Connors, "Poker Play" in Maryann Morrison's *Women's Poker Night*, New York, Kensington Publishing, 2007, p. 26.

and play them well, your EV should be positive, no matter who you are.

Characteristic No. 18: Poker teaches you how to handle losses.
Many people can't cope with losses. A lost job, an argument, or God forbid, a romantic relationship can be a massive tragedy. They can't accept the loss and may even obsess over it. It takes over their lives and can make them look backward rather than forward.

Poker teaches you how to cope with losses because they occur frequently. You lose far more hands than you win, and losing sessions and losing streaks are just normal parts of the game. You also learn that trying to get even quickly is a prescription for disaster. You have to accept short-term losses and continue to play a solid, patient game. You can't be a winner, in poker or life, if you don't learn how to get over losses and move on.

Characteristic No. 19: Poker teaches you to depersonalize conflict. Many people take conflicts too personally. They may want to beat someone so badly that they "win the battle, but lose the war." Worse yet, if they lose, they may take it as a personal defeat and ache for revenge. Anyone who has seriously played games with painful physical contact (such as football, boxing, and soccer) is less likely to take conflict too personally. Getting hurt teaches some athletes that conflict is just part of the game and life. Alas, many people never learn that lesson.

Poker teaches you to depersonalize conflicts because it's based on impersonal conflict. The objective is to win each other's money, and everyone's money is the same. It doesn't matter whether you win or lose to Harry, Susan, or Bob. Everybody's chips have the same value, and everybody's money spends the same.

Poker quickly teaches you that being bluffed, sandbagged, outdrawn, and just plain outplayed are not personal challenges or insults. They are just parts of the game. Poker also teaches you that taking conflicts personally can be extremely expensive.

If you ache for revenge, you may act foolishly and lose a lot of money. Beating "your enemy" can become so important that you play cards you should fold, try hopeless bluffs, and take many other stupid, self-destructive actions. The Chinese have a wonderful saying, "If you set out for revenge, dig two graves: one for him, and one for you." Poker teaches that principle to every open-minded player.

Characteristic No. 20: Poker teaches you how to plan. Many people don't plan well. Instead of setting objectives and planning the steps to reach them, they react impulsively or habitually. Poker develops your planning ability for an extremely wide range of time periods:

- This betting round
- This entire hand
- This session
- This tournament
- This year
- Your entire poker career

Planning for all of these periods requires setting objectives and anticipating what others will do. For example, pocket aces are the best possible hand, and you hope to build a big pot with them. In early position in a loose-passive game, you should raise because your opponents will probably call. In a more aggressive game you might just call, expecting someone to raise and others to call, so that you can reraise.

Poker also teaches you to plan for the entire hand. You use chess-type thinking — "I'll do this, they will do that, and then I'll …". For instance, you may sacrifice some profit on an early betting round to increase your profits for the entire hand.

You can also sacrifice immediate profits for longer-term gains. For example, you may overplay the first few hands to create a "Wild Gambler" image that will get you more action on later hands. Or you may be extremely tight at first to set up later bluffs. Poker teaches you to set clear goals, think of what others are likely to do, plan the actions that will move you toward your goals, and always know why you are doing something.

Good planning requires thinking of multiple contingencies. You should do many "what, if?" analyses. If the next card is a spade, you will bet. If it pairs the board, and Joe bets, you will fold. If it seems innocuous and Harriet bets, you will raise. Most people don't consider nearly enough possibilities. When something unexpected happens, they have no idea what to do.

Planning in real life is so obviously valuable and so rarely done well that we don't need to give any examples. You know that you should do these "what if" analyses and plan your work, finances, and life in general, but many of you probably don't plan well.

Characteristic No. 21: Poker teaches you how to handle deceptive people. Many people are easily deceived. Just look at those late night infomercials that promise you'll quickly get rich, become thin, or relieve all your aches and pains. The promoters wouldn't pay for them if naïve people didn't buy them, and they are only the tip of the iceberg. As Barnum put it, "There's a sucker born every minute."

Because poker players constantly try to bluff, sandbag, and generally deceive each other, you learn how to recognize when it's more likely that someone has a good hand, is on a draw to a good hand, or is flat out bluffing Those skills can help you to spot and react effectively to deceptive people everywhere. A lot of people want to deceive you, and playing poker should help to teach you how to protect yourself.

Characteristic No. 22: Poker teaches you "game selection." Choosing the best games is critically important in both poker and life. Poker teaches you how to evaluate yourself, the competition, and the overall situation, and then to pick the best "games."

Serious poker players recognize that the main reason they win or lose is the difference between their abilities and those of the competition. If they are better than their opponents they expect to win. If they are weaker, they expect to lose.

A secondary consideration is the fit between their style and the game. Let's say that two poker players have equal abilities. Player A will beat a conservative game, but lose in an aggressive one, while Player B will have the opposite results. Obviously, they should choose different games.

Both factors affect your real life results. If you are less talented or have weaker credentials than your competitors, you should switch to a softer game. You should also select a game that fits your style. For example, you and a friend may have similar abilities and credentials, but different temperaments. Perhaps you should work in a large organization, but he should join a small company or start his own business.

Most people don't know how to evaluate themselves and how well they fit into various "games." So they might make a huge mistake that they may not realize for many years. Just think of how many people have changed "games" in their thirties and forties. They finally realized, "I don't belong here."

Characteristic No. 23: Poker teaches you the benefits of acting last. If you act last, you have a huge edge. You know what your opponents have done before acting, but they acted without knowing what you will do. Position is so important that any good player would raise with some cards in last position that he would fold in early position.

Poker is an information-management game, and there are many similar games such as selling and negotiating. The primary rules of all these games are:

1. Get as much information as possible.

2. Give as little information as possible.

For example, when negotiating, you want the other person to go first to learn his position before expressing yours. Let's say you have to sell an unusual house quickly. A licensed appraiser has said that it is worth approximately $250,000, but that it's so unique that he can't put a precise value on it.

Before offering a price, you want to know how this potential buyer feels. He may love, hate, or be indifferent to its unique features. If he makes the first offer, you get some inkling of his feelings. He may even offer $275,000! Since he seems to love its uniqueness, try for an even higher price.

Job interviewers know the value of acting last. Most employment applications contain a question such as: "Approximate starting salary expected." If you answer, you have given the interviewer your position without knowing what he's willing to pay. Since you are unlikely to get more than you ask for, *try to avoid making that first offer.*

Characteristic No. 24: Poker teaches you to focus on the important subjects. Focusing on unimportant subjects causes expensive mistakes at the poker table and in real life. Serious poker players know that all mistakes are not created equal. Trying too hard to avoid small mistakes can cause bigger ones.

Overreacting to any opponent's small mistakes can cause the deadly mistake of underestimating him. For example, you may see that an opponent overplays a mediocre hand such as a small pair. It's a mistake, but a small one, especially because he will get that hand only a few times a night. If he plays the other hands well, don't conclude that he's a weak player.

Your own mistakes should also be analyzed, and some of them can be quite subtle, but still important. For example, you may be so intent on playing "properly" that you seem too serious for the weaker opponents who just want to have a good time. So they avoid you, which reduces your share of the money they give away.

Another error is taking a too conservative approach that can cause strategic mistakes. For example, you could play your cards in a technically correct way, but almost never bluff. You would lose the profit you could gain from good bluffs, and your opponents will not give you much action on your good hands. The same principle applies to always playing hands the same way. The predictability costs you more than you gain by always being technically correct.

A business analogy would be running your organization so rigidly that all the ordinary decisions are made well but:

1. Your employees are not motivated to be creative when the usual routines won't work. In fact, they may fear being punished for violating procedures.

2. Your organization can't respond effectively to the inevitable surprises.

3. Your good employees quit.

4. Your organization becomes a typical bureaucracy, filled with deadwood and unable to achieve its goals.

Characteristic No. 25: Poker teaches you how to apply probability theory. If you are like most people, you don't think in probabilistic terms, or do so very crudely. You think something:

1. Will happen
2. Won't happen
3. Probably will happen
4. Probably won't happen

Thus you are unlikely to make finer distinctions such as between a 30, 20, and 10 percent chance of success.

Poker teaches that these distinctions are important and develops your ability to calculate them. You learn that you should sometimes call a bet if you have a 30 percent chance of winning, but fold with a 20 percent chance. You also learn how to estimate probabilities quickly and accurately.

This neglected skill can be applied to many real life decisions. For example, if you have to fly to Los Angeles for a sales call or job interview, it may be worth the time and expense if the probability of success is 30 percent, but not if it's 20 percent. Hardly anyone thinks this way which can cause many poor decisions.

Characteristic No. 26: Poker teaches you how to conduct risk-reward analyses. These analyses are a more formal way to use probability theory. Since life is intrinsically risky, you probably can't win at poker or life without accurately assessing risks and rewards.

Risk-reward analysis is a form of cost-benefit analysis which also includes the probability of each possible result. Let's say that the pot is $100. You have a flush draw that you expect to win if you make it, but lose if you miss. It will cost you $20 to call the bet. The odds against making your flush are approximately 4-to-1. If you make it, you will win another $20 because you are sure your opponent will call one last bet. You are also sure you cannot bluff. Should you call the $20 bet?

You will certainly lose more often than win, but the potential gain may outweigh the potential loss. Because we are concerned only with the long term, let's do it 100 times:

You will win $120 twenty times for a total win of $2,400
You will lose $20 eighty times for a total loss of $1,600
Your net gain for 100 times will be $800
Your expected value for each call is $8

Thus, you should obviously call the bet.

Poker players constantly do risk-reward analyses, and these analyses are often much more complicated. For example, in deciding whether to semi-bluff, you should estimate the probabilities of:

1. Winning the pot immediately because your opponent(s) fold(s).

2. Winning because you bet again on the next round and your opponent(s) fold(s).

3. Winning because you catch the card you need to make the best hand.

4. Losing because you get called and don't catch your card.

The math can get difficult, but advanced players learn how to estimate these analyses quickly and accurately.

The same sort of analysis should be done whenever you have a real life risky situation. Unfortunately, most people don't do it. They buy stocks or real estate, take a job, open a business, or take personal risks without identifying all the outcomes and estimating the probabilities that each will occur. So bad decisions can be made.

Poker is such an excellent teacher for risky decisions that Peter Lynch, former manager of The Magellan Fund and Vice Chairman of Fidelity, once said that a good way to become a better investor was to "Learn how to play poker."[48]

Characteristic No. 27: Poker teaches you to put things in context and evaluate all variables. People often ask poker

---

[48] "Ten lessons poker teaches great investors," by Christopher Graja, Bloomberg's *Personal Finance*, June, 2001, p. 56

experts, "How should I play this hand?" They are usually frustrated by the standard answer, "It depends on the situation." The expert then asks them about the other players, their own position, the size of the pot, the action on previous betting rounds, the action on the previous hands, and many other subjects. Most people don't want to hear, "It depends on the situation," and they definitely don't want to answer questions.

In fact, they usually can't answer them because they have not counted the pot, thought about the other players, and done all the other things that experts do. They want to know two or three simple rules for playing a pair of aces, or a full house, a flush draw, and the experts won't tell them because there aren't any simple rules.

If you play seriously, you will learn that the KISS formula (Keep It Short and Simple) does not apply to poker. More importantly, it does not apply to most significant real life decisions. KISS has become popular because people want to believe that life is more simplistic than it really is. Poker teaches you to ask the same sorts of questions about investment, career, and other decisions that are necessary to ask at the poker table so that your decision making is much better.

Characteristic No. 28: Poker teaches you how to "Get into people's heads." Poker teaches you to understand and apply psychology because understanding others is absolutely essential. In fact, poker has often been called "a people game played with cards." If you don't understand the other players, you can't expect to do as well as possible,

We have already discussed psychological subjects such as avoiding prejudice and selecting the right games. We will end this long essay by briefly discussing poker's most important psychological lesson: teaching you what other people perceive, think, and want.

The first step is shifting your focus from yourself to them, and poker forces you to make that shift. If you focus on only your own cards, your expectation will decline because poker hands have relative value. That is the important issue is not how good your cards are, it's how they compare to the other players' cards. A flush is a good hand, but it loses to a bigger flush or a full house or better. So poker quickly teaches you to think of what hands other people might hold. It also teaches you to think about what they think you have. And even what they think you think they think.[49]

We and others have written extensively about these subjects, but space limitations allow us to give only two examples. Good players always consider the other player when making any decision. With the same cards and situation, they would be inclined to fold if a conservative player bets, but raise if an aggressive player bets.

Good players would also think about how their opponents think about each other. For example, if a perceptive opponent bets into someone whom he believes is likely to call, he's less likely to be bluffing. If a good player reraises a "maniac," he may have a weaker hand than if he reraised a conservative opponent. Understanding his perceptions of these other players greatly improves your decisions when contesting a pot. And this skill is vital in virtually every area of life since it's difficult to have good personal relationships or to succeed in business without being perceptive about people.

Conclusions

We have described many, but certainly not all, of the skills and personal qualities that poker develops. Most of poker's lessons are variations on one theme: *Think carefully before you*

---

[49] See "Multiple Level Thinking" in David Sklansky and Ed Miller, *No Limit Hold 'em: Theory And Practice,* Henderson, NV, Two Plus Two Publishing, 2006, pp. 168-175.

act. That principle applies everywhere, and far too many people ignore it.

The government's attempts to outlaw Internet poker are based upon a misconception of its nature and value. It's not "just gambling," and it should not be subject to the same rules and penalties as other gambling games. Instead, the government should allow you to play poker in regulated and taxed places because poker is good for you and good for America.

Index

abortion 138, 144-45, 213
academic constraints 4
Acceleration Effect (over-reacting to setbacks/successes) 92-96, 101, 266-67
acting last 287-88
advertising 87
affirming the consequent (logical fallacy) 71-73
AIDS 172-73
AIG 149, 156
airports, lines at 160
alcoholism184-85, 186
American Actuarial Society 2
analogies 206-7
analysis, exploitation/manipulation avoided via 34
annoyances, placing a dollar value on 101-2
anti-abortionists 138, 144-45
Aristotle 71, 73, 85
arrogance 6
The Art of Political Manipulation (Riker) 90
athletes, anti-drug rules for 179
auctions 116-17. *See also* negotiating
baccarat 223-24, 240-41
backers 154, 194-95
bailouts 7, 126-27, 129, 135-36
bank officers' math mistakes 220-21
Barnum, P. T. 286
batting average example 109, 110-11
Bayes Theorem 109, 109n
Bear Stearns 156
A Beautiful Mind (film) 85-86
behavioral cues 243-44. *See also* psychology